# Homol'ovi II: Archaeology of an Ancestral Hopi Village, Arizona

ANTHROPOLOGICAL PAPERS OF
THE UNIVERSITY OF ARIZONA
NUMBER 55

# Homol'ovi II: Archaeology of an Ancestral Hopi Village, Arizona

## E. Charles Adams and Kelley Ann Hays
## Editors

CONTRIBUTORS

E. Charles Adams
Ronald L. Bishop
Patricia L. Crown
Suzanne K. Fish
Lee Fratt
Kelley Ann Hays
Richard C. Lange
John H. Madsen
Charles H. Miksicek
Alan P. Sullivan
Christine R. Szuter
Sharon F. Urban

THE UNIVERSITY OF ARIZONA PRESS
TUCSON
1991

E. Charles Adams is Associate Curator of Archaeology for the Arizona State Museum, University of Arizona, and has been director of the Homol'ovi Research Program since 1985. Upon receiving his doctoral degree from the University of Colorado, Boulder in 1975, he accepted a position as director of the Walpi Archaeological Project for the Museum of Northern Arizona, which he held until 1982. This work on the historic Hopi pueblo of Walpi stimulated his interest in the prehistory and history of the Hopi. The ongoing investigations of late prehistoric pueblos in the Homol'ovi area, which the Hopi consider to be ancestral villages, continues this research interest.

Kelley Ann Hays began working with the Homol'ovi Research Program as a graduate student research assistant in 1984. She served as laboratory director and ceramic analyst for four years, studying the Pueblo IV period ceramics of Homol'ovi II and III. Her doctoral dissertation at the University of Arizona is on early Anasazi design traditions in ceramics, textiles, basketry, and rock art. Her research interests focus on the archaeology of art and symbolic systems in the Basketmaker and Puebloan Southwest.

*Cover*: Whole vessels recovered from Homol'ovi ruins by previous investigators: *back*, Tuwiuca Black-on-orange bowl (Fig. 3.2*e*), Sikyatki Polychrome bowl (Fig. 3.1*b*); *center*, Awatovi Black-on-yellow bowl (Fig. 3.11*a*); *front*, Tuwiuca Black-on-orange jar (Fig. 3.2*f*), Homolovi Polychrome jar (Fig. 3.2*c*), Jeddito Black-on-yellow bowl (Fig. 3.11*b*). Not to scale.

THE UNIVERSITY OF ARIZONA PRESS

Copyright © 1991

The Arizona Board of Regents
All Rights Reserved

This book was set in 10/12 Dutch Roman
⊗ This book is printed on acid-free, archival-quality paper.
Manufactured in the United States of America.

95 94 93 92 91    5 4 3 2 1

Library of Congress Cataloging-in-Publication Data

Homol'ovi II : archaeology of an ancestral Hopi village, Arizona / E.
    Charles Adams and Kelley Ann Hays, editors ; contributors, E.
    Charles Adams ... [et al.].
        p.    cm. -- (Anthropological papers of the University of
    Arizona ; no. 55)
        Includes bibliographical references and index.
        ISBN 0–8165–1265–5 (pbk.)
        1. Homol'ovi II Site (Ariz.) 2. Hopi Indians--Antiquities.
    I. Adams, E. Charles. II. Hays, Kelley Ann, 1960–  . III. Series.
    E99.H7H66   1991
        979.1'35--dc20                          91-12444
                                                   CIP

# Contents

# FIGURES

## TABLES

# Preface

In 1986 Homolovi Ruins State Park was created, the culmination of a seven-year cooperative effort among the citizens of Winslow, professional and avocational archaeologists, the Arizona State legislature, Governor Bruce Babbitt, state and local land managing agencies, the State Historic Preservation Office, and Arizona State Parks. The centerpiece for interpretation for the new park is the site of Homol'ovi II, and the excavated and stabilized rooms reported in this volume are the initial focus of that interpretation.

Although Homol'ovi II has been the subject of vandalism for a century, it remains one of the most significant archaeological sites in Arizona. This importance derives in part from the pueblo's clear ties to modern Hopi culture. Oral traditions of numerous Hopi clans speak of the Homol'ovi area as a final gathering place before the people moved to the modern Hopi villages. This gathering of clans and extensive contact with Hopi already on the mesas in the 1300s is documented in the research summarized in this and subsequent reports on the Homol'ovi area.

The site of Homol'ovi II, AZ J:14:15, was investigated by members of the Archaeology Section, Arizona State Museum, University of Arizona, in the spring of 1984. Excavation and surface collection were conducted from May 7 to 28, 1984 with an average crew size of ten people. Five contiguous rooms and an exterior activity area were completely excavated. Sixty-three systematically placed surface units, totaling 692.6 square meters, were selected and completely collected. Diagnostic and exotic sherds, stone tools, and a sample of ground stone tools were collected from the surface of the entire site. Artifacts were processed each day at a temporary lab and headquarters in Winslow. All materials were then transported to Tucson for further processing and analysis at the Arizona State Museum.

The significance of Homol'ovi II lies in its great size (approximately 700 rooms), late occupation period (to about 1400), and reference in Hopi oral traditions of clan migrations (Fewkes 1904). The gathering of people at Homol'ovi II is recognized in the aggregated pueblos at Homol'ovi and other nearby, contemporary villages. Contacts with neighbors, in particular those on the mesas, is evident in the traded pottery. The project expands upon work conducted by the Museum of Northern Arizona in 1980 and 1981 (Weaver and others 1982). Research goals were the assessment of subsurface damage caused by vandalism, and the collection of surface artifacts and other data useful for the interpretation of site chronology, site and room use, subsistence, and relations with neighboring groups.

The excavated area was stabilized by the Museum of Northern Arizona and a trail was built to the site and around the area of excavation by Soil Systems in 1984. This first excavated area to be opened to the public allows visitors to the Homolovi Ruins State Park an opportunity to understand the value of professional excavations and to visualize when and what activities occurred prehistorically. This report assists the visitor in this interpretation, broadens the research interests in the pueblo for the professional, and furthers our understanding of the late prehistory of the Colorado Plateau in Arizona.

*Acknowledgments*

Mr. Robert Larkin of the Arizona State Land Department was the coordinator for the project and Dr. Paul R. Fish of the Archaeology Section of the Arizona State Museum, University of Arizona, was the principal investigator. John H. Madsen was the field director and Richard C. Lange and Barbara A. Murphy headed mapping, surface collecting, and archaeomagnetic sampling. Appreciation is extended to Davie Saari of the Arizona Archaeological Society who served as field lab director. Louie Curtis and Gordon Pond of Prescott, Arizona offered special support and advice. The Museum of Northern Arizona provided the maps of the architectural layout of the ruin. The successful completion of the Homol'ovi II excavation was insured by the interest and dedication of many volunteers from Arizona and other parts of the country. We wish especially to recognize the Arizona Archaeological and Historical Society of Tucson, and Charles Gilbert and the Arizona Archaeological Society whose members came from Phoenix and other parts of the state to donate their time, energy, and expertise.

Appreciation is expressed to the Field Museum of Natural History, Chicago, Illinois for access to collections illustrated herein, and to the U.S. National Museum of Natural History, Smithsonian Institution.

We are grateful for the support given by the Navajo County Recreation and Parks Department, which provided us with several items of necessity, and by Bill Gibson of the Phoenix District Office of the Bureau of Land Management, who obtained permission to use a BLM trailer for a field office. We extend special thanks to the many individuals and businesses in the town of Winslow who provided equipment and supplies.

Geologist Steve Williams helped identify the type of sandstone used for some of the Homol'ovi II ground stone artifacts and provided information about the morphology of the Shinarump and Moenkopi outcrops around the site. Jenny L. Adams assisted with the design and supervision of the ground stone use-wear replication experiments and provided valuable information on identifying use-wear on the prehistoric artifacts.

In Tucson the laboratory analysis was directed by Kelley Ann Hays, assisted by Lee Fratt, Wendy Jones, Miriam Stark, and Rob Vaitkus.

Ronald Beckwith (Arizona State Museum) drafted all the figures except 3.3 through 3.10, which were drawn by Kelley Ann Hays. Photographs are by Helga Teiwes, photographer for the Arizona State Museum. Carmen Villa Prezelski (Southwest Studies Center, University of Arizona) kindly provided the Spanish translation of the Abstract.

Paul Fish, Richard Lange, John Madsen, and Carol Gifford have commented on previous drafts, resulting in many improvements. We are especially indebted to an anonymous reviewer for lengthy and insightful comments that added immeasurably to improving the content of the entire manuscript.

This publication was made possible in part through the donations of several volunteers who were part of the Earthwatch Research Corps in subsequent seasons at Homol'ovi. We are especially grateful for their contributions.

# CHAPTER ONE

# Regional Prehistory and Research

Kelley Ann Hays, E. Charles Adams, and Richard C. Lange
Arizona State Museum

The prehistoric masonry-walled site of Homol'ovi II is located 6 miles northeast of Winslow, Arizona on a mesa east of the Little Colorado River. Within a 12-mile radius are five other pueblos, Homol'ovi I, III, and IV, Chevelon Ruin, and Cottonwood Creek Ruin. All are late Pueblo period sites dating from A.D. 1250–1400. They are culturally and historically closely related to the modern Hopi villages located 50 miles (80 km) to the north (Fig 1.1).

Although the Homol'ovi sites and Chevelon Ruin were first excavated by Fewkes in 1896, it was not until 1984 that archaeologists turned their attention again to this important complex of 14th-century pueblos. Since Upham's (1982) synthesis of the 14th-century settlement system on the southern Colorado Plateau and western Mogollon Rim, the Homol'ovi sites have been viewed as central to a large, complex interaction system. Adding to the importance of research at these sites is their central role in oral histories of many Hopi clans (Nequatewa 1936; Courlander 1971). It was these oral traditions that first led Fewkes to explore the Homol'ovi ruins and these same oral histories, combined with substantial archaeological evidence, link the Homol'ovi people to the Hopi. Of perhaps greatest significance for the study of Homol'ovi II is the clear indication that this is the specific pueblo referred to in the Hopi oral traditions. The word Hō mōl'ōvē, is derived from the Hopi, Homol = butte(s), ovi = place of. Homol'ovi II is flanked on the west by several buttes. No other pueblo in the Homol'ovi group is situated near any such topographic features.

Archaeologists call the prehistoric inhabitants of the Colorado Plateau the Anasazi, a Navajo word meaning ancient foreigners. The Hopi refer to the people as Hisatsinom, the old people. In the area of the Homol'ovi sites, the central Little Colorado River Valley, is the Winslow branch of the western Anasazi. These inhabitants were strongly influenced by Mogollon people living south along the Mogollon Rim. Together the southern Anasazi and Mogollon forged the tradition referred to here as Western Pueblo that characterized the region after A.D. 1250 (Reed 1948). The Homol'ovi sites, founded after 1250, are better referred to as Western Pueblo, rather than Anasazi, and that usage will be maintained through this and subsequent reports.

The Western Pueblo people were semisedentary to sedentary village dwellers. This sedentism was made possible by their reliance on domestic foodstuffs, especially maize, supplemented with wild plant and animal resources. Domestic turkey and dog may have occasionally furnished a meal but no evidence for consumption of these species has been recovered.

The Pecos Classification developed by Kidder (1927) is used here to discuss the occupation of the central Little Colorado River Valley. Other classifications have been developed by Colton (1939, 1943, 1955) and modified by Gumerman and Skinner (1968). Survey data compiled by Gumerman (1969), Adams (1980), Weaver and others (1982), Andrews (1983), Lange (1989), and Lange and others (1986) form the basis for this discussion of the culture history of the central Little Colorado River Valley in the vicinity of the Homol'ovi sites. The completed intensive survey of a nearly 30-square-mile area generally within about 6 miles (10 km) of Homol'ovi II has recorded over 300 sites (see Lange 1989).

## THE ARCHAEOLOGICAL SEQUENCE

### Paleo-Indian and Archaic

According to Gumerman (1969: 313-317) little is known about the pre-formative cultural horizons in the Homol'ovi area. Clovis points have been found near Winslow (Sims and Daniel 1967); however, no Paleo-Indian sites have been recorded in or near the study area.

Archaic tradition sites are considered under two categories: Tolchaco complex and other (Bartlett 1943). Although the subject of considerable debate, recent

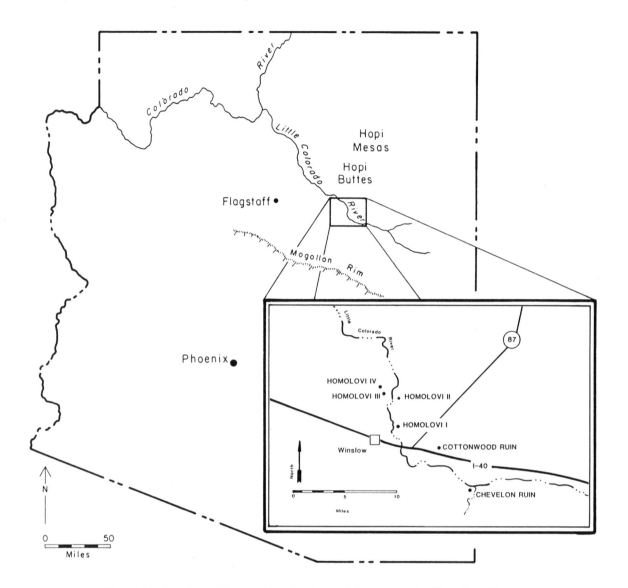

Figure 1.1. Location of late prehistoric sites and features of the Homol'ovi II area.

studies by Keller (1984) and Sullivan (1987) have suggested that Tolchaco sites, which are massive lithic sites that occur along natural terraces of the Little Colorado River, are lithic procurement areas for cultural groups ranging at least from the Archaic throughout the prehistoric occupation along the river valley, or to A.D. 1400.

Other Archaic period locations include a Pinto Basin site east of Winslow (Sims and Daniel 1967) and Pinto Basin-Concho complex projectile points from several sites near the study area. Wendorf and Thomas (1951) defined the Concho complex in the upper Little Colorado River Valley. The only archaic projectile points found near Homol'ovi have been associated with lithic procurement sites in the Little Colorado River gravel terraces.

*Basketmaker II*

Only one site definitely assignable to Basketmaker II has been found near Homol'ovi. Basketmaker II sites on Black Mesa (Gumerman and Dean 1989) and in the Hopi Buttes area (Gumerman 1966) are characterized by shallow, oval pit houses, absence of ceramics, and Basketmaker projectile points. Basketmaker projectile points are common in the area, but are probably the result of the extensive Basketmaker III occupation. Stone working technology typical of earlier Basketmaker II or Archaic people has been found at several nearby sites.

A preceramic component to a Basketmaker III-Pueblo III pit house site (AZ J:14:36) near Homol'ovi I has recently been tested by Lisa C. Young. The

Basketmaker II component had several features, including postholes and firepits, no ceramics, and fragmentary middle Archaic and Basketmaker II points. A single corn cupule yielded a corrected radiocarbon date of 2135 ± 52: 185 B.C. (calibrated at 2 sigma to 365-350 B.C., University of Arizona AA 6110). Other sites within the study area probably also have preceramic components.

*Basketmaker III*

The Basketmaker III period is the first major, datable occupation in the central Little Colorado River Valley near the Homol'ovi ruins. Sites observed on survey that were classified as Basketmaker III had plain-necked gray ware jars and bowls. Decoration was rare and occurred on the unpolished or slightly polished gray surface. The gray ware domination of the ceramics suggests the primary affiliation of the occupants was with the Kayenta Anasazi tradition. Nevertheless, many of the Basketmaker III sites have varying amounts of Alameda Brown Ware or Mogollon Brown Ware ceramics manufactured by the Sinagua people of the Flagstaff area or by Mogollon people south or southeast of the Homol'ovi area.

At least two types of sites are known in the study area. The first is the habitation site. Nearly every finger of gravel terrace protruding toward the Little Colorado River from the east has a pit house hamlet on it. Two lines of evidence lead to this conclusion: the presence of pit house depressions in the terrace and the excavation of two of the hamlets, one about 6 miles (10 km) south of Homol'ovi II (Rippey 1969) and the other 2.5 miles (4 km) south of the pueblo (Young 1989). The Rippey site had 15 pit houses and several features outside the pit structures. Young has excavated 7 pit houses and estimates there are at least 10 more.

The second site type is the sherd and lithic or artifact scatter that may have associated hearth or firepit features. These sites occur north and east of the pit house sites in extensive sand dune areas. The density of artifacts, the presence of features, and the site locations suggest they were used as field houses or to exploit the dunes for dry farming. As suggested by Gumerman and Dean (1989) in their synthesis of the Western Anasazi, paleoclimatic reconstruction indicates stable alluvial conditions that made possible farming of alluvial valleys. Although there are suggestions of this in the side drainages leading into the Little Colorado River from the east in the latest Basketmaker III occupation, erosion and alluviation of the Little Colorado River Valley itself make it impossible to know if the floodplain was used for farming at this time. The Mormon example of the 1870s and 1880s near the Homol'ovi sites would suggest the floodplain probably was not used (Hartman 1978, 1982; Lightfoot 1984). The Mormons were plagued by floods, with as many as six in one year.

Tree-ring dated ceramics from nearby sites and C-14 dates for AZ J:14:36 suggest that the Basketmaker III period in the vicinity of the Homol'ovi sites dates from A.D. 650 to 800. During this period there was a significant, but probably small, population living in the central Little Colorado River Valley. The pit house habitation sites and sand dune farming sites suggest these people spent at least the summer and winter in the area.

*Pueblo I*

The Basketmaker III occupation continues into the early stage of Pueblo I characterized by Kana-a Black-on-white, a polished or white slipped ceramic type with distinctive design styles. All early Pueblo I habitation sites, except one, have high densities of Basketmaker III pottery, suggesting a continued occupation of the gravel terraces and probably a continuation of the settlement pattern started earlier. Although continued reliance on sand dune agriculture is suggested, first definitive evidence of use of the side drainages for farming is indicated during early Pueblo I (Lange and others 1986). Site density is much lower than during Basketmaker III, although this observation is probably skewed by the longevity of the Basketmaker III occupation. Clear association with Basketmaker III sites and very low frequency of Kana-a Black-on-white and Kana-a Gray pottery suggest Pueblo I occupation did not extend past A.D. 850. The ceramic assemblage indicates the Pueblo I occupants were culturally closest to the Kayenta Anasazi to the north.

Apparent abandonment of the area about A.D. 825-850 corresponds with a degraded floodplain regime in the Southwest associated with generally low effective moisture and high variability in precipitation (Dean and others 1985, Fig. 1). Whereas the degraded floodplain may not have seriously affected Pueblo I settlement in the central Little Colorado River Valley and, in fact, could have enhanced it, the low and variable moisture regime in an area receiving only 200 mm a year may have rendered the area too marginal for agriculture. If the side drainages were eroded, floodwater farming may not have been practical. Because degradation of alluvial valleys made the floodplain habitable, it is possible that many Pueblo I sites in the study area have been covered by alluvium.

*Pueblo II*

The Pueblo II period in the central Little Colorado River Valley apparently had a very low density of sites until the transitional period from Pueblo II to Pueblo

III, about A.D. 1100. Adams (1980) notes a few sherd and lithic scatters in the upper sand dunes 3 miles (5 km) south of Homol'ovi II. These probably represent agricultural use of the sand dunes. Whereas this pattern is based on a small sample, at least two other possibilities can be suggested. First, the sand dune areas are botanically the richest and most varied in the study area (Adams 1980, Table 1). Exploitation of the sand dunes could have been for wild plants as well as or instead of domestic ones.

A second pattern is emerging from the survey data that may shed light on the small, dune-associated late Pueblo II sites. About this time or slightly later there was an influx of population into the area. This population established several pit house villages on the same terraces overlooking the Little Colorado River Valley that were utilized by the Basketmaker III populations. The ceramics associated with the pit house dwellers suggest they settled the area about A.D. 1100 and had immigrated from nearby Anasazi communities, perhaps from the Hopi Buttes area. It is probable that prior to resettlement of the central Little Colorado River Valley, forays into the region involved hunting and gathering or planting small agricultural plots. Therefore late Pueblo II sites associated with the sand dunes could represent initial forays into the area antecedent to resettlement rather than occasional seasonal use of the area unassociated with later occupations.

### Pueblo III

Pueblo III is divided into two periods. Based on ceramic evidence, the first period, A.D. 1100–1200, witnessed the resettlement of the central Little Colorado River Valley in the vicinity of the Homol'ovi sites by pit house builders who were local Anasazi immigrants. Four of these pit house villages are located in the study area, three on the gravel terraces north of Homol'ovi I and one on the gravel terrace east of Homol'ovi II. Each settlement apparently contains several pit houses. Excavations by Young (1989) at one of these villages uncovered three Pueblo III pit structures, two small rectangular pit houses, and one circular pit structure 15 m in diameter. The large pit structure was apparently unroofed and is considered an intra- or intervillage integrative structure.

Special use sites associated with this occupation are located both in the sand dunes and within side drainages leading into the Little Colorado River (Lange 1989). These sites suggest a more diversified exploitation of the arable resources of the area than occurred earlier. Whereas the sand dune areas above and on top of the gravel terraces continued to be farmed, the major forms of agriculture occurred in the valleys of the side drainages. These contain a new assemblage of artifacts,

the most notable of which is the "hoe." Hoes are notched, sandstone artifacts ranging from 10 cm to 25 cm long and half that in width. They were either used for traditional hoeing practices of weed removal or for breaking up dirt clods of clay. The side drainage soils are clay derived from Moenkopi Formation and Chinle Formation deposits overlain by alluvial sand deposits of variable depth. The latter served as a mulch keeping the clays moist.

The side drainages are flat, varying only 3 m over a 2 km length. Such topography facilitates floodwater farming. Whether use of the side drainages represents a technological advance in agricultural techniques, a social change involving multiple household cooperation in farming, or a weather pattern more favorable to floodwater farming cannot yet be determined. Maintenance of this land use pattern by Pueblo IV inhabitants of the area through climatic conditions quite different from the early Pueblo III pattern (Dean and others 1985) indicates the ability to use the side drainages was probably the result of cultural change.

The late Pueblo III occupation of the study area has been difficult to characterize. Occasional Tsegi Orange Ware sherds and the presence of two Tsegi Orange Ware-dominated sites ceramically dated to the early A.D. 1200s in upper side drainages indicate both Kayenta Anasazi, possibly from the lower Little Colorado River area, and local Little Colorado Anasazi, makers of Walnut and Leupp Black-on-white, used the area in the early to mid 1200s.

### Pueblo IV

Although Pueblo IV is traditionally dated as beginning at A.D. 1300, for the purpose of research in the central Little Colorado River Valley it is associated with the construction and occupation of the Homol'ovi sites. At least some of these small to large pueblos began in the late 1200s, and 1275 ± 15 years is the probable range for founding dates.

Both Homol'ovi III and Homol'ovi IV were founded in the last quarter of the A.D. 1200s. Ceramics characteristic of the late 1200s are also common at the other four Pueblo IV sites, Homol'ovi I, Homol'ovi II, Cottonwood Creek Ruin, and Chevelon Ruin, indicating their probable establishment by 1300. Homol'ovi III and Homol'ovi IV were abandoned by 1300 and occupants of the pueblos probably migrated the 1.8 miles (3 km) across the river to Homol'ovi II. Ceramics and distinctive architectural patterns from Homol'ovi III and Homol'ovi IV suggest the occupants migrated into the area from the upper Little Colorado River Valley and from the Hopi Mesas area respectively. Whether the area was occupied by a few families or was totally depopulated prior to the establishment of the pueblos, clearly most of the occupants of the Homol'ovi sites migrated to the area. The ceramic data from Homol'ovi III and Homol'ovi IV suggest that immigration was far-reaching, from at least 30 to 60 miles (50–100 km) away.

Most land use patterns did not change between early Pueblo III and Pueblo IV. Both sand dunes and side drainage valleys and slopes were used for agriculture. Moreover, Pueblo IV agricultural sites are found in upper side drainage areas over 3 miles (5 km) from the pueblos, representing expanded exploitation of the drainage areas over Pueblo III use. The principal difference between the early Pueblo III and the Pueblo IV land use pattern involved agricultural use of the floodplain. Establishment of the Homol'ovi pueblos is apparently coincident with a shift in Little Colorado River stream flow to significantly below normal (Adams 1989b; Kolbe 1991). This apparently made the floodplain less flood prone and suitable for some form of irrigation. Canal irrigation is not indicated; however, the over 1 m of alluvium that has accumulated since 1938 would have covered the remains of any such features (Kolbe 1991).

Population decline seems to have set in by the late A.D. 1300s. By 1400, or shortly thereafter, Homol'ovi II and the surrounding area were abandoned. Cause of the abandonment is unknown. Paleoclimatic reconstruction indicates the late 1200s to 1400 were characterized by severe erosion and periodic drought (Dean and others 1985). Distribution of agricultural sites in the side drainages is discontinuous, showing higher use of the upper sections of the valley and avoidance of sections of the lower valleys. Perhaps erosion of the top sandy mulch was taking place in the lower valleys, removing them from agricultural production. If this pattern expanded, the agricultural base for the pueblos could have failed, forcing abandonment and resettlement elsewhere. Whether the abandonment was piecemeal or sudden is a subject for future investigation. Many of the Homol'ovi people migrated to the Hopi mesas, although some may have moved east to Zuni.

## PREVIOUS ARCHAEOLOGICAL WORK

Jesse Walter Fewkes conducted extensive excavations at Chevelon and Homol'ovi I in 1896 for the Smithsonian Institution (Fewkes 1904). He spent one day testing for the burial area at Homol'ovi II and produced a map of the site. J. Wattron, an amateur from Holbrook, excavated at both Homol'ovi I and Homol'ovi II in 1901. His collections and field notes were purchased by Stanley McCormick for the Field Museum of Natural History in Chicago. Many ceramic vessels from this collection appear in a publication by Martin and Willis (1940). In 1937, Colton and Hargrave conducted a survey and surface collection of sites in the area. Gordon Pond excavated a kiva in the west plaza of Homol'ovi II in 1962 and discovered a partial wall mural depicting katsina-like figures (Pond 1966: 555–558). The Museum of Northern Arizona (MNA) conducted investigations near highway I-40 south of the Homol'ovi ruins in 1967, and in the vicinity of Homol'ovi I in 1978. In 1979, E. Charles Adams (then of MNA) investigated Homol'ovi I itself and the area between Homol'ovi I and II (Adams 1980). An assessment of Homol'ovi II and further survey work were conducted by Donald E. Weaver (Weaver and others 1982). An assessment of Homol'ovi III and Chevelon Ruin was conducted by Michael Andrews (1982). Jeffrey Hantman (1982) prepared a long term management plan for the Pueblo IV site group around Winslow that included an assessment of Homol'ovi IV and Cottonwood Creek Ruin. Steven Dosh (1982) reported on backfilling and stabilization of Homol'ovi I and later on Homol'ovi II (1984).

Several studies of nearby and adjoining regions are crucial to the understanding of the Homol'ovi sites in their regional context. These include research by the Museum of Northern Arizona on the Hopi Buttes (Gumerman 1969), by the Peabody Museum at Awatovi (Smith 1971), by the Museum of Northern Arizona at Walpi Pueblo (Adams 1982), by Arizona State University at Chavez Pass (Upham 1982), by UCLA in the Chevelon Drainage (Plog and others 1976), by Northern Arizona University around Chevelon Ruin (Andrews 1983), by the Museum of Northern Arizona (Jennings 1980) and the Western Archeological and Conservation Center in Tucson (Burton 1990) at the Pueblo IV period Puerco Ruin in the Petrified Forest National Park, and by the Navajo Nation Archaeology Division at Bidahochi Ruin (Gilpin 1988).

Gumerman (1969) and Gumerman and Skinner (1968) concentrated their survey and excavations in the Hopi Buttes area to the north of the Homol'ovi sites and along the Little Colorado River to the east. Their research identified and refined the archaeological sequence for the area, which was applied to the central Little Colorado River Valley, although no work was done in the immediate area of Homol'ovi. Very few Pueblo IV sites contemporary with the Homol'ovi occupation were found. All of these were small scatters often associated with earlier sites. Absence of habitation sites suggests seasonal use of the Hopi Buttes area after A.D. 1300.

With the exception of the UCLA work and the work at Walpi, the other research programs have emphasized excavation or survey on or around large pueblos built and occupied between A.D. 1300 and 1400. The Walpi research concentrated on the Hopi pueblo subsequent to its establishment on First Mesa after 1680.

## INVESTIGATIONS AT HOMOL'OVI II

### Environment

Homol'ovi II is located near the southwestern edge of the Colorado Plateau physiographic province. It is on a low sandstone and conglomerate mesa capped by the Shinarump Conglomerate at an elevation of 4920 feet (1504 m). The Little Colorado River, presently 1.25 miles (2 km) to the west, lies at 4825 feet (1470 m). It is flanked by low bluffs of Moenkopi Sandstone and Shinarump Conglomerate overlain by gravels derived from the Shinarump Conglomerate. The Shinarump, which overlies the Moenkopi, contains cobbles of chert, petrified wood, and quartzite. These are excellent raw materials for the manufacture of stone tools. Both formations also contain strata of clay, useful for ceramic manufacture and for construction, and strata of straight-fracturing sandstone, an excellent building material. Sherd and lithic scatters indicate nearby sand dunes were probably used for dry farming (Lange 1989). Soils on the Homol'ovi II mesa itself are too thin for agriculture and consist mainly of eolian sand.

Due to its large drainage area, the Little Colorado River is nearly a perennial stream. It is occasionally dry, but water can always be reached by digging in the stream bed (Adams 1980: 3). Field houses and artifact scatters in side drainages and near the river indicate the prehistoric inhabitants of Homol'ovi II practiced flood-water farming, probably using spreaders and arroyo mouth (ak chin) techniques. They may have used irrigation canals. No examples of such agricultural features have yet been located, with the exception of a possible checkdam or water diversion feature in a small arroyo just below the site (Weaver and others 1982: 7). Such features, if present, may have been buried in alluvium or washed away by the river (Adams 1980: 10). Winslow area Mormon settlers of the 1870s experienced difficulty with raging floods that destroyed their irrigation works (Hantman and Lightfoot 1978: 64).

Hopi farming along a similar semipermanent stream, Moenkopi Wash, in the late 1800s was accomplished by using diversion dams. These earthen works were constructed or repaired annually, and they simply diverted stream flow from the main channel into nearby fields. A similar technique used along the Little Colorado River by Homol'ovi occupants would probably leave no traces for archaeologists to discover. Colton notes that in 1880 the Little Colorado's streambed was much narrower than it is now; cottonwood trees grew along the banks, and pools supported beaver colonies (Colton 1937: 17). At present the river meanders through a broad streambed. Tom Kolbe and Thor N. V. Karlstrom of the Quaternary Studies Program at Northern Arizona University have sectioned the salt cedar, or tamarisk,

choking the terraces along the modern streambed and have determined that the recent terraces began forming in 1930.

Flora and fauna of the Little Colorado region are varied. Extensive lists of species can be found in Adams (1980: 7) and Weaver and others (1982: 5). Antelope, deer, elk and water fowl are mentioned in early historic accounts (Adams 1980: 9; Szuter, Chapter 9). Numerous wild edible plants were present in addition to native cultigens such as corn, beans, and squash grown during the site's occupation (Miksicek, Chapter 8). Vegetation is xerophytic, typified by grasses and low shrubs, and is probably much sparser now than it was before depletion by overgrazing in the historic period (Weaver and others 1982: 4).

Climate is classified as warm steppe. The region is within the Great Basin Desert Province of the Upper Sonoran Life Zone. Winslow, 3.7 miles (6 km) upstream from Homol'ovi II and at 4880 feet (1487 m) elevation, has a mean annual temperature of 12.7° C (54.9° F), with a mean maximum of 21.7° C (71.0° F) and mean minimum of 3.6° C (38.4° F). The growing season averages 172 days, long enough for the maturation of corn and other crops in an arid climate. Annual precipitation averages 206 mm (8.1 inches). Over half falls in summer thundershowers, the remainder in mild winter showers and snows.

Paleoenvironmental reconstruction (Euler and others 1979; Dean and others 1985) suggests a major environmental transformation between A.D. 1275 and 1300 characterized by a severe drought and degradation of alluvial valleys. Degradation apparently persisted until 1475 with highly variable precipitation patterns. These conditions would have characterized the time of major occupation at Homol'ovi II, from 1300 to 1400, based on tree-ring dated ceramics and radiocarbon dates (Breternitz 1966, Tables 2.2 and 2.3). The effect of the environment on the Homol'ovi II occupants is the subject of on-going research in the area.

### Research Themes and Methods

Prior to excavation, the extent, distribution, and depth of undisturbed deposits at Homol'ovi II were largely unknown. An evaluation of the potential subsurface cultural material was essential for the planning of future data recovery. The results presented herein allow researchers to structure directions for future study.

A cluster of rooms was selected for excavation because it was believed that stabilization and interpretation of a contiguous set of rooms would be easier than several discontinuous rooms. Relationships of rooms in terms of their use, abutment and bonding data for chronological control, and methods of vandalism could all be better understood through excavations of connected rooms.

*Site Chronology*

The sequence of construction proposed for Homol'ovi II is tentative (Weaver and others 1982: 12) and is based primarily on architecture and small surface collections of artifacts. Therefore, refinement of the construction sequence for the entire pueblo is necessary. The identification of the final period of occupation was also an essential goal for the project, because there was disagreement as to whether or not the site was occupied at Spanish contact in 1540. As a result, based on surface collections by the Museum of Northern Arizona and a study of architecture (Weaver and others 1982: 14), five rooms in the south roomblock of the western plaza were chosen for excavation as potentially representing the latest occupation at the site.

*Excavation Methods*

Five rooms and an extramural activity area were excavated in a cluster to ease logistical problems and to produce an interpretable unit (see Fig. 1.2). The cluster is located in the Western Plaza, south roomblock. Excavation proveniences included the room unit as horizontal control and room fill, roof fall (sometimes arbitrarily assigned to the fill 20 cm above the floor), and floor as primary vertical control. The area chosen for excavation was surface collected before excavation began. The walls of most rooms were already partially exposed; therefore, surface artifacts from each room were bagged separately. Exterior spoil on the south side of the roomblock, almost entirely pothunters' backdirt, was also excavated and screened. Artifacts were bagged and labeled by general provenience (for example, exterior spoil: Room 217).

Rooms 216 and 217 were excavated first, followed by Room 212, Activity Area 221, and exterior Room 217, then Rooms 215, 211, and a small section outside of Room 206.

Room fill consisted mostly of rock rubble and was extremely mixed due to vandalism, and no information was to be gained by excavating disturbed deposits in levels. Deposits that appeared to be undisturbed were excavated by cultural or natural strata. In most rooms, only one such level, or less, remained on and above the floor.

The fill from the east half of each room was removed by shovel, crowbar, and trowel (except Room 215 in which the west half was removed first). Trowels were used near the walls to ensure preservation of any existing plaster. All fill was screened through one-fourth inch mesh. Main backdirt piles were located 20 m south

of the roomblock. The backdirt area was surface collected before use and appears as Collection Unit 2 in the analysis of surface material.

All artifacts and other cultural materials were bagged as general fill from the east or west half of each room. In all cases, both halves of rooms were equally disturbed and therefore the distinction between halves has not been preserved in the artifact analysis. When floor was defined, all artifacts within 20 cm of the floor were bagged separately from general fill and labeled "floor fill." Undisturbed deposits, such as roof fall, were occasionally discerned (roof fall in Room 215 and fill in Area 221), and the arbitrary 20 cm level was replaced by natural strata in all procedures. All floor contact artifacts were left in position until they were mapped and photographed.

Once a profile map was drawn of the section left by the unexcavated half of each room, the exposed floor and associated features were protected by partial backfilling. The remaining half was excavated to 20 cm above floor, or to roof fall, then the entire floor was carefully exposed.

Floors were drawn to scale and photographed in both color and black and white. Fortunately, most floor features were undisturbed. All features were drawn to scale and photographed. The contents of each feature were bagged and then sifted through a series of fine screens for subsequent analysis. Precise sample location data were recorded on ASM excavation records and have been retained for future reference. Pollen samples were taken in undisturbed areas such as beneath sandstone rubble on floors and under roof fall where present. No samples were taken from general fill due to extensive disturbance. Wall dimensions were measured and are shown in Table 2.1.

Archaeomagnetic dating samples were taken from five features: two hearths, a burned pit, a clay-lined pit, and a fire pit or ash pit. Soil and clay for sampling were sparse or nonexistent in most hearths and the naturally colored red clay made it difficult to determine whether clay-lined pits had been fired. Results from these samples are given in Table 2.2.

No wood samples suitable for dendrochronology were recovered. Three samples for radiocarbon dating were taken from corn cobs or saltbush in the hearths of the rooms. Flotation samples were taken from Activity Area 221. An abundance of carbonized vegetal material stimulated the collection of a sample comprising approximately 100 gallons of soil. This was reduced to 20 to 25 gallons of carbonized plant remains after flotation at the Winslow lab. The remaining fill from Area 221 was screened through one-fourth inch mesh. Artifacts and additional carbonized materials were collected.

Evidence of vandalism was generally easy to

recognize. Modern trash and refuse that appeared to date from about 1900 to 1930 was found throughout the area excavated. Aluminum cans were found on the floors of Rooms 212 and 217. The floors of all rooms (except Room 215) and Area 221 were damaged, broken, or partly removed by vandals. Some of the worst examples of vandals' work appear in Rooms 211 and 216, where large portions of the floors were disturbed and exhibit shovel marks.

The excavated portion of the roomblock was mapped with a transit. By using a Museum of Northern Arizona datum position as a reference point, it was possible to refine the MNA maps. The location of the surface collection units and baselines were also mapped with respect to the MNA datums.

## Surface Collection

The surface collection sampling strategy addressed two major concerns. First, while recognizing that unaccountable numbers of artifacts had been collected, it was felt that an extensive detailed collection should be made prior to backfilling and stabilization and before opening the ruin to visitors and further impacts. Second, the assessments made by the Museum of Northern Arizona based on architecture and a 0.15 percent sample collection of the site (Weaver and others 1982: 14, 24) could be further evaluated. Conjectures about development of the pueblo and period of occupation could be more closely examined with a larger collection.

The collection of a larger sample of surface artifacts would produce a database that could be statistically evaluated to characterize the variability in surface remains across the site. Although variation will be affected by vandalism and previous surface collecting, these effects may be standardized across a site as thoroughly vandalized as Homol'ovi II. Thus variation may be due to cultural factors such as period of occupation, nature and extent of exchange, and others. Such trends can then be used in making decisions about where to conduct future excavations.

Surface collection units were placed systematically as opposed to the previous (MNA) random stratified sample. A systematic sampling strategy was chosen to ensure even coverage of a large pueblo suffering from the effects of extensive vandalism. Although vandalism will tend to blur distinctions in surface remains, a systematic collection approach should mitigate the problem more than a random or stratified random sample. Initial collections from 10-m diameter circles produced large quantities of artifacts; however, the collections resulting from a 10-m diameter circle (78.5 square meters) produced more artifacts than could be reasonably analyzed. A 5-m diameter circle was tried and also found to

**Table 1.1. Homol'ovi II Surface Collection Material**

Collection unit sizes:

| | | |
|---|---|---|
| Unit 1 = 78.5 square meters | diameter = 10 m |
| Unit 2 = 78.5 square meters | diameter = 10 m |
| Unit 3 = 19.6 square meters | diameter = 5 m |
| Units 4–30 = 3.1 square meters | diameter = 2 m |
| Units 31–50 = 19.6 square meters | diameter = 5 m |
| Units 51–63 = 3.1 square meters | diameter = 2 m |

Collection unit locations:
   Units  1–20 = southern periphery
   Units 21–30 = northern periphery
   Units 31–36 = West Plaza
   Units 37–44 = Central Plaza
   Units 45–50 = East Plaza
   Units 51–63 = northern periphery

Sherd density:
| | | |
|---|---|---|
| * West Plaza Area collected | = | 117.6 square meters<br>3897 sherds<br>33.1 sherds per sq. m |
| Central Plaza Area collected | = | 156.8 square meters<br>2925 sherds<br>18.7 sherds per sq. m |
| East Plaza Area collected | = | 117.6 square meters<br>2882 sherds<br>24.5 sherds per sq. m |
| Exterior Pueblo Area collected | = | 300.6 square meters<br>7550 sherds<br>25.1 sherds per sq.m |
| All areas collected | = | 692.6 square meters<br>17,254 sherds<br>24.9 sherds per sq. m |

*West Plaza Units 31 and 34 have very few sherds and Units 32 and 33 have twice as many as would be expected if density were uniform. This discrepancy is probably the result of mislabeled bags in the field, not of uneven sherd distribution.

produce numbers of artifacts too large for the general goals of the surface collection. Consequently, collection units were limited to 2-m diameter circles on the north and south sides of the pueblo. Units were systematically spaced 10 m apart along baselines established by using the mapping datums located by MNA. In the plazas, 5-m diameter circles were used: 6 units in the West and East plazas, 8 units in the Central Plaza. In all, 63 units were collected, representing 692.6 square meters. Collection units were located as listed in Table 1.1 and shown on Figure. 1.2. This sample represents a collection of 3.8 percent of the site (compared to MNA's original collection of 27 square meters, or 0.15 percent

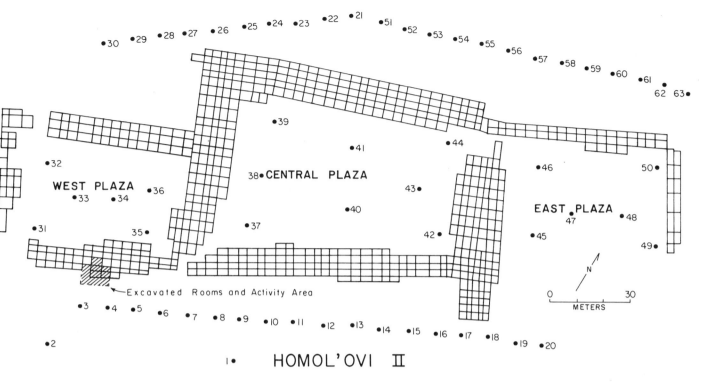

Figure 1.2. Plan of Homol'ovi II showing location of surface collection units and excavated area.

of the site), based on a site area of 18,200 square meters.

Collection units were marked at the center with a wooden stake. A radius was measured with a tape and the boundary of the circle was scuffed into the surface. All artifacts and cultural materials within the boundary of the circle were recovered. All visible artifacts that could be picked up were collected. Decisions concerning the sizes of artifacts to be disregarded in the analysis were made in the laboratory. All lithic material was kept, but sherds smaller than 1 square centimeter were not analyzed.

Nonsystematic collections of artifacts were also made from the three plazas and the south side of the pueblo. The nonsystematic collection of artifacts was made to increase recovery of types of artifacts with traditionally low counts and recovery of diagnostic artifacts. Artifacts with low counts included ground stone, lithic tools, shell, large ceramic sherds with designs or rims, and others. Diagnostic artifacts included items that added chronological control, such as projectile points or some pottery types, or added information about trade, such as some pottery, shell, obsidian, turquoise, and others. Generally ground stone was counted, but not collected. The plazas were each quartered for greater control over artifact location for the nonsystematic collections. Approximately 64,000 artifacts were recovered from the collection units, including 42,000 sherds.

Within this framework of regional prehistory and current investigations, the archaeological story of Homol'ovi II is outlined. Although pothunters and vandals may have compromised the integrity of the Homol'ovi II Ruin, the site still contains extremely important information about the people who lived at Homol'ovi II, their culture, and environment. The following chapters provide analyses of the cultural, botanical, and faunal materials recovered from the Homol'ovi II excavation.

# CHAPTER TWO

# Architecture

John H. Madsen and Kelley Ann Hays
Arizona State Museum

Five rooms and an outside work area were excavated at Homol'ovi II (Fig. 2.1). The rooms are contiguous to one another and are part of a larger unit of 60 or more rooms forming the southern roomblock of the West Plaza. Rooms 211 and 215 are interior units of the roomblock, and Rooms 212, 216, and 217 are exterior pueblo rooms with at least one wall exposed to sunlight. Area 221, the work area, is adjacent to Room 216 and outside the roomblock. Architecturally the five rooms are similar; they were built from unmodified blocks and platy slabs of rock obtained primarily from the local Shinarump Conglomerate. The mortar used to reinforce the walls is comprised of a calichified silty soil. We suspect the mortar was obtained from the red silty clay deposits in the Moenkopi Formation. Mixed into the mortar were charcoal, pottery fragments, and other cultural material. All of the walls were chinked and most were plastered with a clay mixture. The floors appeared to be plastered with the same silty clay soil used as mortar in the walls. A Munsell Color Chart was used to assess the color range of the dry room plaster and was useful in determining replastering episodes. Table 2.1 provides the dimensions and condition of each wall exposed during excavation.

## EXCAVATED AREAS

### Room 211

Room 211 is rectangular, of sandstone slab and block construction (Figs. 2.1, 2.2). Vandals had thoroughly disturbed the integrity of the upper fill and damaged the walls. Those portions of the interior east and west walls that still stand have remnant wall plaster. The plaster on the east wall is pinkish gray (5YR 6/2 dry) and is smoke blackened from an adjacent firepit (Feature 2). The interior west wall was plastered at least twice; here the inner or older plaster appears to be similar to the outer plaster on the east wall. The last application of plaster on the west wall was with a light reddish brown (5YR 6/4 dry) clay mixture.

The north wall had a doorway at one time but this entrance was later sealed. The sealed entrance is 117 cm west of the northeast corner of Room 211 and measures 68 cm high and 51 cm wide, with the threshold about 35 cm above the floor. Sandstone wall footings can be seen in areas where vandals broke through the plastered floor.

Although the west half of the floor was removed by vandals, the east half was covered with a blocky brown soil from 5 cm to 20 cm deep. This blocky layer probably represented roof fall, and although it had been disturbed by pothunters, it had never been totally penetrated. It capped an intact rectangular hearth (Feature 1), an oval firepit (Feature 2), and a variety of artifacts.

Feature 1 is a rectangular hearth located in the northeast quarter of the room. This hearth is set 10 cm from the north wall. It measures 39 cm long, 28 cm wide, and ranges from 10 cm to 18 cm deep. There is thick plaster on the floor around the east and south sides of the hearth. Five small sandstone slabs were fitted in the 10-cm space between the north wall and the edge of the hearth to form a narrow shelf. Scorched sandstone slabs line the bottom and sides of the rectangular box. Small patches of remnant plaster on the inside of this hearth suggest it may have been completely plastered at one time. An arrangement of 13 rocks inside Feature 1 probably served as support for a cooking vessel or perhaps a piki stone.

Pieces of a partially restorable Homolovi Corrugated cooking jar were found inside Feature 1, and additional fragments of this vessel were clustered with other sherds and mammal bone between the hearth and the east wall of the room. In addition, a piki stone fragment, a chert flake with edge damage, and two pieces of chert debitage were recovered from inside the hearth. Botanical remains from the ashy fill include maize kernels, cob fragments, and a variety of woody materials and seeds from such plants as cotton and yucca.

Feature 2, a rectangular pit with rounded corners and baked plastered sides, is in the southeast quarter of the room, nearly against the east wall. One upright

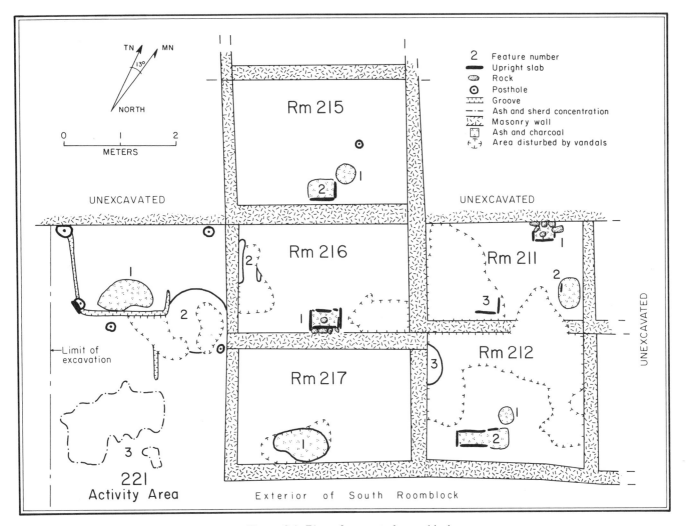

Figure 2.1. Plan of excavated roomblock.

sandstone slab was incorporated into the west wall of the pit. Feature 2 is 50 cm long north to south, 35 cm wide, and approximately 15 cm deep. Two small sandstone slabs were on the floor near its northeast edge. The interior of the pit was filled with ash, wood charcoal, maize kernels, cob fragments, numerous types of seeds, and rabbit and rodent bone.

Feature 3 is a damaged, slab-lined hearth situated along the south wall just west of center. The upright stone slabs forming the south and east walls were still in place, with a single sandstone slab on the bottom. The hearth was severely impacted by pothunting and had no contents.

It seems likely that Features 1 and 2 were used at the same time. Feature 3, on the other hand, was so disturbed that it was impossible to determine its association with the other features. Although there was no visible evidence, Feature 3 could have been sealed

under the floor of Room 211 during the use of Features 1 and 2.

The east half of the floor was intact and covered in places by a blocky brown soil. A number of artifacts were on the floor in what appeared to be an original in situ context. Artifacts included a mano fragment; two sandstone slabs, one of which is ground; two bone fragments; a piece of red ochre; one obsidian fragment; and a variety of potsherds. Broken pottery in contact with the floor included pieces of the Homolovi Corrugated jar, Jeddito Yellow Ware (including a Jeddito Engraved bowl), Winslow Orange Ware, and Alameda Brown Ware, in addition to Tusayan Corrugated.

The botanical content of Features 1 and 2 and the artifact assemblage, which included a piki stone fragment and mano, suggest that food was processed and prepared in Room 211. Other domestic activities were not discernible from the assemblage.

Table 2.1. Wall Data

| | | Room 211 | Room 212 | Room 215 | Room 216 | Room 217 |
|---|---|---|---|---|---|---|
| North Wall | Condition | Damaged West end | Poor, extensive damage | 65% intact, West end missing | 95% intact, minor damage to center | 6-7 courses intact |
| | Horizontal | 3.00 m | 2.94 m | 3.28 m | 3.20 m | 3.16 m |
| | Vertical | 0.70-1.5 m W-E | 0.30-0.60 m W-E | 0.50-1.40 m W-E | 1.15-1.25 m W-E | 0.50-0.60 m W-E |
| | Width | Unknown | 0.21-0.26 m W-E | 0.23 m | 0.35-0.43 m W-E | 0.30 m |
| South Wall | Condition | Damaged West end | 3-4 courses intact | 95% intact | 4 courses intact | 4-6 courses intact |
| | Horizontal | 3.00 m | 3.03 m | 3.24 m | 3.18 m | 3.18 m |
| | Vertical | 0.20-0.60 m W-E | 0.18-0.10 m W-E | 1.10-1.25 m W-E | 0.30-0.60 m W-E | 0.30-0.25 m W-E |
| | Width | 0.21-0.26 m W-E | 0.28-0.24 m W-E | 0.35-0.43 m | 0.30 m | 0.27-0.28 m W-E |
| East Wall | Condition | Good 8-10 courses intact | 5-8 courses intact | 90% intact, 5 end missing | 6-10 courses intact | 6-7 courses intact |
| | Horizontal | 1.93 m | 2.49 m | 2.23 m | 2.02 m | 2.12 m |
| | Vertical | 1.0-0.80 m N-S | 0.80-0.20 m N-S | 1.40-0.80 m N-S | 0.70 m | 0.60-0.20 m N-S |
| | Width | Unknown | 0.26 m | 0.27 m | 0.25-0.26 m N-S | 0.29-0.30 m N-S |
| West Wall | Condition | Good 7 courses intact | 4-6 courses intact | 30-40% intact, poor, most missing | 4-6 courses intact | 4-6 courses intact |
| | Horizontal | 1.82 m | 2.39 m | 2.35 m | 1.90 m | 2.16 m |
| | Vertical | 0.70-0.80 m N-S | 0.80-1.0 m N-S | 0.80-1.0 m N-S | 0.70-0.05 m N-S | 0.40-0.30 m N-S |
| | Width | 0.25-0.26 m N-S | 0.29-0.30 m N-S | Collapsed | 0.21 m | 0.27 |

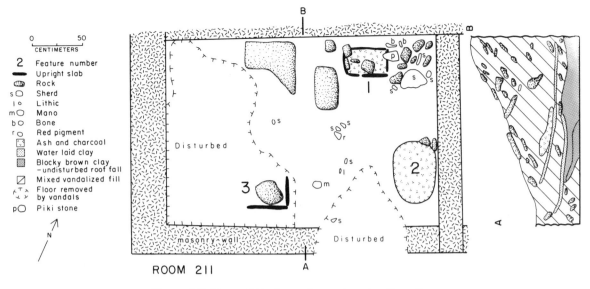

Figure 2.2. Room 211, floor plan and west soil profile.

The room fill contained sherds from vessels found on the floor of Room 211. Predominant in the disturbed fill were Jeddito and Awatovi Yellow wares, with Winslow and Homolovi Orange wares well represented.

Two radiocarbon samples (Beta 12913 Feature 1 and Beta 12914 Feature 2) and an archaeomagnetic sample (HV005 Feature 2) were taken from hearths in Room 211 (Table 2.2). Radiocarbon sample 12913 provided a date of A.D. 1340 ± 85. This sample was calibrated at 1285-1333, 1340-1397, and provided a maximum date range of 1256-1442 for two standard deviations (see Chronology below).

**Table 2.2. Archaeomagnetic and Radiocarbon Dates from Homol'ovi II**

| | ARCHAEOMAGNETIC DATES* | | | |
|---|---|---|---|---|
| Provenience | Sample No. | 95% | 68% | alpha 95 |
| Room 216, Feature 2 | HV002 | 700-1450 | 700-1450 | 17.1 |
| Room 216, Feature 1 | HV003 | 1170-1450 | 1350-1450 | 11.1 |
| Room 212, Feature 1 | HV004 | 1300-1450 | 860-1020 | 9.6 |
| Room 211, Feature 2 | HV005 | 920-1450 | 1060-1450 | 6.4 |
| Area 221, Feature 1 | HV001 | Not Datable | Not Datable | 11.8 |

| | RADIOCARBON DATES | | | | |
|---|---|---|---|---|---|
| Provenience | Sample No. | Maize Corrected | Date | Calibrated 1 sd | probability | Calibrated 2 sd |
| Room 211, Feature 1 | Beta 12913 | 610 ± 85 | 1340 ± 85 | 1285-1333 / 1340-1397 | (0.46) / (0.54) | 1256-1442 mean = 1349 |
| Room 211, Feature 2 | Beta 12914 | 1160 ± 85 | 790 ± 85 | | | |
| Room 215, Feature 2 | Beta 12915 | 600 ± 75 | 1350 ± 75 | 1299-1334 / 1337-1373 / 1379-1405 | (0.36) / (0.38) / (0.26) | 1276-1436 mean = 1356 |
| Combined Beta 12913 and 12915 | | | | 1298-1333 / 1241-1374 / 1378-1397 | (0.40) / (0.38) / (0.21) | 1281-1416 mean = 1349 |

* (Archaeomagnetic Program, Arizona State Museum, University of Arizona)

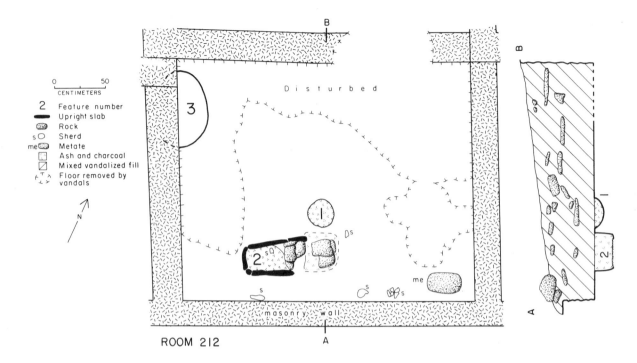

Figure 2.3. Room 212, floor plan and west soil profile.

## Room 212

Room 212 is attached to the south side of Room 211 and adjoins Room 217 to the west (Figs. 2.1, 2.3). The walls of this room incurred serious demolition over the years from pothunters and thus there was no physical evidence to indicate whether or not the room walls were plastered or contained doorways or windows. The mortar used to bond the building stone is a light reddish brown (5YR 6/4 dry). It is one of three rooms studied with a south wall that defined the outside or exterior wall of the pueblo. The south wall of Rooms 212 and 217 is continuous. Fortunately, the lower courses of the four walls that make up this room were intact and it was possible to outline and define the extent of the room.

Like the majority of rooms at Homol'ovi II, the integrity of room fill was compromised by years of vandalism. Approximately half of the floor in Room 212 had been destroyed. That portion of floor that remained was in poor condition but still contained evidence of being plastered at least twice. It also contained floor features, including an ash or firepit, a remodeled hearth, and a clay-lined pit (Fig. 2.3).

Feature 1 is a shallow circular pit containing fine ash located midway between the east and west walls and just north of a rectangular slab-lined hearth (Feature 2). The position of this shallow pit near the formal hearth and the abundance of fine ash in it suggest Feature 1 is an ash pit.

The rectangular slab-lined hearth (Feature 2) appears to have been remodeled. It is 25 cm away from the south wall and was originally centered between the east and west walls. The east end of the original hearth was abandoned and covered by floor, and the west end of the original hearth was incorporated into the new hearth that extends west. Slabs from the old bottom were left in place and a new stone slab was added to the bottom of the new extension. The upright sandstone slabs, which make the north, south, and west walls of the new hearth, were plastered. The remodeled hearth is 32 cm wide and 56 cm long. An additional 33 cm of old hearth bottom (covered by floor) extends east, making the overall length of this feature 89 cm. The original hearth and remodeled portion were filled with a mixture of ash, charcoal, corn kernels, cob fragments, beans, a variety of seeds, and a few fragments of rodent and larger mammal bone.

Feature 3 is a clay-lined pit that extends under the west wall. It was probably located immediately below the floor plaster of Room 212 prior to pothunting activity. The shallow basin was exposed by vandals and

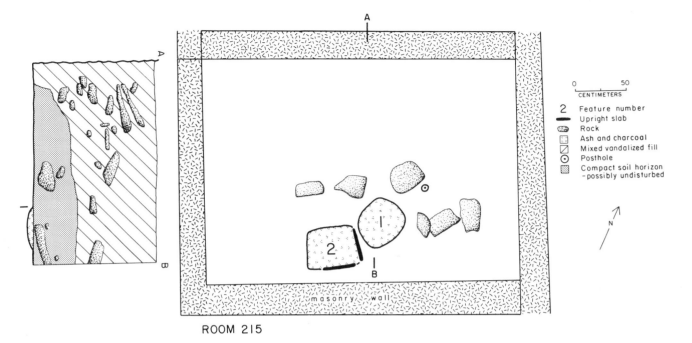

Figure 2.4. Room 215, floor plan and east soil profile.

at the time of our discovery had no contents. The clay lining appeared slightly fired, although there was a consensus among the crew that this feature represented a mixing pit for mortar and plaster used during room construction in the immediate area.

Five partially restorable vessels were in Room 212, and pieces from each vessel were found in both disturbed and undisturbed context (see Hays, Chapter 3). An undisturbed deposit along the south wall contained two partially restorable vessels in contact with the floor and wall. In addition, a metate was slightly above the floor in the southeast corner of the room. These artifacts appear to be in situ and were never disturbed by pothunting activity. Numerous pottery fragments were found toward the center of the room. Although they were on and within 20 cm of the intact floor, their context is questionable because of sporadic shoveling at this level by pothunters. The artifacts from this 20-cm level were called floor-fill and included Awatovi or Jeddito Black-on-yellow, black-on-white (Cibola and Tusayan White Ware of the Pueblo II time period), Tusayan Plain and Corrugated, Jeddito Plain and Corrugated, Homolovi Corrugated, Alameda Brown Ware, Chavez Pass Orange (undecorated), a wide variety of Winslow Orange Ware types, and Kinnikinick Brown. General disturbed room fill (excluding the 20 cm above

the intact floor) reflects a similar range of ceramics and also includes White Mountain Red Ware, Zuni types, Roosevelt Red Ware, and Tsegi Black-on-orange.

Because damage to this room extended over much of the floor, an interpretation of room function is difficult. The presence of a hearth with carbonized domestic and wild plant seeds and mammal bone suggests food was processed and prepared in this room. The whole metate, although slightly above the floor, is probably directly associated with food processing in this particular room.

An archaeomagnetic dating sample was taken from Feature 1 (sample HV004) and suggests this room was used during the 14th century. The hearth sample had a 95 percent confidence level and dated to A.D. 1300 through 1450.

### Room 215

Room 215 is slightly larger than the four other excavated rooms (Figs. 2.1, 2.4). It is rectangular, built with sandstone block, and bonded by a gray (2.5YR 5/4 dry) mortar. Gaps between blocks were well chinked. Although the upper walls were broken down by vandals, standing portions contain excellent examples of wall plaster. Two episodes of plastering are evident on a segment of the east wall. Here the earliest plaster coat is reddish brown to red (2.5YR 5/4 to 5/6 dry). The outside layer on the east wall and all other wall surfaces in this room are gray (5YR 5/1 to 6/1 dry). The sequence of plastering episodes in this room suggests that two different clay sources were used in the original construction. That is, clay from a gray source was used to bond the walls and a red clay was used to plaster the interior walls. Later the walls were replastered with gray clay. Although two clay sources should not be ruled out, it is also possible that the original wall plaster was gray as well but baked red by an unintentional fire in the room.

Some clay daub with reed impressions was recovered from this room but in disturbed context. Whether any of the daub is actually associated with the original superstructure of Room 215 is unknown. There are no obvious signs of a doorway into this room, but one may have been sealed and hidden by wall plaster. Vandalism to the center of the south wall is severe and may have removed evidence of an opening there. A "posthole" was found in the center of the floor toward the east wall and although its function (if any) is uncertain, it could have been the support for a single-pole ladder extending through a roof entrance.

Although the floor of Room 215 is generally compact and smooth, it is eroded in many places revealing at least two episodes of plastering. The last coat of floor plaster curved gently up the walls and appears continuous with the latest coat of wall plaster. A test pit through the floor on the west wall revealed a culturally sterile gray sand deposit. The sand is so fine that it appears wind blown, suggesting this part of the pueblo may rest on an old stabilized dune. The west wall extends 20 cm below the floor to act as a footing in this sand.

The original deposit in this room was extensively disturbed by pothunters but at least 20 cm of undisturbed cultural fill covered the floor. Therefore the artifacts on the floor were presumed to be in situ.

Feature 1 is a shallow basin in the floor 10 cm from the northeast corner of Feature 2, a rectangular hearth. Feature 1 is 7 cm deep and 49 cm in diameter. A large quantity of ash, charcoal, and artifacts was found in and around the basin. The interior clay lining of Feature 1 is not baked, nor is the surrounding floor, but there is sufficient evidence to suggest that this feature was used as a hearth immediately before abandonment of the room. More is said below about this feature and its associated artifacts.

Feature 2 is a rectangular hearth set in the floor near the center of the south wall. It is 58 cm long, between 35 cm and 39 cm wide, and 19 cm deep. The hearth is lined on the south and east by upright, scorched sandstone slabs. Slabs lining the north and west sides of the box have slumped inward. Three slabs form the bottom of the hearth.

When discovered, Feature 2 was covered with four thin sandstone fragments that helped preserve and protect numerous items. The hearth contained corn kernels, bone, partially charred piñon seeds, two varieties of squash, and other seeds (Miksicek, Chapter 8). In addition, the ash fill contained two sherds and a retouched piece of obsidian.

The rectangular hearth (Feature 2) was used until the ash reached the top of the feature and then, instead of being cleaned out for further use, it was covered with sandstone slabs. The shallow basin labeled Feature 1 in Figure 2.4 continued to be used after abandonment of the hearth, and the ash from the shallow basin began to overflow onto the floor, covering Feature 2 as well as a 1-meter diameter area of the floor. This lens of ash contained numerous sherd fragments from at least four vessels (Chapter 3).

In situ (apparently undisturbed) artifacts from the floor of Room 215 included sherds from at least four partially restorable bowls of polished yellow ware. One, a Paayu Polychrome bowl (type description in Chapter 3), has a katsina face depicted on its interior surface that Emory Sekaquaptewa (Department of Anthropology, University of Arizona) has identified as the Sun (Tàawa) katsina. The Sun Forehead Clan (Qalangyam) is one of the largest clans on Second and Third Mesas. Other sherds in floor contact included Jeddito and Awatovi Black-on-yellow, Jeddito Black-on-orange, Jeddito Corrugated, Homolovi Polychrome, Tusayan Corrugated, and Homolovi Corrugated. Disturbed room fill contained, in addition to the above ceramic types, one Cibola White Ware sherd.

A single radiocarbon sample (Beta 12915 Feature 2) from the rectangular hearth suggests this room was in use in A.D. 1350 ± 75 years (calibrated at 1276–1436 for two standard deviations). This date is consistent with the presence of both Jeddito and Awatovi Black-on-yellow in the ceramic assemblage (Chapter 3).

## Room 216

Room 216 is south of Room 215 and was obviously built after Room 215 was constructed. Both rooms share the same continuous east wall, which separates Room 215 from an unexcavated room to the east, and Room 216 from Room 211, which is also located to the east. The walls of this room were severely damaged by pothunting activity, but fortunately the majority of interior fill near the floor was intact. Beneath this layer was a hearth, a storage pit, and a number of artifacts presumably in their original floor contact positions (Figs. 2.1, 2.5).

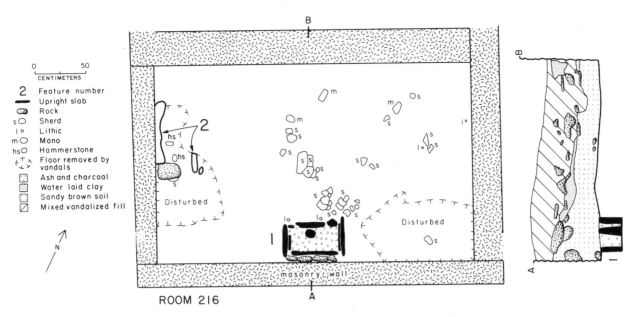

Figure 2.5. Room 216, floor plan and west soil profile.

The walls of Room 216 are a single-course wide with some minor double-course work. The north, east, and south walls were standing between 0.30 m and 1.25 m high. These standing segments are sufficiently high to indicate there were no entrances built into these walls. The west wall was too low to make any judgment as to possible entries. The walls of Room 216 were chinked and then plastered at least twice. The inner layer is light reddish brown (5YR 6/3 dry). The outer plaster is similar in color but the chroma was toward 5YR 6/4 when dry. The mortar that bonds these walls is similar to the light reddish brown (5YR 6/4 dry) outer wall plaster.

Lenses of water-deposited clay were found sporadically throughout the upper fill and they represent areas opened up by vandals. Mixed into these areas were tin fragments, wood lathing, and tinfoil. General fill in the southwest corner of Room 216 contained carbonized ears of corn and other floral remains fused together by intense heat. All of this material is out of its original context and comes from an outside area referred to as Activity Area 221. It was tossed into Room 216 by pot hunters. As excavation proceeded downward, the general fill gave way to a hard, blocky, light brown soil that contained fragments of burned reed and clay impressions of reed and other floral materials indicative of roof fall. Embedded into this deposit at different angles were sandstone slabs that were probably part of the superstructure. Vandals penetrated the roof fall in several places and went through the floor in the southeast corner of the room and near the west wall.

The floor of Room 216 had been plastered at least three times. Overlying the latest floor (between the roof fall and the top plaster) was a lens of fine sand and a thin layer of dry, cracked clay that probably blew into the room after it was abandoned. A rectangular hearth and the artifact assemblage on the floor were covered in part by this sand and clay. Once the hearth and floor assemblage were documented, the floor plaster was removed to expose two earlier floors. The second or middle floor contained a thin, ashy veneer with burned reed fragments, suggesting that the room was burned and later rebuilt. Although there is evidence of an earlier or original plaster floor, it was bonded to the floor above and could not be exposed.

Feature 1 is a slab-lined hearth centered and set in the floor against the south wall. It measures 62 cm long east to west, 25 cm wide, and is 21 cm deep. The sides and bottom are lined with sandstone slabs that are scorched to a dark gray. The gaps between these stone slabs were filled with clay. The hearth went through at least one episode of remodeling or repair when the north wall of the box was moved inward, making the hearth smaller.

The hearth interior contains a number of protruding stones that probably represent supports for cooking vessels. Upright sandstone slabs are placed inside the east and west walls of the fire box and a third upright stone stands in the center of the hearth (see Feature 1, Room 211 for a similar example). Four small cobbles are bound together by plaster between the south wall and the edge of the hearth to complete the vessel supports.

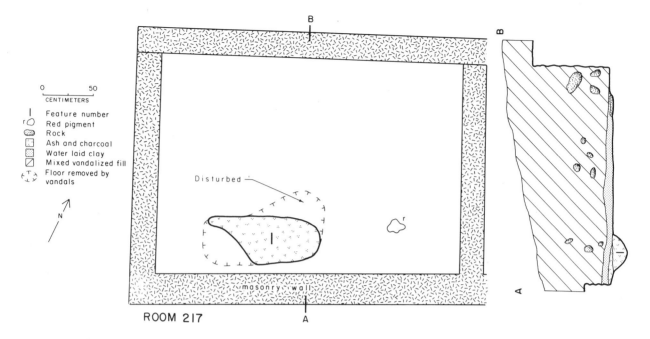

Figure 2.6. Room 217, floor plan and west soil profile.

Feature 2 is a shallow storage pit that had been exposed by vandals and refilled. Fragments of a gray clay plaster remain on its surface. The interior plaster of the pit extends up the west wall, indicating that it was a room feature and not an extramural feature created before Room 216 was added to the pueblo. Several artifacts, including two hammerstones, one sherd, and one bone fragment, were recovered from the pit. Their context is questionable because this feature is located at the very bottom of a pothunter pit. Feature 2 was probably built during the first or second plastering of the floor because a portion of the pit protruded under the latest floor plaster. Whether the pit was completely covered by the last plastering and exposed by vandals or whether a portion of the pit was in use during the last plastering could not be determined.

Floor contact artifacts in Room 216 consisted of two manos, an abrader, several lithics, and a number of sherds of Jeddito and Awatovi Black-on-yellow, Paayu Polychrome, Kinnikinick Plain, Jeddito Corrugated, and Homolovi Corrugated. Disturbed fill also contained small amounts of Tsegi Polychrome (one sherd), a variety of white wares, Jeddito and Homolovi Plain, Tusayan Corrugated, and one vitrified (unidentifiable) sherd.

Two archaeomagnetic samples came from Room 216. Sample HV002 was taken from Feature 2, and sample HV003 was removed from Feature 1. The statistical results were disappointing. The sample reading from

Feature 1 had a statistical confidence level of 95 percent; however, it placed the hearth at A.D. 1170–1450. At a 68 percent statistical level of confidence the data indicate that the hearth was last used somewhere in the vicinity of 1350 to 1450.

## Room 217

Room 217 is an exterior room that abuts the south side of Room 216 and shares a continuous south wall with Room 212, which is to the east. This room forms the west end of a three-room section that protrudes from the main south wall in this part of the pueblo (Figs. 2.1, 2.6). The walls of Room 217 have been seriously damaged by pothunting activity and there is little that can be said about them. They are a single-course wide with some minor double-course work included. The mortar bonding the sandstone block is in the pink range (5YR 7/4 dry). The interior walls today show little evidence of having been plastered, but this is likely a result of postoccupation deterioration.

The floor was plastered at least twice. The earlier layer is red and appears to have been burned. Charcoal fragments embedded in the upper margin of this floor support this notion. The later episode of plastering averages about 3 cm thick. This floor is largely intact, but shows scars from vandals' shovels. An aluminum can and one copper wire terminal were found in contact

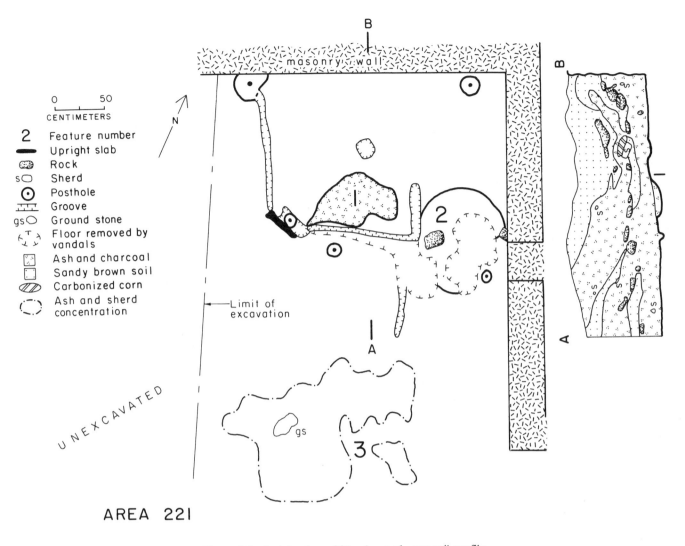

Figure 2.7. Activity Area 221, plan and west soil profile.

with the floor, which put most of the prehistoric artifacts on the floor in questionable context.

A vandalized firepit (Feature 1) is west of center along the south wall of Room 217. A part of this feature can be identified by a baked clay outline, but the degree of damage done to this feature by vandals renders it impossible to discern whether the hearth was a simple circular depression or a sandstone slab-lined rectangular box. The artifacts found inside Feature 1 were in questionable context and included several pieces of lithic debitage and sherds of indeterminate corrugated and Jeddito Yellow Ware. The floor around the feature is burned.

Although one piece of bone and two sherds were embedded slightly into the floor suggesting they were in situ, most of the floor assemblage was in questionable context, as indicated earlier. The floor contact pottery

included black-on-yellow (intermediate between Awatovi and Jeddito), unidentified white wares, Jeddito and Homolovi Corrugated, and Winslow Orange Ware. Fill contained, in addition, a variety of white wares, Jeddito Plain, Homolovi Plain, a variety of brown wares, and three unidentified plain polished gray sherds.

### Exterior Activity Area 221

Area 221 is west of and adjacent to Room 216. The Museum of Northern Arizona had designated this area as Room 221, but excavation showed it to be an extramural activity area with a number of interesting features (Figs. 2.1, 2.7).

Two kinds of structural evidence are present. Three floor grooves, averaging 3 cm in depth, may have supported a low wall or a deflector of wood or, more likely, of sandstone slabs. The grooves outline a squarish floor area adjacent to the south wall of unexcavated Room 222. Five postholes surround this enclosure. Two are associated with the west floor groove. The southernmost posthole contains sandstone slabs that may have aided in supporting a post. Two holes are near the west walls of Rooms 216 and 217, and a fifth is situated outside the center of the south floor groove. Some grooves contained fragments of rotten wood, probably remnants of posts supporting a ramada-like structure.

Two features are within the floor that was evidently sheltered by this ramada. Feature 1 is an irregular hearth located just inside the south floor groove. It measures approximately 90 cm east to west by 60 cm north to south and averages 5 cm deep.

Feature 2 is a large shallow circular pit whose eastern edge extends under the wall of Room 216, indicating an earlier construction date than that of Room 216. It was filled with reddish compact clay that had probably not been fired. The feature measures 1.25 m east to west by 1.00 m north to south. The depression probably served as a puddling pit for preparing mortar. Color of its contents is similar to the color of mortar in the north and east walls of the ramada area. Archaeomagnetic dating samples were taken from Feature 1 and Feature 2 but were undatable.

Immediately south of the ramada is Feature 3, an irregular-shaped concentration of potsherds lying in a thin bed of ash that measures 1.5 m north to south and 2 m east to west. Beneath the sherd concentration is a fire-blackened surface with four small circular pits. None of these pits appear to have been used as hearths, and their interiors are not prepared in any way. They range from 10 cm to 25 cm in diameter. Evidence of rodent disturbance is present and one pit contained an active rodent nest with grass and leaves.

Feature 3 contained a variety of pottery that included Jeddito and Awatovi Black-on-Yellow, Huckovi Black-on-orange, Jeddito Plain and Corrugated, Homolovi Plain and Corrugated, Chavez Pass Black-on-red, MacDonald Corrugated, Kwaituki Black-on-red, Kinnikinick Plain, Little Colorado White Ware, Homolovi Polychrome, and Bidahochi Polychrome. Many sherds were badly burned and remain unidentified.

Depth of fill overlying the surface of this activity area ranged from 1 m near the exterior of Room 222's south wall, to approximately 20 cm at points 5 m south of the roomblock. The fill was mixed by pothunters and rodent activity but was largely undisturbed. It contained quantities of carbonized corn kernels and cobs. Many were fused together; some retained their husks. Vitrified sherds, soil, and probably floor plaster fragments were abundant, as well as many fragments of roof daub displaying the impressions of reeds.

The concentration of potsherds in Feature 3 and the fill above it included eight partially reconstructible vessels. It is possible that this area was used for firing pottery, which would account for the blackened surface and the concentration of broken and sintered pottery here. But most of these reconstructible vessels show use wear, indicating that they were not broken in manufacture, but were dumped here after having been used. The fill above this feature and the pottery in it most probably is debris cleared from a burned storeroom and dumped here. It is possible, of course, that some activity involving burning, such as cooking or pottery firing, occurred on this surface before the dumping took place.

In summary, interpretation of this area is more complex than that of the rooms. There are at least three possible components. The clay puddling pits probably represent the first use of this area. Next, either the hearth or the ramada was constructed; possibly both were constructed at the same time. The hearth was never used intensively, because the soil around it is not well fired. At the same time, the area south of the ramada may have been used for firing pottery. Last, probably after the ramada was taken down, the whole area was covered with trash that consisted, for the most part, of fill cleaned out of one or more burned storerooms. Corncobs were broken rather than whole as they should be if they had burned in situ and remained undisturbed. Considerable burned roof daub showing impressions of reeds (*Phragmites communis*) was mixed with the corn as well as some unfired clay daub of similar form. The rooms that burned should be easy to locate with further excavation, because the fire was hot enough to fuse and severely vitrify sherds. It also would have baked floor and wall plaster. Although this scenario is favored, it is also possible that the corn was being stored either on top of or beneath the ramada when the ramada caught fire, and that the burned clay daub was from the roof of the ramada.

## CHRONOLOGY

The yellow ware pottery found in contact with the floors of the five rooms excavated has been tree-ring dated. Among the most common types in floor context were Awatovi Black-on-yellow, Jeddito Black-on-yellow, and Paayu Polychrome, an antecedent type to Sikyatki Polychrome. The frequencies of these types suggest the five rooms were occupied between A.D. 1300 to 1450 and probably more precisely from 1350 to 1375. A detailed description of Homol'ovi II pottery types and further discussions of chronology are in Chapter 3.

Although five archaeomagnetic samples and three radiocarbon samples were submitted for dating, the results for interpreting the occupation period of the rooms are less than satisfactory (Table 2.2). Three archaeomagnetic samples, HV001, HV002, and HV005 could not be interpreted because their plots against the archaeomagnetic curve were highly imprecise (Alpha 95 value greater than 10.0). Similarly, radiocarbon sample Beta 12914 must have been taken from old wood because it is not even close to the tree-ring based ceramic dates for the excavated area.

Archaeomagnetic sample HV003 from Room 216 (Feature 1) and sample HV004 from Room 212 (Feature 1) generally place the occupation of the five rooms as between A.D. 1300 and 1450 or later. The archaeomagnetic curve extends only to 1450 and samples extending beyond that date are assigned 1450 ending dates.

Charred specimens of maize from Room 211 (Feature 1) and from Room 215 (Feature 2) were submitted to Beta Analytic, Inc. for radiocarbon dating analysis. Due to the nature of the carbon-14 curve for this period, calibrated dates at a 68 percent confidence level are invariably split into two or even three groupings. The 95 percent confidence level gives a broader date range. By combining the broad range dates from Rooms 211 and 215 (Beta 12913 and Beta 12915), we get a date of 1281 to 1416. The radiocarbon dates correspond well with the ceramic date provided above and are suggested, or at least not disproved, by the archaeomagnetic dates. As a result, the correspondence of ceramic, radiocarbon, and archaeomagnetic dates supports the conclusion that the five excavated rooms probably date to the middle or late 14th century.

## SUMMARY

The five excavated rooms share similar architectural characteristics. A simple style of wall construction was used in this part of the pueblo. Here walls are primarily a single-course wide and are built with unmodified tabular sandstone rock in all shapes and sizes. Each layer of stone is mortared in place with adobe and heavily chinked to level each upward course. Although we cannot determine the original height of the walls, the amount of rubble suggests that this part of the pueblo was no more than one story high.

Four rooms have rectangular hearths with tabular stones lining their sides and bottoms. The fifth (Room 217) also contains evidence of a hearth but its characteristics could not be determined because of extensive damage from vandals. The hearths may have been used in a variety of food preparation activities. The hearths contained maize kernels, cob fragments, beans, squash, and a variety of seeds. The seeds included, but were not limited to, yucca, cotton, piñon, and ricegrass. A piki stone fragment was found in Room 211 near Feature 1,

suggesting that this particular hearth may have been used as a piki oven. In addition to the piki stone fragment, pieces of a scorched corrugated utility jar were found in and near this same hearth, suggesting this vessel also may have been used in food processing activities.

A clay-lined basin filled with ash is immediately northeast and adjacent to the rectangular hearth in Room 212. A similar feature is in the same position next to a hearth in Room 215. Feature 2 in Room 211 was filled with ash and is located southeast of the rectangular hearth along the north wall of that room. Although the term ash pit may be a misnomer, it was used to distinguish these three features from formal rectangular hearths. These shallow basins may have been filled with warm coals to preheat the bottoms of cooking vessels, or used to prepare foods in a manner similar to a rectangular hearth. The ash pits in Rooms 212 and 215 contained only fine ash, whereas the pit in Room 211 contained not only ash but an abundance of charred plant remains.

Miscellaneous floor features included a clay-lined storage pit in Room 216, which contained two hammerstones, bird bone, and an unworked piece of sandstone. A puddling pit was protruding under the west wall of Room 212. A larger puddling pit was in Activity Area 221 and was filled with reddish clay that appeared identical to mortar and plaster found on the walls and floors in the five excavated rooms. These puddling pits were probably associated with various building episodes in the immediate area; however, both seem to predate the excavated rooms.

Each room contained evidence of reconditioning work and repair activity but there is little evidence for major remodeling. The rectangular hearth in Room 212 was repositioned slightly west of center and the north wall of the hearth in Room 216 was obviously repaired. Based on room wall abutments it seems likely that Room 210 (unexcavated) and Room 211 shared a common west wall and therefore may have been built at the same time. A sealed doorway between these two rooms is the only evidence for true remodeling. Perhaps the most common type of reconditioning work was plastering walls and floors. Remnant coats of plaster were found on all interior walls except in Room 212. Based on the overall thickness of these patches, which was usually quit thin, replastering seems to have been an infrequent event, unlike Hopi rooms today where the ideal is to replaster walls annually. As with the walls, replastering of floors was also infrequent. No room has more than three layers of plaster on either floor or walls.

Wall corner bonding and abutment patterns were examined in an attempt to determine the building sequence of the five excavated rooms (see Fig. 2.1). Room 210 (unexcavated) and Room 211 shared a common west wall that was made stronger by bonding the south wall of Room 211 to it, creating a solid L-shape design. The south and north walls of Room 215 are abutted against Room 210, suggesting that perhaps it was added onto the pueblo after Rooms 210 and 211 were built. Assuming that construction of rooms continued in a grid block pattern, it is likely that Room 216 was built later than the previously mentioned rooms. It was formed by building a west wall that abuts Room 215, and a south wall that abuts both this new west wall and the south wall of Room 211. Rooms 212 and 217 followed later in the building sequence. Both of these rooms (and unexcavated Room 206) share a common south wall. Without knowing the entire wall abutment pattern of Room 206, however, it is difficult to determine whether Room 217 came before Room 212. In any event, since they share a common south wall they were probably built together in a short period of time.

The excavation of five contiguous rooms in a pueblo that contains hundreds of rooms certainly limits the range of interpretations one might make about the indigenous people, their use of the local environment, and their associations and dealings with their neighbors. Such interpretations must wait until a larger set of data can be gathered from the surrounding environment, from rooms and features throughout this pueblo, and from other nearby prehistoric pueblo communities. The five excavated rooms at Homol'ovi II, however, share similar architecture, artifacts, and floor features, and overall it seems that food processing and preparation were important room activities. For interpretive purposes one might categorize the five rooms as habitation

structures. Activities related to tool and craft production and those artifacts that might represent social or religious activities were not found, but certainly they exist elsewhere at Homol'ovi II.

One observation that should be mentioned and that may be important to later assessments of Homol'ovi II abandonment is the condition in which the rooms were left by their occupants. Each hearth contained abundant botanical remains and was completely filled with compact ash. In one instance, there was no attempt to clean out and reuse a rectangular hearth. Once it was filled, it was covered with small sandstone slabs and someone continued to build fires in the shallow ash pit adjacent to it. Ash from the fires eventually overflowed onto the sandstone slabs that covered the rectangular hearth. If people using these particular rooms had abandoned them in a hurry one might expect not only a larger household artifact assemblage but differentiation in the ash from one hearth to the next. It seems unlikely that the hearths would be cleaned out at the same time and then refilled at the same rate.

In conclusion, our objective at Homol'ovi II was twofold. The first goal was to determine the extent, distribution, and depth of undisturbed cultural deposits in rooms that appeared from all surface indications to have been totally destroyed by vandals. Pothunters had indeed contributed substantially to the degradation of walls and upper room fill; however, most rooms still contained large segments of intact floors, features, and in situ artifact assemblages. Our second aim was to expose a small block of contiguous rooms that would ultimately be incorporated into a proposed archaeological and cultural interpretation program for the Homolovi Ruins State Park.

# CHAPTER THREE

# Ceramics

Kelley Ann Hays
Arizona State Museum

As is typical of Pueblo IV period sites, Homol'ovi II has a high density of potsherds on its surface and in subsurface deposits, and the ceramic assemblage includes a high proportion of decorated wares. Yet this assemblage is unusual in that sherds presumed to have been imported to the region, particularly Jeddito Yellow Ware, vastly outnumber sherds of locally produced Winslow Orange Ware.

With the exception of some partial floor assemblages and part of Area 221, described in Chapter 2 and discussed below, the ceramics recovered at Homol'ovi II must be considered to come from deposits disturbed by vandalism. Nonetheless, the excavated sherds probably came from the same general area of the site. Even though room fill was subsequently mixed, general characterizations of the ceramic assemblage yield interesting information about the excavated roomblock and the site as a whole. Some partial floor assemblages appear to have been minimally disturbed, and they offer insights into chronology and room function. Surface sherds yield general information on the occupation span of the pueblo and on trade relationships with other regions. The large number of sherds examined here made it possible to refine the pottery typology for the Pueblo IV period in this area and to broaden the known ranges of variation for many wares. Comparisons with ceramics of the western mound at Awatovi (Smith 1971), a large Hopi village contemporaneous with Homol'ovi II, are useful in this regard. Some limited comparisons with the pottery of nearby Homol'ovi III (AZ J:14:14), a smaller and for the most part earlier site, provide information about change in local ceramic manufacturing and trade relationships.

## METHODS OF ANALYSIS

Sherds were sorted first by ware, then by type. Examination of temper, texture, and fracture of a fresh break with a 10x hand lens aided ware identifications. Descriptions follow Colton (1956) as much as possible, and are supplemented by the work of Smith (1971), Carlson (1970) and Kintigh (1985). Colton based many of his type descriptions on small samples, which do not describe a reasonable range of variation. I have expanded some of Colton's type descriptions, defined a new type in the Jeddito Yellow Ware, defined a new locally produced utility ware, and noted many variations.

This report does not debate the merits of the ware-type system. Ware and type names provide a common language for comparing Homol'ovi ceramics with those from other sites in the Southwest. Ware designations refer to characteristics of paste and manufacturing techniques, and they encompass both chronological and spatial information. The type names used here summarize information about colors of decoration and slips. These characteristics have chronological significance. Stylistic features such as design repertoire and line width have no relevance in discriminating types among the dominant decorated wares at Homol'ovi II. Therefore, classification by type in this assemblage is not as subjectively based as is the case in many other assemblages in which stylistic features are given great weight.

## DESCRIPTIONS OF WARES AND TYPES

The following descriptions summarize the dominant characteristics and ranges of variation in the Homol'ovi II ceramic assemblage. The term temper is used here to refer to any nonplastic inclusions in the paste that may or may not have been deliberately added. Sand and angular rock inclusions could have been naturally present in the clays used to make pottery. Sherd temper, on the other hand, would have been deliberately added.

### Decorated Wares

Jeddito Yellow Ware accounts for about 65 percent of sherds on the site's surface (Table 3.1) and about 90 percent of decorated sherds. These figures are intriguing because on many Anasazi sites the most predominant

**Table 3.1. Percentages of Ceramic Wares by Provenience**

| Wares | (No. of sherds) | Surface Collection | | | | | Excavation | |
|---|---|---|---|---|---|---|---|---|
| | | West Plaza (5036) | Central Plaza (2931) | East Plaza (2884) | Exterior Areas (7417) | All Surface (18,268) | All Rooms (2342) | All Excavations[1] (6592) |
| Jeddito Yellow | | 67.06 | 62.13 | 65.63 | 64.90 | 65.17 | 52.43 | 43.11 |
| Tsegi Orange | | 0.02 | | 0.14 | 0.09 | 0.10 | 0.51 | 0.44 |
| White Wares | | 0.71 | 1.71 | 2.46 | 1.16 | 1.33 | 1.07 | 1.46 |
| Winslow Orange | | 1.71 | 2.01 | 3.60 | 2.67 | 2.45 | 2.43 | 2.29 |
| Imports[2] | | 0.40 | 0.65 | 0.94 | 0.61 | 0.61 | 0.73 | 0.55 |
| Unknown decorated and polished | | 1.45 | 2.15 | 3.74 | 2.24 | 2.24 | 2.56 | 1.62 |
| Awatovi Yellow | | 7.90 | 7.37 | 4.99 | 4.92 | 6.15 | 14.73 | 9.31 |
| Homolovi Orange | | 2.70 | 2.56 | 2.57 | 1.63 | 2.22 | 8.41 | 7.68 |
| Gray Wares | | 1.93 | 2.80 | 2.43 | 1.40 | 1.93 | 3.37 | 4.60 |
| Brown Wares | | 1.13 | 4.50 | 1.11 | 1.36 | 1.62 | 1.75 | 2.68 |
| Unknown Utility | | 14.85 | 14.09 | 12.24 | 18.93 | 15.97 | 11.96 | 24.70 |
| Tooled | | | 0.03 | 0.14 | 0.03 | 0.02 | | |
| Vitrified | | | | | | 0.05 | 0.04 | 1.56 |

1. All excavations = all rooms + Activity Area 221.
2. Includes White Mountain Red Ware, Zuni pottery types, and Roosevelt Red Ware (Salado).

pottery types are locally made. For reasons detailed below, Jeddito Yellow Ware is presumed to have been manufactured on the Hopi Mesas, 80 km (50 miles) north of Homol'ovi. The remainder of the decorated sherds from the surface of Homol'ovi II consists of locally manufactured Winslow Orange Ware (about 3.4% of decorated sherds on the surface), a wide variety of imported pottery (Zuni, Salado, Tsegi Orange Ware, and White Mountain Red Ware, less than 1% each), a variety of white wares dating from the Pueblo I through the early Pueblo IV periods (1.85%), and a range of unidentified sherds that may be locally made or imported (3.12%).

## Jeddito Yellow Ware

Jeddito Yellow Ware was almost certainly made on the Hopi Mesas. Neutron-activation results on five black-on-yellow sherds from Homol'ovi II match these sherds with clay sources at Awatovi on Antelope Mesa (Bishop and others 1988). Dilatometer tests to determine firing temperature show that black-on-yellow sherds from Homol'ovi II must have been coal-fired (Block 1985), also suggesting manufacture on the Hopi Mesas where the nearest coal deposits to Homol'ovi are found. Smith (1971), Hack (1942b), and Sullivan (1988), describe extensive ceramic manufacturing areas near prehistoric coal mines on Antelope Mesa.

Most of the Jeddito Yellow Ware from Homol'ovi II conforms to Colton's 1956 description (Ware 7B). All types are well fired, well polished, and have fine paste, strong walls, and a clean, shattering fracture. Colton states that temper is "rarely quartz sand; usually not visible without a glass; occasional reddish angular fragments." Smith (1971) notes that the earlier Jeddito Yellow Ware type, Awatovi Black-on-yellow, contains fine sherd temper as well as sand, and the later Jeddito Black-on-yellow type contains very sparse fine sand that is not visible, or barely visible, even with a 10x lens. All types contain red ferruginous particles, possibly a natural component of the clay (Smith 1971: 479). Sherd fragments were not identified in the paste of Homol'ovi pottery using a handlens, but may be present. Decorated sherds have brown to black iron-manganese paint (Smith 1971: 478).

Smith states that at Awatovi, Jeddito Yellow Ware bowls and ladles were much more common than jars. Examination of the Field Museum of Natural History collections of whole vessels from Homol'ovi I and II results in the same conclusion, and the same range of vessel shapes. The most common bowl shape is an oblate hemisphere, with an incurved rim, and the maximum diameter occurs 2 cm to 3 cm below the rim (see Fig. 3.11a, b). Bowls tend to be just over twice as wide as they are deep (Smith 1971: 480). Most have decoration on the exterior as well as the interior. Exterior designs tend to be isolated geometric figures.

**Table 3.2.  Classification Sequence of Jeddito Yellow Ware**

| Colors of decoration | More temper ⟶ Less temper<br>Early 1300s* | Mid to late 1300s | 1400s |
|---|---|---|---|
| Black only | Awatovi-black-on-yellow | Awatovi and Jeddito black-on-yellow | Jeddito black-on-yellow |
| Black with white outline | Bidahochi Polychrome | Bidahochi Polychrome | (no longer occurs) |
| Watery black and solid black | (does not occur) | Paayu Polychrome | (no longer occurs?) |
| Black with red outline | (does not occur) | Sikyatki Polychrome | (no longer occurs) |
| Black with massed red | (does not occur) | ? | Sikyatki Polychrome |
| Black with massed red and engraved | (does not occur) | (does not occur) | Awatovi Polychrome |
| Black with massed red and massed white | (does not occur) | (does not occur) | Kawaika-a Polychrome (very late) |
| Black engraved | (does not occur) | ? | Jeddito Engraved |
| Black spattered and stippled | (does not occur) | ? | Jeddito Stippled |

*A general temporal ordering is based on the observation that temper generally becomes less abundant through time in large samples of sherds, but any amount could occur at any time. The "periods" shown refer to which configuration of attributes (types) one should expect to co-occur, and dates are a general guideline. Question marks refer to possible but undocumented overlap between time periods.

**Table 3.3.  Distinctive Paste and Decoration Features of Jeddito Yellow Ware Variants**

| Decoration features | Paste and surface features | | |
|---|---|---|---|
| | Orange paste<br>No slip<br>With or without sand temper | Yellow paste<br>Orange (red) slip<br>Sand temper (abundant) | Yellow paste<br>Orange (red) slip<br>No temper (fine) |
| No decoration | Huckovi Orange | Kwaituki Orange | Kokop Orange |
| Black design | Huckovi Black-on-orange | Kwaituki Black-on-orange | Kokop Black-on-orange |
| Black with white outline | Huckovi Polychrome | Kwaituki Polychrome | Kokop Polychrome |

*Note*: Because of the small sample size and the wide variability within it, it was not possible to determine whether the Kwaituki types belong in Jeddito Yellow Ware or in Winslow Orange Ware.

The most common Awatovi Black-on-yellow jar shape is "approximately globular, markedly oblate" (Smith 1971: 505). The height of jars tends to be half or two-thirds the width (see shape of Fig. 3.1a). Seed jars and jars with flattish shoulder and wide, short neck also appeared at Awatovi and in the Field Museum collections from Homol'ovi. Awatovi Black-on-yellow jars are more squat than the earlier globular Jeddito Black-on-orange jars, but the later Jeddito Black-on-yellow jars are yet more squat and often have a high, sharply curving shoulder. Both Awatovi and Jeddito Black-on-yellow jars have designs bounded above and below by broad framing lines with a "ceremonial break."

Most types in Jeddito Yellow Ware are named on the basis of paste color and paint colors. All types are characterized by a fine, hard paste, sharp fracture, and little or no temper. Two kinds of clay are used, resulting in two different colors. Most commonly used was a gray clay that fires yellow in an oxidizing atmosphere. This series includes many types defined on the basis of colors of decoration and presence or absence of slip. Less common is orange-firing pottery made from a yellow clay, designated the Huckovi series. Nomenclature and distinctive features of the Jeddito Yellow Ware types are presented in Tables 3.2 and 3.3. Their temporal spans are listed in Table 3.4. Only types that are useful for temporal resolution of the Homol'ovi occupation are discussed in detail here.

About 70 percent of the excavated Jeddito Yellow Ware at Homol'ovi II is yellow with black or brown

**Table 3.4. Chronological Relationships of Homol'ovi II Ceramics: Jeddito Yellow Ware**

| Date A.D. | Awatovi Black-on-yellow | Jeddito Black-on-yellow | Early Sikyatki Polychrome | Late Sikyatki Polychrome | Bidahochi Polychrome | Huckovi types |
|---|---|---|---|---|---|---|
| 1500 | | * | | * | | |
| | | * | | * | | |
| 1475 | | * | | * | | |
| | | * | | * | | |
| 1450 | | * | | * | | |
| | | * | | * | | |
| 1425 | | * | \| | * | | |
| | | * | \| | * | | |
| 1400 | | * | * | * | | |
| | | * | * | \| | \| | \| |
| 1375 | \| | * | * | | \| | \| |
| | \| | * | * | | * | \| |
| 1350 | * | \| | \| | | * | * |
| | * | \| | \| | | * | * |
| 1325 | * | \| | \| | | * | * |
| | * | | | | * | * |
| 1300 | * | | | | \| | * |
| | | | | | \| | |
| 1275 | | | | | | \| |

* = best dates; | = possible extent.

*Note.* Huckovi Orange series: in the Western Mound at Awatovi, Huckovi Black-on-orange was concentrated in the same levels as Awatovi Black-on-yellow and early Jeddito Black-on-yellow. Huckovi may have originated somewhat earlier than Awatovi Black-on-yellow (Smith 1971: 539).

decoration, and 25 percent is from undecorated vessels or undecorated portions of vessels. The remaining 5 percent includes a variety of polychrome types, and proportions of types in the surface assemblage are similar (Table 3.5). Most sherds have some visible quartz sand and many have red angular fragments also. These sherds conform most strongly to Smith's (1971) definition of Awatovi Black-on-yellow. Awatovi Black-on-yellow tends to be a strong or darker yellow (Munsell range 7.5YR to 10YR, "yellow, reddish yellow, very pale brown"), have visible temper, and geometric designs. Paint may bleed at the edges. In contrast, the chronologically later Jeddito Black-on-yellow tends to be light yellow (10YR to 2.5Y), have no visible temper or only occasional inclusions, and a freer treatment of design, including looser, less precise brushwork, and

depiction of life forms. These two types represent the two ends of a continuum, and all phases of this continuum appear in the Homol'ovi assemblage. Due to the extensive disturbance and possible mixing of trash deposits from different time periods, it was determined that sorting the relative amounts of Awatovi and Jeddito Black-on-yellow in the sherds recovered would yield little useful information and would be extremely time-consuming. Hence, only partially reconstructible vessels were classified to this level. Bichrome sherds in this ware are typed as Awatovi or Jeddito Black-on-yellow.

Sikyatki Polychrome (Colton's Type 9) has yellow paste with black (or brown) and red (or orange) painted decoration. Colton distinguishes an early style, in which designs are geometric, and the red paint is used to outline black solid areas (Fig. 3.1a). The later style employs more "life forms and free treatment," and red is used in solid areas outlined by black (Fig. 3.1b). Most sherds of Sikyatki Polychrome in this assemblage were small and not distinctive, but both red outlining and solid areas of red occur. Whole Sikyatki Polychrome vessels excavated at Homol'ovi I and II by Fewkes (U.S. National Museum) and Wattron (McCormick Collection, Field Museum of Natural History) include both styles. But the design repertoire of these vessels is more limited and geometric than the free, flamboyant decoration of vessels from the Sikyatki site itself and from late 15th- and 16th-century deposits at Awatovi (Fig. 3.1c). In short, although Sikyatki Polychrome as a type dates to a long period of about A.D. 1375 to 1629, there is stylistic change over time. The Homol'ovi examples appear to date from 1375 to no later than 1450 based on these stylistic criteria.

The Homol'ovi assemblage corroborates Colton's and Smith's conclusion that Bidahochi Polychrome predates Sikyatki Polychrome. Bidahochi Polychrome, which has solid black designs with white outlining, is more abundant than Sikyatki in the East Plaza, presumed on the basis of surface ceramics collected by Weaver and others (1982) to be the earlier part of the site. In the excavated area, Bidahochi Polychrome appears only in Area 221, which seems to have been used as a trash area for the disposal of the contents of a burned room. Sikyatki Polychrome is rare in this deposit. This disposal evidently took place before the abandonment of the adjoining roomblock. Sikyatki Polychrome appeared in the fill of some excavated rooms, and Bidahochi is absent in room fill except in the heavily disturbed fill of Room 211 (see Table 3.5).

Kawaika-a Polychrome (Type 11, spelled Kawaioku in Colton 1956), is a post-1450 yellow ware that uses white paint in massed areas in addition to black, and sometimes red. Only two yellow ware sherds with all three paint colors were found at Homol'ovi II. They

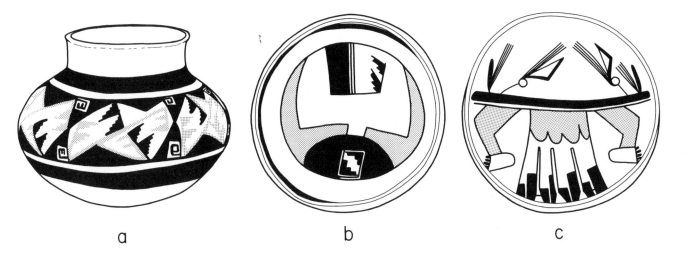

Figure 3.1. Sylistic sequence of Sikyatki Polychrome: *a*, Early Sikyatki Polychrome, late 1300s, geometric designs with thin red outlines; *b*, Middle style, late 1300s through early 1400s; *c*, Late style, mid to late 1400s through about 1629. Stippling represents reddish orange paint. (Provenience and vessel diameters in Appendix B.)

**Table 3.5.  Percentages of Jeddito Yellow Ware Types**

| | | IN EXCAVATED AREAS | | | | | | | |
| | | Room | | | | | All Rooms | Area 221 | All Excavated |
| Type | (Number of sherds) | 211 (278) | 212 (207) | 215 (217) | 216 (293) | 217 (233) | (1228) | (1614) | (2842) |
|---|---|---|---|---|---|---|---|---|---|
| Plain polished | | 25.90 | 25.00 | 11.98 | 26.96 | 23.18 | 23.05 | 26.27 | 24.88 |
| Black-on-yellow | | 66.91 | 75.00 | 80.64 | 69.28 | 72.96 | 72.39 | 69.33 | 70.65 |
| Paayu Polychrome | | 1.44 | | 6.91 | 2.39 | 1.72 | 2.44 | | 1.06 |
| Sikyatki Polychrome | | 1.44 | | 0.46 | 0.34 | 0.43 | 0.57 | 0.25 | 0.39 |
| Bidahochi Polychrome | | 2.16 | | | | | 0.49 | 2.91 | 1.86 |
| Huckovi types | | 0.72 | | | 1.02 | 0.43 | 0.49 | 1.12 | 0.84 |
| Kwaituki types | | | | | | 1.29 | 0.24 | 0.12 | 0.18 |
| Jeddito Engraved | | 1.44 | | | | | 0.33 | | 0.14 |

| | IN SURFACE PROVENIENCES | | | | |
| | West Plaza (3377) | Central Plaza (1821) | East Plaza (1893) | Exterior areas (4814) | All Surface (11,905) |
|---|---|---|---|---|---|
| Plain polished yellow | 44.24 | 35.37 | 36.66 | 36.46 | 38.52 |
| Black-on-yellow | 54.27 | 62.22 | 60.01 | 60.74 | 59.02 |
| Sikyatki Polychrome | 0.56 | 0.77 | 0.69 | 0.54 | 0.60 |
| Bidahochi Polychrome | 0.24 | 0.44 | 0.85 | 0.23 | 0.36 |
| Huckovi types | 0.62 | 0.93 | 1.69 | 1.82 | 1.33 |
| Kwaituki types | 0.06 | 0.05 | 0.05 | | 0.03 |
| Jeddito Engraved | | 0.16 | | 0.02 | 0.03 |
| Jeddito Stippled | | 0.05 | 0.05 | 0.12 | 0.07 |
| Kawaika-a? (3 colors) | | | 0.05 | 0.02 | 0.02 |
| Antelope Black-on-straw? | | | | 0.04 | 0.02 |

have black and red in massed areas, but white is used only as outlining. Therefore, they do not conform to Colton's description of sherds dating to the post-1450 period and do not serve as evidence for dating the site. These sherds, tabulated as unknown decorated, are most aptly described as a hybrid of Bidahochi and Sikyatki polychromes. Absence of true Kawaika-a Polychrome supports an abandonment date before 1450.

### Paayu Polychrome
### (New type)

Paayu Polychrome is a new type in Jeddito Yellow Ware. It is distinguished from Jeddito Black-on-yellow in that paint density is manipulated to produce the illusion of two different colors. Similar to watercolor technique, one color is watery and the other dense, but they are produced with the same pigment. Dark brown is used for outlining and for some solid areas. The other solid areas are filled with a watery light brown, through which the yellow paste is visible. Sometimes brushstrokes are clearly visible, sometimes there is a mottled effect due to pooling of watery paint before drying. In certain lighting conditions, this light brown appears somewhat orange. Stylistically, Paayu Polychrome seemingly fits at the beginning of Colton's "free-treatment" design style, but precedes the late-style Sikyatki Polychrome. It probably appears at about the same time as other variants such as Jeddito Engraved, which has fine lines engraved through the black paint, and Jeddito Stippled, on which paint is spattered and scumbled. The appearance of these new decorative techniques in the mid-1300s is one manifestation of a broadening of the potters' stylistic repertoire.

Paayu is the Hopi word for the Little Colorado River. This term was chosen to reflect the type's Hopi origins, but also, as required by Colton's rules for naming new types, to refer to the area in which the type is first recognized and defined. With considerable trepidation, I follow also Colton's rule of defining a new type, rather than a variety, for this distinctive decorative technique. Two partially reconstructible Paayu Polychrome bowls, but no reconstructible Sikyatki Polychrome vessels, were recovered in the 1984 excavation of Homol'ovi II (see Figs. 3.5c, 3.6b).

### Antelope Series

Antelope Black-on-straw and Antelope Polychrome are types defined by Smith (1971) in the Awatovi assemblage. They have buff to pink paste, multicolored sand temper, and a crumbling fracture. Smith noted their similarity to types in Colton's description of Winslow Orange Ware, but decided they were distinct on the basis of color. Investigations at Homol'ovi have shown that pink, buff, and yellow are common colors for Tuwiuca Black-on-orange and Homolovi Polychrome. It seems likely that at least some of Smith's Antelope series sherds from Awatovi are the same as some sherds we call Winslow Orange Ware at Homol'ovi. Until a hands-on comparison of Awatovi and Homol'ovi sherds is made, judgement must be reserved. A few of the Homol'ovi II surface sherds were typed as Antelope Black-on-straw. These had a lighter color and sharper fracture than is normal in Winslow Orange Ware, but a coarser paste and more crumbling fracture than is usual for Jeddito Yellow Ware.

### Tsegi Orange Ware

Tsegi Orange Ware (Colton Ware 5B) comes from a wide area north of Homol'ovi and is associated with the Kayenta Anasazi from A.D. 1050 to 1300. The Tsegi series has a dull orange surface color and often has a gray core. Temper includes quartz sand and light-colored angular fragments of crushed sherds. It often has mineral paint. Several small sherds of untyped polychromes and black-on-orange of this series were recovered on the surface of Homol'ovi II.

By far the majority of Tsegi Orange Ware sherds from Homol'ovi are of the Jeddito Orange series (types 14 and 15). Jeddito Orange, Black-on-orange, Polychrome, and Jeddito Black-on-orange Slipped Variety were presumed by Colton (1956) to have been made on the Hopi Mesas from about A.D. 1275 to 1400. Smith (1971) refined dates for these types to 1250–1350. The best tree-ring dates for traded Jeddito Black-on-orange are 1276 to 1320 (Breternitz 1966: 78). Temper of Jeddito Orange types consists of varying proportions of sand and light-colored angular fragments of crushed sherds. Jeddito Orange types lack a carbon streak and have well-polished surfaces. The fracture is usually sharper than the Tsegi series, and in hardness and finish the Jeddito Orange series more closely resembles Jeddito Yellow Ware and Bidahochi Black-on-white, also made on the Hopi Mesas. Smith (1971: 592) suggests these types are all coal-fired based on the fact that sherds and wasters of this type are found in pottery firing areas near prehistoric coal mines on Antelope Mesa. Jeddito Black-on-orange differs from Huckovi Black-on-orange in having at least some sherd temper.

Sherds of the Jeddito Orange Series at Homol'ovi II were rare, small, and virtually all bichrome. These types are more common at Homol'ovi III, and very common at Homol'ovi IV, both smaller sites dating to the late 1200s. Percentages of decorated pottery at the site are shown in Tables 3.6 and 3.7.

## White Wares

White wares from all periods, Basketmaker III to Pueblo III, were recovered in the surface collection of Homol'ovi II. They include Tusayan White Ware (organic paint, sand temper), Cibola White Ware (mineral paint, sherd and sand temper), Little Colorado White Ware (organic paint, sherd temper), and some sherds with mixtures of these attributes. All rooms contained at least some white ware sherds in the fill, and the fill of Area 221 contained many sherds from all three white wares. Little Colorado types were especially common in this area, and Pueblo II design styles predominated. Several white and black-on-white sherds with a fine paste similar to Jeddito Yellow Ware were also recovered from surface and excavations. These conform well to Smith's (1971) description of Bidahochi Black-on-white, which he found to be contemporaneous with Awatovi Black-on-yellow.

Except for Bidahochi Black-on-white, none of the white wares date to the major occupation of the pueblo, and the types present are common at surrounding sites dating to Basketmaker III through Pueblo III times. There are probably earlier components having white wares underneath the Pueblo IV occupation.

Table 3.6. Percentages of Decorated Pottery by Level

| Pottery | (Number of sherds) | Floor Contact[1] (390) | Total Excavated[2] (3261) | Surface[3] (13,135) |
|---|---|---|---|---|
| Jeddito Yellow Ware | | 84.62 | 87.15 | 90.63 |
| Tsegi Orange Ware | | 0.77 | 0.89 | 0.14 |
| White Wares | | 1.79 | 2.94 | 1.85 |
| Winslow Orange Ware | | 6.41 | 4.63 | 3.40 |
| White Mountain Red Ware | | 0.77 | 0.61 | 0.21 |
| Zuni pottery types | | | 0.15 | 0.32 |
| Roosevelt (Salado) | | | 0.33 | 0.31 |
| Unknown decorated | | 3.33 | 1.26 | 0.84 |
| Unknown plain polished | | 2.31 | 2.02 | 2.28 |

1. Includes Area 221 floor contact and ash layer contact.
2. Includes floor, floor fill, and fill.
3. Numbered surface units.

Table 3.7. Percentages of Decorated Pottery in Excavated Areas and on Each Floor

### IN EXCAVATED AREAS

| Pottery | (Number of sherds) | Room 211 (310) | 212 (244) | 215 (259) | 216 (318) | 217 (268) | All Rooms (1399) | Area 221 (1862) | All Excavated (3261) |
|---|---|---|---|---|---|---|---|---|---|
| Jeddito Yellow Ware | | 89.97 | 84.84 | 83.78 | 92.14 | 86.94 | 87.78 | 86.68 | 87.15 |
| Winslow Orange Ware | | 4.84 | 6.15 | 4.25 | 2.52 | 2.99 | 4.07 | 5.05 | 4.63 |
| Tsegi Orange Ware | | | 0.82 | 3.09 | 0.31 | 0.37 | 0.86 | 0.91 | 0.89 |
| White wares | | 1.29 | 3.69 | 0.39 | 1.57 | 2.24 | 1.79 | 3.81 | 2.94 |
| White Mountain Red Ware | | 0.97 | 2.05 | | | 0.37 | 0.64 | 0.59 | 0.61 |
| Zuni types | | 0.32 | 0.41 | | | 0.37 | 0.21 | 0.11 | 0.15 |
| Salado | | 0.32 | 0.41 | | | 1.12 | 0.35 | 0.32 | 0.34 |
| Unknown decorated | | 1.29 | 0.41 | 6.56 | 1.26 | 2.99 | 2.43 | 0.38 | 1.26 |
| Unknown plain polished | | 1.29 | 1.23 | 1.93 | 2.20 | 2.61 | 1.86 | 2.15 | 2.02 |

### ON FLOORS

| Pottery | Room 211 (9) | 212 (23) | 215 (113) | 216 (16) | 217 (9) | All Rooms (170) | Area 221[a] (3) | Area 221[b] (217) | All Floors (390) |
|---|---|---|---|---|---|---|---|---|---|
| Jeddito Yellow | 44.44 | 100.00 | 84.07 | 100.00 | 55.56 | 84.12 | 100.00 | 84.79 | 84.62 |
| Winslow Orange | 11.11 | | 5.31 | 100.00 | 11.11 | 4.71 | | 7.83 | 6.41 |
| Tsegi Orange | | | 2.65 | | | 1.76 | | | 0.77 |
| White wares | | | | | 22.22 | 1.17 | | 2.40 | 1.79 |
| White Mountain Red | 33.33 | | | | | 1.76 | | | 0.77 |
| Unknown decorated | 11.11 | | 6.19 | | 11.11 | 5.29 | | 1.84 | 3.33 |
| Unknown plain polished | | | 1.77 | | | 1.17 | | 3.22 | 2.31 |

a. Floor contact.   b. Ash layer contact.

**Table 3.8.  Diagnostic Features of Winslow Orange Ware**

| Decoration features | Paste and surface features | | |
| --- | --- | --- | --- |
| | Orange (tan, pink, grayish yellow)<br>No slip | Orange (tan, pink, grayish yellow)<br>Slip | Red<br><br>No slip |
| No decoration | Tuwiuca Orange | Chavez Pass Red | Black Axe Red |
| Black paint | Tuwiuca Black-on-orange | Chavez Pass Black-on-red | Homol'ovi Black-on-red |
| Black and white paint | Homolovi Polychrome | Chavez Pass Polychrome | Black Axe Polychrome |

## Winslow Orange Ware

Winslow Orange Ware is the most common decorated ceramic ware at the site of Homol'ovi III, and the second most common at Homol'ovi II. In the Homol'ovi II assemblage, it makes up almost 5 percent of decorated ware in the excavated portion of the site and only about 3.4 percent of decorated ware on the surface (Table 3.6).

Winslow Orange Ware is characterized by coiled construction, a relatively soft, crumbling paste with abundant temper, and a wide range of colors. Type names are based on colors of decoration and presence or absence of slip (Table 3.8).

Winslow Orange Ware displays a remarkable range of color, probably due to a variety of clay sources and a poorly controlled firing process. Based on a sample of about 100 Tuwiuca Black-on-orange and Homolovi Polychrome sherds from the late occupation of Homol'ovi III in the mid-A.D. 1300s, Munsell color values have the following range: 2.5YR 5/4–6/8 and 5YR 5/2–8/6, with some specimens of 7.5YR 6/2–8/2 and 10YR 5/1–8/3. Most sherds are Munsell colors pink, reddish yellow, light red, or light reddish brown. Brick-red sherds, those with a Munsell hue of 10R, are placed in Colton's (1956) Black Axe series, a designation of unknown temporal and spatial value. Black Axe sherds are very rare at Homol'ovi.

Many examples of Winslow Orange Ware have a gray, gray-brown, or greenish gray color. The relationship between incomplete oxidation and low chroma values is discussed by Rice (1987: 343–345). Many vessels are only partially oxidized, and most have extensive fire clouding. Frequent misfiring may be due to the use of unsuitable fuel such as cottonwood and driftwood; high quality fuel was scarce in the Homol'ovi area. A few vessels are reduced, resulting in a type that might best be described as a white ware. In the sample from Homol'ovi III, 15 percent of bichrome and 30 percent of polychrome sherds were misfired, colored gray, white, very pale brown, light brownish gray, and pinkish gray.

The Winslow Orange Ware sherds from Homol'ovi II resemble those from Homol'ovi III in every way, although no indepth analysis of them was made.

Winslow Orange Ware is presumed to have been locally manufactured in the Homol'ovi area, because this is its area of greatest abundance and because we have been able to replicate it using local materials. Results of experiments by Robert Vaitkus (1986) in the University of Arizona's Laboratory of Traditional Technology suggest that local Homol'ovi primary clays were used with the addition of about 40 percent temper. Examination of thin sections of Winslow Orange Ware sherds from Homol'ovi III by geologist Steven Williams confirms that temper content is about 40 percent. Temper materials from various local sources were used, primarily water- and wind-deposited sands and crushed sherds. All thin-sectioned sherds contained sherd temper, varying in quantity from predominant to very sparse. A major source of temper was angular sand from colluvial deposits in the Shinarump member of the Chinle Formation. Quartz is the primary mineral in this sand, with lesser amounts of a wide variety of minerals. Most Winslow sherds contain feldspar, chert, and microcline. Some also contain chalcedony, augite, basalt, olivine, pyroxene, carbonate, and mica. The source of the red angular fragments that are so common in Winslow Orange Ware has not yet been located in samples of local sand and clay, but does appear to be some sort of local mudstone that may be part of the original clay matrix (according to Steven Williams). Rounded and angular fragments occur, often together in the same example.

The exterior surface of jars and both surfaces of bowls are smooth and polished, but rarely shiny. They have a slightly gritty feel and often show minute crazing.

The addition of a thin, often watery red or orange slip defines the Chavez Pass series. Although Colton named the Chavez Pass series of Winslow Orange Ware for Chavez Pass (Nuvakwewtaqa Pueblo), these types were almost certainly made at Homol'ovi and traded to

Chavez Pass, where the local ceramics are primarily Alameda Brown Ware.

Paint is usually dark brown, thinly applied, and flat. It appears to be a mixture of mineral and organic components. White paint used for outlining is quite variable, but often thick and somewhat fugitive.

Decorative style combines features of Jeddito Black-on-orange and Awatovi Black-on-yellow with features of Pinedale and Fourmile polychromes. Judging by examples from Homol'ovi II and III and whole vessels in museum collections, as well as Homol'ovi sherds, the most common design elements on Winslow Orange Ware vessels are thick black lines sectioning the design field, separated by undecorated spaces from areas bounded by thin lines and filled with hatchure and corbelling (Fig. 3.2). Also common are triangles, serrate lines, interlocking keys, interlocking hatched and solid spirals, terrace and half-terrace shapes. Less common are life forms; flagged triangles; "mosquito bar" or trellis combinations of hatching, dots and corbelling; ticking; dotted lines; and dot filled areas.

Vessel forms are predominantly bowls, jars, and ladles. Bowls almost always share the same round-sided, inverted rim shape found in Jeddito Yellow Ware and Fourmile Polychrome bowls. Jars are usually somewhat squat and may have a high shoulder or a rounded sidewall. Globular jars also occur. Ladles vary, but the range of shapes resembles that found in Jeddito Yellow Ware (Smith 1971). Solid or hollow cylindrical handles

predominate and are attached to a round cup. Modeled animal forms appear occasionally as handles. Several examples of bird-shaped vessels were recovered at Homol'ovi III.

Chronological relationships among types of Winslow Orange Ware can be ordered as an increasing preference for polychrome designs across time and a decrease in the use of slip. The Chavez Pass types are much more common in the early component of Homol'ovi III (late 1200s), are less abundant in the late component (mid-1300s), and very rare at Homol'ovi II (mid to late 1300s; Table 3.9). The most abundant types in all these components are unslipped Tuwiuca Orange, Tuwiuca Black-on-orange, and Homolovi Polychrome. Homolovi Polychrome is more abundant in the late component of Homol'ovi III than in the early trash levels.

Breternitz (1966: 78) notes that Colton's dates of A.D. 1300-1400 for Homolovi Polychrome could not be improved by the scarce tree-ring evidence then available. Now excavations at the Homol'ovi sites suggest that Winslow Orange Ware does appear at least as early as 1275, is manufactured through the early 1300s, but is rare or nonexistent after 1350. It probably ceased to be manufactured sometime in the mid 1300s. Winslow Orange Ware makes up only about 5 percent of decorated ware in the excavated assemblage, thought to date to about 1350-1375 based on the Jeddito Yellow Ware chronology and radiocarbon dates from the hearths. The possible reasons for the replacement of Winslow

**Table 3.9. Percentages of Winslow Orange Ware Types**

| | | IN EXCAVATED AREAS | | | | | | | |
| | | Room | | | | | All | Area | All |
| Type | (Number of sherds) | 211 (15) | 212 (15) | 215 (11) | 216 (8) | 217 (8) | Rooms (57) | 221 (94) | Excavated (151) |
|---|---|---|---|---|---|---|---|---|---|
| Tuwiuca Orange | | 53.33 | 46.67 | | 37.50 | | 31.58 | 11.70 | 19.21 |
| Tuwiuca Black-on-orange | | | | | | 12.50 | 1.75 | 2.13 | 1.98 |
| Homolovi Polychrome | | 40.00 | 40.00 | 100.00 | 37.50 | 50.00 | 52.63 | 84.04 | 72.19 |
| Chavez Pass Black-on-red | | 6.67 | 6.67 | | 12.50 | 12.50 | 7.02 | 1.06 | 3.31 |
| Chavez Pass Polychrome | | | 6.67 | | 12.50 | 25.00 | 7.02 | 1.06 | 3.31 |

| | IN SURFACE PROVENIENCES | | | | |
| | West Plaza (85) | Central Plaza (59) | East Plaza (104) | Exterior areas (198) | All Surface (447) |
|---|---|---|---|---|---|
| Tuwiuca Orange | 5.81 | 1.69 | 1.92 | 14.14 | 8.05 |
| Tuwiuca Black-on-orange | 40.70 | 42.37 | 36.54 | 29.29 | 34.90 |
| Homolovi Polychrome | 46.51 | 52.54 | 59.62 | 54.04 | 53.69 |
| Chavez Pass Black-on-red | 3.49 | 3.39 | | 2.02 | 2.01 |
| Chavez Pass Polychrome | | | | 0.51 | 0.22 |
| Homolovi Black-on-red | 2.33 | | 0.96 | | 0.67 |
| Black Axe Polychrome | 1.16 | | 0.96 | | 0.45 |

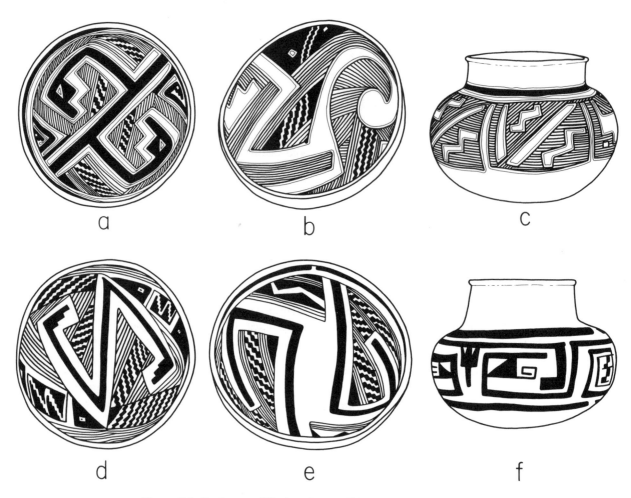

Figure 3.2. Designs on Winslow Orange Ware vessels: *a-c*, Homolovi Polychrome; *d-f*, Tuwiuca Black-on-orange. (See Appendix B.)

Orange Ware by imported Jeddito Yellow Ware at Homol'ovi are discussed below.

### White Mountain Red Ware

At Homol'ovi II small amounts of White Mountain Red Ware appeared regularly and these examples conformed to Carlson's (1970) descriptions. This ware is characterized by thick red slip and mineral paint. The slip is much thicker than that on the Chavez Pass series of Winslow Orange Ware, and the paint is much denser and blacker and is sometimes shiny. Paste is usually gray or white, but is sometimes oxidized to buff or yellow. Sherd temper is always present, sometimes with the addition of sand. Most sherds of this ware could not be assigned to a specific type because of their small size. Not enough decoration was present on them, and most of the types in this ware are distinguished on the basis of design style. Of those that were typable,

Fourmile Polychrome was most common, followed by Cedar Creek, Pinedale, and St. Johns polychromes. Percentages of White Mountain Red Ware by level are given in Tables 3.6 and 3.7, and dates for the types are in Table 3.10.

### Zuni Pottery Types

Zuni pottery types are distinguished from White Mountain Red ware on the basis of glaze paint. Later types have a white slip on one or both bowl surfaces and on many jar exteriors. This slip has an eggshell color and texture. The most common type at Homol'ovi II was Pinnawa Glaze-on-white (dating A.D. 1300–1630), followed by Kechipawan Polychrome (1375–1630). Also present were Heshotauthla Polychrome (1300–1500) and Kwakina Polychrome (1275–1630). Absence of Matsaki Polychrome, a post-1400 Zuni imitation of the later Sikyatki Polychrome style, at Homol'ovi II supports the

**Table 3.10. Chronological Relationships of Trade Wares**

| Date A.D. | White Mountain Red Ware and Roosevelt Red Ware types[1] | | | | | | Zuni pottery types[2] | | | | |
|---|---|---|---|---|---|---|---|---|---|---|---|
| | Pinto Polychrome | Gila Polychrome | Tonto Polychrome | Pinedale Polychrome | Cedar Creek Polychrome | Fourmile Polychrome | Kwakina Polychrome | Heshotauthla Polychrome | Pinnawa Glaze-on-white | Kechipawan Polychrome | Matsaki Polychrome |
| 1500 | | | | | | | \| | \| | \| | \| | \| |
| 1475 | | | | | | | \| | \| | \| | \| | \| |
| 1450 | | | | | | | \| | \| | \| | \| | \| |
| 1425 | | | | | | | \| | \| | \| | \| | * |
| 1400 | | \| | \| | | | \| | \| | \| | \| | | * |
| 1375 | | \| | \| | | \| | \| | \| | \| | \| | \| | |
| 1350 | \| | \| | \| | | \| | \| | \| | \| | \| | | |
| 1325 | \| | \| | \| | \| | \| | \| | \| | \| | | | |
| 1300 | \| | \| | \| | \| | \| | \| | \| | \| | | | |
| 1275 | \| | | | \| | | | \| | | | | |
| 1250 | * | | | | | | | | | | |
| 1225 | * | | | | | | | | | | |
| 1200 | * | | | | | | | | | | |

*Rare.
1. Crown 1981:32; Carlson 1970; Breternitz 1966.
2. Kintigh 1985: 15.

inference that the site had been abandoned by 1400 (Tables 3.6, 3.7).

## Roosevelt Red Ware

Roosevelt Red Ware sherds at Homol'ovi II consist mainly of Gila Polychrome with a small amount of Tonto Polychrome. Most sherds of this ware were not typable. The ware is distinguished by a cream-colored slip on bowl interiors and a dark brick-red exterior slip. Temper in the Homol'ovi II examples is usually sand with white and gray crushed sherds in brown paste with dark gray core. Organic black paint is often grayish and bleeds at the edges. Tonto Polychrome bowls and jars have all three colors on their exteriors. Gila Polychrome bowls have a broad, broken banding line at the rim. Gila Polychrome is dated from A.D. 1300 to 1400 by Crown (1981) and Wood (1987). Tonto Polychrome, often considered to be a late variety of Gila, nonethe-

less is no later than some Gila. Sherds in this ware come from the Salado culture area, but neutron activation studies of a sample of the Homol'ovi Roosevelt Red Ware failed to match them with any known source of this ware (Crown and Bishop, Chapter 4).

## Unknown Decorated

Most of the unidentifiable sherds were small, burned, or badly weathered. They were placed in the category of unknown decorated if they had vestiges of painted designs, and in unknown plain polished if there was no evidence of decoration. Obviously, plain polished sherds may simply be undecorated portions of the same vessels. Sherds were not placed in the Jeddito Yellow or Winslow Orange wares unless type could also be determined. Types in these wares are based on paint colors, so for the most part, even small sherds can be typed. Undecorated body sherds of these wares are classified as Plain Polished Yellow, Tuwiuca Orange, Chavez Pass Red, and so on. For the other wares, sherds were classified by ware for the data presentation in the tables and types are described above in order of relative frequency.

As inevitably must occur when a large number of sherds are examined, and especially when potters from diverse traditions interact with each other and pots and people are moving long distances, some sherds display characteristics of several wares that "should not go together." These could not be identified even though they were in excellent condition, and space does not allow for their individual description.

Unidentified sherds make up 2.28 percent of decorated ware sherds on the surface, and 3.29 percent in excavated areas. The higher figure for excavated sherds is due to burning.

## Utility Wares

Utility wares are here defined as corrugated and plain pottery with unpolished surfaces, no painted decoration, and abundant temper. There is some question about the appropriateness of the term "utility ware" and whether it implies functional distinctions that may not have existed. Judging by sooting and patterns of heat-related fractures, many corrugated and rough plain vessels were used for cooking. Many were probably used for storage, as were some decorated vessels. Nonetheless, the distinction we are making here is between relatively thin-walled vessels with small temper particles, polished surfaces, and, usually, decoration on the one hand. Bowls, jars, and other forms appear, which probably served a variety of functions, seemingly excluding cooking. On the other hand, we have relatively thick-walled vessels with abundant, large temper particles,

**Table 3.11. Characteristics of Decorated and Utility Wares**

| Decorated Ware | Utility Ware | Origin and characteristics |
|---|---|---|
| **Little Colorado White Ware** (Organic paint) | **Little Colorado Gray Ware** (Plain and corrugated) | Gray paste, white sherd temper. Probably local to Winslow area during Pueblo II and III. |
| **Tusayan White Ware** (Organic paint) | **Tusayan Gray Ware** (Plain and corrugated) | Gray or white paste, sand temper. From Kayenta and Hopi areas. Basketmaker III through Pueblo III. |
| **Winslow Orange Ware** (Mixed pigments) | **Homolovi Orange Ware** (Plain and corrugated) | Orange to yellowish paste, temper of multicolored sand, sherds, sometimes red angular fragments. From Homol'ovi area. |
| **Jeddito Yellow Ware** (Mixed pigments) | **Awatovi Yellow Ware** (Plain and corrugated) | Hard yellow paste and sharp fracture, quartz sand temper (very fine in decorated ware), occasional red angular fragments. From Hopi Mesas and is coal fired. |

**Table 3.12. Percentages of Utility Sherds by Ware and Surface Treatment**

| Ware | Excavated sherds (n = 3228) | | Surface collected sherds (n = 5129) | | |
|---|---|---|---|---|---|
| | Corrugated | Plain | Corrugated | Plain | Tooled |
| Awatovi Yellow Ware | 16.76 | 2.26 | 17.61 | 4.29 | |
| Homolovi Orange Ware | 14.56 | 1.12 | 5.34 | 2.57 | |
| Gray Wares | 8.21 | 1.18 | 4.56 | 2.32 | |
| Brown Wares | 1.18[a] | 4.31[b] | 3.59[a] | 2.69[b] | |
| Unknown, including burned | 43.12 | 7.31 | 50.20 | 6.69 | 0.14 |
| | 83.83 | 16.18 | 81.30 | 18.56 | 0.14 |

a. At least half Mogollon Brown Ware.    b. Virtually all Alameda Brown Ware

rough surfaces, and with no painted decoration. It is these that have been termed utility ware. Over 99 percent of all utility ware vessels are jars; many but by no means all have sooted exteriors. Relationships between specific decorated and utility wares are summarized in Table 3.11.

Utility ware sherds make up 69 percent of sherds on room floors, 55 percent of sherds in the fill and ash layer contact levels of Area 221, 42 percent of sherds in room fill, and 43 percent of surface sherds. Floor counts are elevated by the presence of numerous large, shattered cooking pots in several of the rooms. But these figures could also reflect an increase in the proportion of discarded decorated ceramics after the roomblock was abandoned and filled with later trash, or a higher breakage rate for decorated vessels.

Proportions of various utility types in the surface and excavated assemblages are shown in Table 3.12. The most common utility wares at Homol'ovi II are Awatovi Yellow Ware, Homolovi Orange Ware, Tusayan Gray Ware, and another unidentified gray ware that is probably locally made. It is a version of Homolovi Orange Ware fired in a reducing atmosphere, discussed below as Homolovi Gray Ware. Utility ware as defined here also includes Mogollon and Alameda brown wares, and a large number of unidentifiable sherds. Most of these are burned, but some sherds included in the unknown utility category may be a locally produced imitation of Alameda Brown Ware. Some of these sherds do have polished surfaces, but none have painted decoration.

**Awatovi Yellow Ware**

Awatovi Yellow Ware (Ware 7A) is the utility equivalent of Jeddito Yellow Ware. It includes Jeddito

Corrugated, Jeddito Plain, and Jeddito Tooled. The three have the same hard, yellow paste with abundant quartz sand temper. Temper particles are usually large, with sand grains exceeding 0.5 mm in diameter. Occasional red angular fragments appear, as in Jeddito Yellow Ware. These types differ in surface treatment, as their names imply. Surface and core color do not contrast and are yellow unless fire clouded, burned, or misfired. Many corrugated sherds in the Homol'ovi assemblage are burned and many contain soot on one or both surfaces. As color was used as a diagnostic feature of this type, there is probably a higher percentage of Jeddito Corrugated than indicated in the sherd counts. Coil size and treatment of Jeddito Corrugated is extremely varied and resembles the same wide range found in Tusayan Gray Ware (Gifford and Smith 1978).

### Homolovi Orange Ware

Homolovi Orange Ware (Ware 6A) differs from Awatovi Yellow Ware mainly in temper, but also in fracture, which is less sharp and often crumbling. The softer paste is probably a result of lower firing temperature. In addition to sand, temper almost always includes red angular fragments and sometimes includes yellowish white angular fragments, possibly sherd, and black fragments. The yellow or orange core color usually contrasts with the orange surface color. Pinkish and tan colors also occur. Color is extremely variable even on a single sherd. Coil treatment on Homolovi Corrugated is variable, but seems to be less variable than that of Jeddito Corrugated.

Homolovi Plain has a rough, unpolished surface with coils entirely obliterated and is otherwise the same as Homolovi Corrugated.

In the Homol'ovi II assemblage are numerous sherds with attributes between Homolovi Plain, which should have large temper particles and a very rough surface, and Tuwiuca Orange, which should be polished. These are counted in the Unknown Plain Unpolished category. They are variable in their temper content and density and have no core-surface color contrast. They are well smoothed but not polished. Some contain light-colored angular fragments, possibly crushed sherd, possibly a mineral that is not found in Homolovi Plain. Sherd temper in Tuwiuca Orange is usually orange or pink. When yellow or white fragments occur in Tuwiuca Orange, orange or pink fragments are also present.

One surface sherd (Fig. 3.3c) has Homolovi Plain paste and is decorated with four crescent-shaped impressions. Most of the surface is plain and rough. The impressions were probably made with a fingernail.

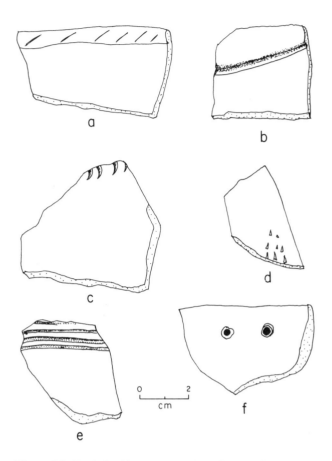

Figure 3.3. Tooled utility ware sherds. *a*, Jeddito Corrugated rim sherd with an indented fillet around the flare of the rim. *b*, Jeddito Plain sherd has a groove and ridge across it; the groove appears to be the impression of a cord or thin twig made when the clay was wet. *c*, Homolovi Plain sherd with crescent-shaped indentations. *d*, Unidentified plain ware sherd with small wedge-shaped impressions on the exterior surface, black smudged interior, abraded. *e*, Plain gray sherd with a series of grooves made when the clay was wet. *f*, Perforated plate rim fragment.

### Gray Ware

Gray Plain and corrugated sherds were counted, but only floor contact sherds were typed. This decision was made due to the intensive examination necessary to distinguish gray ware types, and to the impossibility of knowing whether a burned sherd was originally fired in an oxidized or reduced atmosphere, an important distinction between some wares. For example, a reduced Jeddito Corrugated is Tusayan Corrugated, and a reduced Homolovi Corrugated is Homolovi Gray Corrugated (new ware, described below).

Virtually all gray corrugated sherds had sand temper. The few with sherd temper are classified as Little

Colorado Corrugated. Most appeared to have almost pure quartz sand temper and are typable as Tusayan Corrugated. Those with mixed quartz and other colored sand particles are Homolovi Gray Corrugated. These were almost certainly locally made, and have a softer fracture like Homolovi Orange Ware.

Gray ware with rough, unpolished surfaces, quartz sand temper, and no corrugation are categorized as gray plain with no type designation given. They best fit the type Kiet Siel Gray (A.D. 1200–1300; Colton 1955, Type 13 in Ware 8A)). In the late 1200s through 1400s, the use of corrugation was waning. Jeddito Plain is a common type at Homol'ovi II. In sherd form it resembles an oxidized Tusayan Gray Ware that lacks corrugation.

*Homolovi Gray Ware*
*(New Ware)*

Homolovi Gray Ware is here defined as a coarse, gray utility ware found in the Winslow area with the following characteristics: abundant multicolored sand temper, crumbling fracture, usually dark gray surface and core, occasionally light gray surface. There are three types. Homolovi Gray Plain is the plain and rough-surfaced noncorrugated counterpart of Homolovi Gray Corrugated. Several plain, polished gray sherds have abundant, rounded, coarse sand temper particles of varied colors that protrude on the vessel surfaces. These sherds do not match the description of any named type and are probably locally manufactured. Because only surface treatment distinguishes them from Homolovi Gray Plain and Corrugated, this new type has been placed in the Homolovi Gray Ware and called Homolovi Gray Polished. The type is much more common at Homol'ovi III than at Homol'ovi II and may date to the A.D. 1275–1300 period, extending to the mid-1300s. Influence from the Alameda Brown Ware tradition is probable, based on rim form, a greater wall thickness than most decorated wares, and a surface appearance that often shows polishing streaks and large dents or flat areas. Because of the small size of sherds of this type recovered so far, it is not known whether these flat areas are caused by some limited local use of paddle and anvil construction.

### Brown Corrugated

A wide variety of corrugated sherds was placed in this category, although the overall proportion of brown corrugated sherds was very small. Some are Mogollon Brown Ware with fine paste and small, delicate indentations. One of these has broad, white designs painted over the corrugation and was typed as MacDonald Corrugated. Others are similar but undecorated.

A second broad class of brown corrugated sherds has a brown or reddish brown surface and a core of the same color or black. These sherds have coarse, unsorted sand temper, including many well-rounded opaque grains of white and greenish chert, as well as somewhat angular clear and translucent grains of quartz. Temper protrudes on the surface. The coil indentations are usually partly obliterated.

### Alameda Brown Ware

All sherds of a brown color and undecorated, noncorrugated surface were placed in this category. Virtually all of these can be typed within the Alameda Brown Ware, but because types within this ware are distinguished by temper, the process of typing all sherds of this category was deemed too time-consuming. The most common types of Alameda Brown Ware at Homol'ovi II appear to be Chavez and Kinnikinick, followed by Grapevine, Young's, Diablo and Sunset Brown. They have plain, rough or polished exterior surfaces and scraped or wiped interiors. Virtually all are jars. Exteriors are brown or reddish brown, and interiors are black. Larger sherds show the faceting characteristic of paddle and anvil construction. Temper ranges from shiny black volcanic cinders in Sunset Brown, limestone in Grapevine, to a mixture of gray tuff and sand in Kinnikinick and Chavez Brown.

### Unknown Corrugated

Many corrugated sherds from all proveniences were burned, weathered, or misfired and were not securely typable using criteria outlined above. For example, burning obscures surface color, changes fracture characteristics, and seems to render colored angular fragments in the paste invisible.

### Unknown Tooled

Several plain ware sherds were recovered that have unusual surface treatments (Fig. 3.3). The variety of texturing in utility ware at Homol'ovi may be related to the elaboration in decorative techniques, such as stippling and engraving, in the painted wares.

*Perforated Plate Fragment*

A rim sherd (Fig. 3.3f) from a plate or shallow bowl is perforated at intervals of 1.5 cm. These perforations were made from the inside out while the clay was wet. The paste is fine, porous, soft, and orange. The sherd resembles perforated plates from Black Mesa and other Kayenta Anasazi areas described by Christianson (1987).

## Unknown Plain Utility

In addition to the plain orange sherds with attributes between Homolovi Plain and Tuwiuca Orange, described above, this category included many accidentally burned and weathered sherds. Also included are a number of orange and brownish orange sherds. Some have gray cores. They are hard and have a sharp fracture. Temper consists of opaque white angular fragments and white rounded fragments that do not appear to be ground sherds. Most also included some sand and although quartz is not the only material present, the remainder has not been identified. The surface of these sherds is rough, but a polished version occurs and is included in tabulations under unknown plain polished. They are not Chavez Brown, but sherds of this sort are found at Chavez Pass. They may be a variety of Alameda Brown Ware or an imitation of Chavez Brown from some area other than Chavez Pass.

## Vitrified Sherds

Many sherds from Area 221 and several from other proveniences were fired at an extremely high temperature, probably when rooms were burned rather than in accidents during the manufacturing process. They are glassy and discolored, and some have bubbly, slaglike adhesions. Most are probably Jeddito Yellow Ware, based on observable characteristics of style and shape, but positive identifications were not attempted and may not be possible.

## Glazed Sherd

One sherd from Surface Unit 35 (West Plaza) has a glassy green glaze on both surfaces and a hard fine paste. Lee Fratt of the Arizona State Museum has tentatively typed this sherd as Awatovi Green, which was made in Mexico, probably between about 1700 and 1800 (Caywood 1972). It should be considered a postabandonment, intrusive artifact and it does not appear in tables and tabulations.

Three other sherds, all from Area 221 fill, also appear to be glazed, but only on one surface. They differ from the Awatovi Green sherd and from all other kinds of Mexican glaze ware. They are dark olive green and appear to be warped. They are probably yellow ware that was highly fired and came into contact with some sort of fluxing material during the burning of the room in which the vessels were stored. These sherds are tabulated as "vitrified."

## PARTIALLY RECONSTRUCTIBLE VESSELS

Twenty-five partially reconstructible vessels were recovered from excavated areas, and one was collected from the surface. Few of these vessels are more than 50 percent reconstructed; many described here are only large fragments. The criterion for deciding if a fragment was to be considered a sherd or a partially reconstructible vessel was an arbitrary size cutoff at about 100 square centimeters. Because so few vessels were recovered, most are illustrated and described in order to offer information on the range of variation.

Of these vessels, 17 are bowls, 1 is a ladle, 7 are jars; 22 are Jeddito Yellow Ware, 1 is Winslow Orange Ware, and 2 are portions of corrugated vessels. The following vessels and fragments are described in detail below or in captions: a Jeddito Corrugated jar (Room 216: Specimen 3), a Homol'ovi Corrugated Jar (211:1), a Homolovi Polychrome bowl (221:9), two Bidahochi Polychrome vessels (bowl 221:8; jar 221:2), two Paayu Polychrome bowls (215:1; 216:1), a Jeddito Engraved bowl (211:2), a Huckovi Black-on-orange bowl (221:4), nine Awatovi Black-on-yellow bowls (212:2, 4, 5, 6; 215:2; 216:2; 221:1, 6, 7), an Awatovi Black-on-yellow ladle (221:10), three Awatovi black-on-yellow jars (212:3; 221:3, 5), two Jeddito Black-on-yellow bowls (215:3, 4), and a plain yellow jar base reworked as a plate or scoop (212:1).

As noted above, Jeddito and Awatovi Black-on-yellow types are not distinct, but represent clusters of attributes arranged on a continuum. These vessels were typed according to Smith's (1971) description, summarized as follows: Jeddito Black-on-yellow vessels tend to have a light yellow color, a fine paste with no visible temper, although occasional inclusions of sand or red angular fragments are allowable. Awatovi Black-on-yellow tends to have a darker yellow paste and surface color, some visible temper, and rectilinear geometric designs. Paint on Awatovi Black-on-yellow sometimes bleeds at the edges. Most of the Homol'ovi II vessels do not fall squarely in either category, and the type assignments do not necessarily reflect a temporal difference. Most of the vessels are types thought to date to the 1300s (Smith 1971; Breternitz 1966; Colton 1956), consistent with the transitional period between Awatovi and Jeddito Black-on-yellow (Smith 1971). The primary criterion to distinguish the two types is presence of visible temper.

Each vessel is described in detail and most are illustrated to approximately the same scale unless otherwise indicated (Figs. 3.4–3.8). Munsell color measurements of vessel surfaces are given in the captions, with maximum dimension in centimeters. Additional provenience information is in Appendix B.

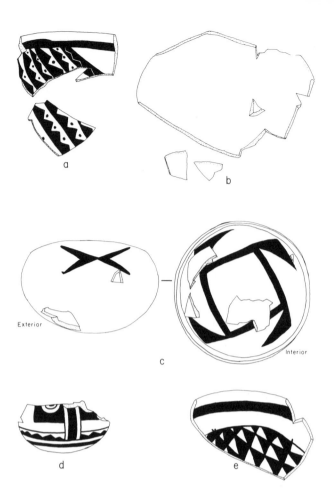

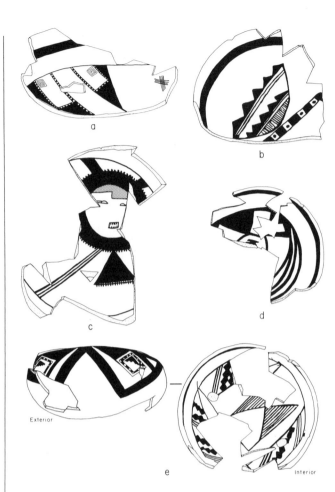

Figure 3.4. Partially reconstructible vessels from Rooms 211 and 212. *a*, Jeddito Engraved bowl (211:2) with sparse sand temper and red angular fragments; light yellow (10YR 8/4), light brown paint; diameter of largest fragment is about 15 cm. *b*, Broken jar base reworked as a shallow plate (212:1); undecorated yellow paste (10YR 8/4); ground edges, heavy wear on interior and exterior surfaces; diameter is about 26 cm. *c*, Atypical Awatovi Black-on-yellow bowl (212:2); color closer to buff than yellow (7.5YR 8/4); paste is finer than Winslow Orange Ware and contains sand and rounded opaque fragments the same color as the clay; possibly locally manufactured rather than imported from the Hopi Mesas; diameter is about 20 cm. *d*, Small Awatovi Black-on-yellow jar base (212:3); light yellow (10YR 8/3) paste tempered with sparse, fine sand and varicolored angular fragments; highly polished exterior; base shows some wear; diameter is about 15 cm. *e*, Awatovi Black-on-yellow bowl fragment (212:4); partially burned or badly fire clouded in the firing process; unclouded surface is light yellow (2.5YR 8/4); diameter is about 20 cm.

Figure 3.5. Partially reconstructible vessels from Rooms 212 and 215. *a*, Awatovi Black-on-yellow bowl fragment (212:5); fine yellow (10YR 8/4) paste; the vessel appears oval rather than round; diameter is about 20 cm. *b*, Awatovi Black-on-yellow bowl (212:6); fine, hard paste containing sparse gray angular fragments; surface color is dark yellow (10YR 7/4) and the core is a lighter shade; base shows slight wear; paint is dense, dark brown, and bleeds at the edges; diameter is about 20 cm. *c*, Paayu Polychrome bowl (215:1) depicting a katsina face; fine yellow (2.5Y 8/4) paste with no visible temper; base is worn; interior surface is slightly worn in the center of the bowl; diameter is about 20 cm. *d*, Awatovi Black-on-yellow bowl (215:2); very hard, fine paste; yellow (2.5Y 8/4); temper is abundant sand and red angular fragments that stick out on the surface; paint on interior surface is dark brown but watery in many areas and bleeds at the edges; vessel shows no wear; diameter is about 20 cm. *e*, Jeddito Black-on-yellow bowl (215:3); fine, light yellow paste (2.5Y 8/2) containing sparse, fine quartz sand temper; exterior base is slightly worn but interior shows no wear; diameter is about 20 cm.

Illustrations are tracings of slide transparencies and distortion of design resulting from rendering a three-dimensional object in two dimensions is retained. In some cases oblique views of bowl exteriors, drawn to show designs, have resulted in illustrations that make the bowls look deeper than they are.

## Room 211

Two partially reconstructible vessels were found in Room 211, including one of only two utility ware vessels. Feature 1, a hearth, contained conjoinable sherds of a sidewall section of a Homolovi Corrugated jar (not

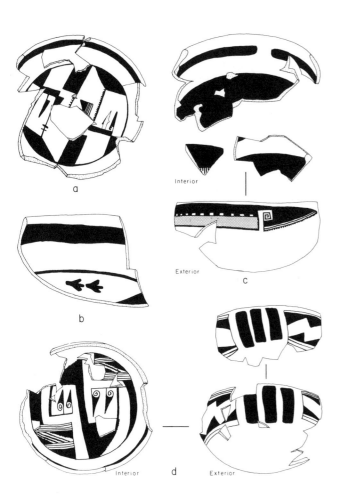

Figure 3.6. Partially reconstructible vessels from Rooms 215, 216, and Activity Area 221. *a*, Jeddito Black-on-yellow bowl (215:4); very fine, light yellow (2.5Y 8/2) paste, watery brown paint that bleeds slightly at the edges; no visible temper; exterior base is worn, interior is not; diameter is about 20 cm. *b*, Paayu Polychrome deep bowl (216:1); fine light yellow (2.5Y 8/2) paste containing sparse red angular fragments; no visible temper; diameter is about 20 cm. *c*, Awatovi Black-on-yellow bowl rim (216:2); light pinkish yellow (10YR 8/4) paste includes some sand and red angular fragments; interior paint bleeds at edges, exterior does not; diameter is about 10 cm. *d*, Awatovi Black-on-yellow bowl (221:1), nearly complete, burned; exterior base is worn from use; diameter is about 20 cm.

illustrated; specimen 211:1). Coils on the uppermost portion of the vessel wall are indented, and those on the lower portion are partially obliterated. Both surfaces are mottled orange and gray, and parts of the exterior are sooted. The second vessel is a Jeddito Engraved bowl, specimen 211:2 (Fig. 3.4*a*). The design includes rows of triangles with dots in between them, and a broad line with an engraved zigzag. The design is unusual in that it proceeds directly from the broad subrim framing line rather than from the more typical thinner line lower on the vessel sidewall that defines the design field.

## Room 212

There were five partially reconstructible vessels in Room 212. Sherds from two of them were found outside the room in the vandal's backdirt and both inside and outside Room 217, which probably indicates that vandals threw backdirt from Room 212 into 217 as well as outside the walls.

Two vessels from this room are unique in the assemblage. Specimen 212:1 appears to have been the base of a broken jar (Fig. 3.4*b*) that was reworked to make a shallow plate. This item also could have been used for scooping flour, or as a puki for molding the bases of new clay vessels. The edges are ground, and both interior and exterior surfaces are very worn, scratched, and abraded, presumably from use. The largest sherd (18 cm across) was propped against the south wall of the room, just above the floor, with two small sherds nearby.

Specimen 212:2 is an atypical Awatovi Black-on-yellow bowl (Fig. 3.4*c*). Designs are unusually simple for Jeddito Yellow Ware, and any other decorated ware common at the site. The surface is somewhat gritty like Winslow Orange Ware, the fracture is not as sharp as most yellow ware, and the color is somewhat closer to buff than yellow (7.5YR 8/4). The paste is finer than Winslow Orange Ware and contains sand and rounded opaque fragments the same color as the clay. It would not be surprising if neutron activation results were to show this vessel was locally manufactured rather than imported from the Hopi Mesas. Some local Winslow clays do fire to a yellowish color, and the softer paste of this vessel resembles local Winslow Orange Ware.

## Room 215

Four vessels were recovered from Room 215. They are among the most complete of the recovered vessels, which supports the excavator's observation that this is the least vandalized of the five rooms. Sherds from some of the vessels appeared in Rooms 216 and 217, showing that there has been some mixing of fill, either by vandals or prehistoric trash disposal, but probably the former. The ceramic assemblage in this room may possibly be later than that of the other rooms, based on the absence of Bidahochi Polychrome and the presence of Jeddito Black-on-yellow and Paayu Polychrome.

The most unusual vessel recovered in the excavation is a Paayu Polychrome bowl, specimen 215:1 (Fig. 3.5*c*), depicting a katsina face. The figure most closely resembles the Hopi Sun Forehead Katsina (Taawa), according to Emory Sekaquaptewa of the Department of Anthropology, University of Arizona. The central figure is offset from the center of the bowl. It has a toothed

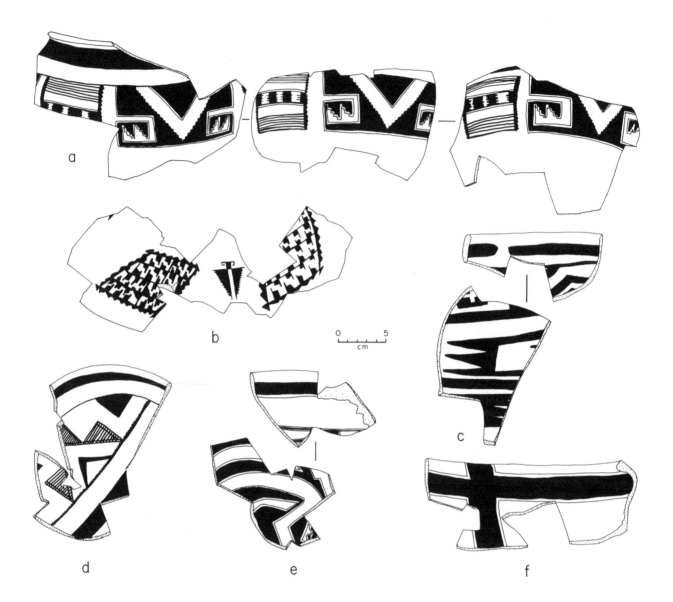

Figure 3.7. Partially reconstructible vessels from Activity Area 221. *a*, Bidahochi Polychrome jar (221:2); paste is fine, mottled, reddish yellow (10YR 8/6 to 7.5YR 7/8) containing abundant red angular fragments; fine temper is visible on surface; one side burned; rim is sharply outflaring and sidewall is everted, not globular; diameter is about 20 cm. *b*, Awatovi Black-on-yellow jar (221:3); fine yellow (10YR 9/6) paste containing sparse red angular fragments; diameter is about 30 cm. *c*, Huckovi Black-on-orange bowl (221:4); very hard, fine paste containing sparse red angular fragments; orange (5YR 6/6) paste; base fragments show small amount of wear; dark brown paint has an almost glassy surface in places but is not a true glaze; diameter is about 15 cm. *d*, Awatovi Black-on-yellow bowl body fragment (221:6); fine yellow (2.5Y 8/2) paste with dark brown paint that bleeds slightly at the edges in a few places only; the sand temper is visible only with handlens; exterior base is worn, partially burned; diameter is about 15 cm. *e*, Bidahochi Polychrome bowl (221:8); light yellow paste (10YR 8/4) with red angular and sand inclusions; light brown watery paint, outlining in thin white paint; diameter of largest piece is about 12 cm. *f*, Homolovi Polychrome bowl rim fragment (221:9); misfired or burned to a dull gray-brown (5YR 4/1); broad brown (5YR 3/2) bands outlined in white that meet at right angles below the rim; paste contains abundant varicolored angular fragments and sand; in some breaks the core is incompletely reduced and retains an orange color (7.5YR 7/6); diameter is about 20 cm.

mouth, an asymmetric watery brown stepped design on the forehead, squinting eyes, and a ticked ruff around the face. It resembles masklike faces often found on Fourmile Polychrome, Sikyatki Polychrome, Jeddito and Awatovi Black-on-yellow, Gila Polychrome, and other 14th-century types (Ferg 1982; Hays 1989). The vessel consists of nine body sherds all found in contact with the floor. It has a fine, yellow (2.5Y 8/4) paste with no visible temper. The base is worn, and the interior surface is somewhat worn in the center of the bowl.

## Room 216

Three partially reconstructible vessels were recovered in this badly vandalized room. Additional sherds from the first vessel came from Room 211 floor fill and floor contact, Room 217 fill, surface, and vandals' exterior backdirt.

The second Paayu Polychrome vessel in the assem-assemblage (216:1; Fig. 3.6*b*) is a deep bowl with a strongly incurving sidewall and a fine paste. The interior design of the reconstructed portion is a light, watery brown, massed area below the broken subrim framing line. Paint density is varied in this area, and brush strokes are visible. Several sherds that do not conjoin this portion certainly belong to the vessel, but offer few clues to what the whole design looked like. Three of these sherds were engraved, then were painted over the engraving to produce thin dark brown parallel lines in the light brown surface. The effect is somewhat like intaglio. To my knowledge, such a technique has not been noted before in prehistoric Southwestern ceramics. Jeddito Engraved and Awatovi Polychrome, as defined by Colton, are engraved after being painted so that the light paste shows through the dark paint in the engraved designs. This example is painted after engraving in order to pool paint in the scratches. Hence, this is another way of manipulating paint density, the characteristic that defines Paayu Polychrome. The exterior design on this vessel also shows manipulation of paint density to produce different colors. A dark brown, rectilinear design encloses a broad, watery stripe of light orange-brown, almost, if not exactly, the same chroma as the outlining and solid brown areas.

The second partly reconstructible utility vessel in the assemblage is a Jeddito Corrugated jar (216:3; not illustrated). Large sherds from the neck and rim were found beside the hearth. More sherds were found in the hearth fill, floor fill, and general fill. Not enough contiguous fragments were recovered to allow a volume estimate. The neck opening measures approximately 21 cm in diameter. Only the interior of the rim has a yellow color; the rest is mottled gray. Part of the exterior surface is sooted.

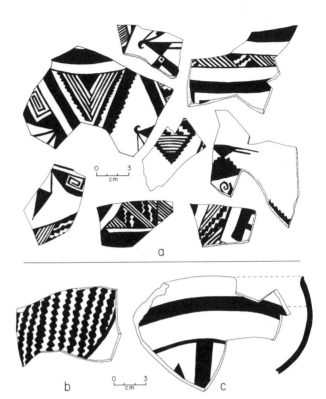

Figure 3.8. Partially reconstructible vessels from Activity Area 221. *a*, Large Awatovi Black-on-yellow jar sherds (221:5); fine yellow paste (10YR 8/7) with fine sand and fine red angular fragments; birds probably represent parrots; diameter of largest sherd is about 12 cm. *b*, Awatovi Black-on-yellow bowl body fragment from between base and sidewall (221:7); paste is fine, with sparse red angular inclusions and a carbon streak; interior is orange (7.5YR 7/6) with some gray and reddish staining; exterior shows slight wear; diameter is about 10 cm. *c*, Awatovi Black-on-yellow bowl rim fragment from the East Plaza; light yellow (2.5Y 8/4) paste with abundant, very fine, sand temper; light brown paint bleeds at the edges in the interior design.

## Activity Area 221

Eight partially reconstructible vessels were recovered from exterior Activity Area 221. Five are at least partially burned and probably were part of the contents of a storeroom that burned and then were thrown into the area where they were recovered. The other three are not visibly burned; they may have come from other trash or merely sustained less damage in the burning event. Most have worn bases, suggesting that they were used before being burned and discarded, and that they did not break while being manufactured.

The Area 221 assemblage includes two Bidahochi Polychrome vessels (221:2 and 221:8), one Huckovi

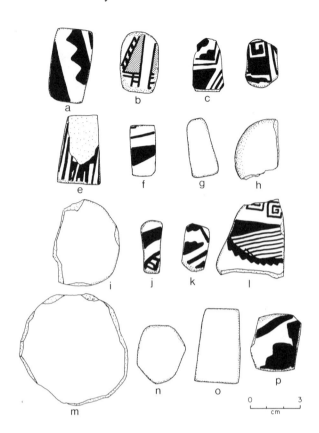

Figure 3.9. Shaped sherds (see Table 3.13).

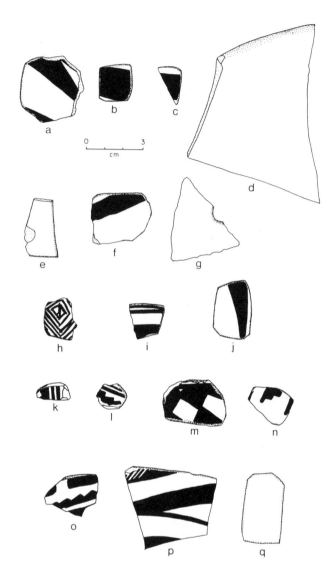

Figure 3.10. Shaped sherds (see Table 3.13).

Black-on-orange bowl (221:4), and a Homolovi Poly-chrome bowl (221:9), all rare types in the overall assem-blage. These vessels present several interesting features. The surface of vessel 221:2 (Fig. 3.7*a*) is mottled with small splotches of light yellow and dark orange, sug-gesting that two kinds of clay were mixed in making this vessel, but that mixing was not done thoroughly.

Vessel 221:9 (Fig. 3.7*f*) is a Homolovi Polychrome bowl rim fragment that has been misfired or burned to a dull gray-brown (5YR 4/1). In some breaks the core is completely reduced and retains an orange color (7.5YR 7/6), perhaps caused by wood that produced a smoky, but hot, firing or by later burning. The bowl has broad brown (5YR 3/2) bands outlined in white that meet at right angles below the rim. This is not a typical Homolovi Polychrome design, and it most closely resembles northern Tsegi Orange Ware polychromes, especially the type Tusayan Polychrome (Smith 1971: 296).

The only partially reconstructible ladle (specimen 221:10; not illustrated) was burned and shattered; it was recovered in the general fill of Area 221. It is Awatovi Black-on-yellow, and has a round cup and a tubular handle. The end of the handle appears to have been shaped like an animal head, with pointed ears and nose.

## SHAPED SHERDS

Shaped sherds are defined as pieces from broken ceramic vessels that have been modified by grinding, flaking, or both, on one or more edges. The 33 shaped sherds in the Homol'ovi II assemblage (Figs. 3.9, 3.10; Table 3.13) range from about 1 square centimeter to 250 square centimeters in surface area. Most were formed by flaking the sherd with a hammerstone to shape it, then grinding the edges. Those that are ground on all sides tend to have regular shapes, for example rectangular and trapezoidal. Many are ground on only one edge; they may be broken from more heavily modified pieces or may have functioned as tools. It is difficult to tell if these are whole or fragmentary artifacts. Three perhaps served as scrapers or other tools, based on a relatively large size and a single ground edge that is bevelled. The remaining 30 appear

**Table 3.13. Inventory of Shaped Sherds**

| Provenience | Form | Shaping | Length cm | Width cm | Thick-ness cm | Condition; type and vessel form |
|---|---|---|---|---|---|---|
| **FIGURE 3.9** | | | | | | |
| *a*  217 f | Rectangular | G-4 | 4.1 | 2.2 | 0.5 | Whole; Roosevelt Red Ware jar |
| *b*  221 f | Rectangular | G-4 | 3.2 | 2.2 | 0.6 | Whole; Sikyatki Polychrome bowl |
| *c*  #1 SP | Irregular | F-4, G-1 | 2.9 | 1.8 | 0.4 | Whole; Black-on-yellow jar |
| *d*  #1 SP | Irregular | G-4 | 2.6 | 1.9 | 0.5 | Whole; Tusayan White Ware jar |
| *e*  #36 WP | Trapezoidal | G-4 | 4.0 | 2.3 | 0.4 | Whole; Cibola White Ware jar, surface partly spalled |
| *f*  #38 CP | Rectangular | G-4 | 3.0 | 1.6 | 0.4 | Whole; Cibola White Ware bowl, surface partly spalled |
| *g*  #44 CP | Trapezoidal | G-4 | 3.2 | 1.7 | 0.6 | Whole; Tuwiuca Orange jar |
| *h*  #48 EP | Round | G-all? | 4.0 | 2.5 | 0.6 | Fragment; unknown plain ware, unknown form |
| *i*  CP SW | Round | F-all | 4.8 | 3.8 | 0.6 | Fragment; unknown form, worn on convex surface |
| *j*  CP SW | Irregular | G-3 | 3.0 | 1.0 | 0.5 | Whole; black-on-yellow bowl |
| *k*  CP SW | Rectangular | G-3, UW-1 | 2.6 | 1.5 | 0.5 | Whole; black-on-yellow jar |
| *l*  CP SW | Irregular | G-2, UW-2 | 4.0 | 3.2 | 0.5 | Whole; black-on-yellow bowl |
| *m*  CP SW | Round | F-all | 6.7 | 6.0 | 0.6 | Whole; plain yellow, abraded surface? |
| *n*  CP NE | Round | G-all | 3.2 diameter | | 0.6 | Whole; plain yellow, unknown form, both surfaces abraded |
| *o*  CP NE | Trapezoidal | G-4 | 4.1 | 2.4 | 0.4 | Whole; plain, polished yellow jar |
| *p*  CP NE | Square | G-3, F-1 | 3.2 | 2.7 | 0.4 | Whole; Tuwiuca Black-on-orange jar |
| **FIGURE 3.10** | | | | | | |
| *a*  EP NE | Irregular | G-2, UW-2 | 3.7 | 3.6 | 0.5 | Whole; Cibola White Ware jar |
| *b*  Unknown | Square | G-4 | 2.1 | 1.8 | 0.4 | Whole; black-on-yellow jar |
| *c*  216 s | Irregular | G-2, UW-1 | 2.1 | 1.0 | 0.5 | Fragment; black-on-yellow bowl |
| *d*  206 ext. | Irregular | G-1, UW-3 | 10.2 | 7.0 | 0.6 | Fragment?; plain polished yellow jar |
| *e*  #34 | Rectangular | G-3, UW-1 | 3.3 | 1.5 | 0.5 | Whole?; plain polished yellow jar |
| *f*  #34 | Irregular | G-1,F-2,UW-1 | 3.5 | 2.5 | 0.5 | Fragment; black-on-yellow bowl |
| *g*  CP SW | Irregular | G-1, UW-3 | 4.7 | 4.0 | 0.6 | Fragment; Tuwiuca Orange jar |
| *h*  211 fc | Irregular | G-1, UW-3 | 2.4 | 1.9 | 0.6 | Fragment; black-on-yellow bowl |
| *i*  211 f | Irregular | G-1, UW-3 | 2.1 | 2.0 | 0.5 | Fragment; black-on-yellow jar |
| *j*  212 fc | Rectangular | G-4 | 3.2 | 2.0 | 0.5 | Fragment; black-on-yellow jar |
| *k*  217 f | Irregular | G-3, UW-1 | 2.0 | 0.8 | 0.6 | Fragment; black-on-yellow jar |
| *l*  221 f | Irregular | G-2, UW-2 | 1.6 | 1.5 | 0.3 | Fragment; black-on-yellow jar |
| *m*  211 f | Irregular | G-4 | 3.7 | 2.0 | 0.6 | Fragment?; black-on-yellow bowl |
| *n*  211 ff | Trapezoidal | G-2, UW-2 | 2.5 | 1.5 | 0.5 | Fragment; black-on-yellow jar |
| *o*  216 f | Irregular | G-1, UW-2 | 3.1 | 2.0 | 0.3 | Fragment; black-on-yellow jar |
| *p*  206 ext. | Irregular | G-1, UW-3 | 5.4 | 4.5 | 0.7 | Fragment; black-on-yellow jar |
| *q*  206 ext. | Rectangular | G-3, UW-1 | 3.9 | 2.0 | 0.5 | Whole?; plain polished yellow jar |

Provenience: EP = East Plaza; CP = Central Plaza; WP = West Plaza; SP = south of pueblo; Ext. = exterior fill, vandals' backdirt; f = fill; fc = floor contact; ff = floor fill (20 cm above floor); s = surface.
Shaping: G = ground; F = flaked; UW = unworked; numbers indicate how many sides are so modified.
Vessel type: black-on-yellow may be Jeddito or Awatovi Black-on-yellow.

to have been intentionally shaped for other purposes, such as ornaments, toys, or gaming pieces.

Although none of the sherds found at Homol'ovi II were drilled, similarly shaped sherds at other sites (for example, Adams 1979) are drilled and used as pendants and spindle whorls. Some worked sherds had been used as scrapers and shaping tools in making pottery. Small,

regularly shaped pieces were used as dice or other gaming pieces.

Characteristics of the Homol'ovi pieces include: 24 decorated and 9 plain; 23 Jeddito Yellow Ware, 5 white ware, 3 Winslow Orange Ware, 1 Roosevelt Red Ware, and 1 unknown plain ware. The high incidence of yellow ware reflects its predominance on the site as a whole, but there are a disproportionately large number of shaped white ware sherds. It is possible that these earlier sherds were curated as tools into the later, yellow ware period, or that white sherds found in earlier trash were later recovered and shaped for an aesthetic or symbolic reason.

Of the 18 shaped sherds from surface collections, 11 came from the Central Plaza. As this is the largest of the plazas and the one with the most collection units, this is not a significant fact. Excavated shaped sherds are fairly evenly distributed among rooms, with the exception of Room 215, which has none. Room 215 also had the least variety in its ceramic and lithic assemblages, appeared to represent the latest assemblage, and was the least disturbed by vandalism. In addition, its hearth was sealed before abandonment, suggesting it may have been last used as a storage room. In short, the distribution of shaped sherds does not contribute to an understanding of activity areas at Homol'ovi II. Information on shaped sherds is summarized in Table 3.13. Other small artifacts are discussed in Appendix A.

## SUMMARY AND CONCLUSIONS

The percentages of ceramic wares present in each plaza and the exterior areas of the pueblo are summarized in Table 3.1. Jeddito Yellow Ware is the most common ware in all areas, and it is evenly distributed.

There are some differences among the three plazas. Most notable is that sherd density is higher in the West Plaza than in the other plazas. Additional evidence suggests that rooms adjoining the West Plaza were the latest to be occupied, assuming that trash was deposited nearest inhabited rooms. First, the concentration of both Jeddito and Awatovi yellow wares is highest in this plaza. These types are assumed to date to the post-1300 period. Second, the percentages of white wares and gray wares, which for the most part date prior to A.D. 1300, are lowest here. The East Plaza, on the other hand, shows some indications of having been occupied early and abandoned before the West Plaza. Winslow Orange Ware is most common in the East Plaza and Awatovi Yellow Ware is least common. Additionally, the East Plaza has slightly higher percentages of Bidahochi Polychrome and Huckovi types, which seem to date to the earlier 1300s.

Exterior areas differ from the plazas primarily in having a higher percentage of unidentified sherds. This difference is probably due to a higher proportion of burned sherds in these areas, perhaps reflecting a tendency to dispose of burned trash outside the pueblo rather than inside the plazas, but this hypothesis has not been tested. No conclusions about activity areas can be presented at this time from surface ceramics.

The most important conclusions that can be drawn from the surface assemblage are about trade, overall site occupation span, and abandonment date. Trade in yellow wares was obviously important in the local economy and is discussed below. In addition to these Hopi ceramics, there are small, but consistent, amounts of White Mountain Red Ware, assumed to have been manufactured in the Show Low area (Carlson 1970); Zuni pottery types; and Roosevelt Red Ware, from unknown locations but presumably made in central Arizona. Like Jeddito Yellow Ware, sherds of these types are fairly evenly dispersed over the site. Such dispersal may reflect equal access to exotic pottery and a lack of "ethnic neighborhoods" that expressed their origins and identities with imported pottery. Or dispersal may be a result of extreme disturbance due to vandalism. Only further excavation can tell us more about the role of exotic pottery in the lives of the pueblo inhabitants.

Many of the types of exotic decorated pottery that appear at Homol'ovi are well-dated by tree rings (Table 3.10). The most abundant types in these wares, Fourmile Polychrome, Pinnawa Glaze-on-white, Kechipawan Polychrome, and Gila Polychrome fit well with the 14th-century dates obtained by examination of the yellow ware types (Table 3.4).

A few sherds of northern polychromes, Tsegi Black-on-orange, and a variety of white wares dating from the A.D. 600s into the 1300s suggest a long, though not necessarily continuous, use of the locality. A small but consistent appearance of Jeddito Black-on-orange (about 1250-1350), and the abundance of Awatovi Black-on-yellow, which is most common at Awatovi from about 1300 to 1350, suggest the site was occupied in the late 1200s and had a relatively large pottery-using and pottery-breaking population by the early or mid 1300s.

Absence of types known to date post–1400, such as Matsaki Polychrome, Kawaika-a Polychrome, and late-style Sikyatki Polychrome, suggest that Homol'ovi II was abandoned about A.D. 1400. A few early historic sherds, including one of Awatovi Green (Spanish period), one possible Polacca Polychrome sherd (1800s), and several possible 15th-century Zuni sherds, suggest that the site was revisited occasionally.

### Excavated Materials

Many sherds fit with sherds from adjoining rooms to form partially reconstructible vessels. Because most of the rooms had been severely vandalized, such mixing of fill is not surprising. Rather it is surprising that we were able to reconstruct any partial vessels, and in many cases we found parts of these vessels on or near minimally undisturbed floors.

Floor assemblages (Table 3.7, and descriptions of partially reconstructible vessels) consisted primarily of

Jeddito Yellow Ware and types datable to the period from A.D. 1300–1400. Assuming all households had equal access to Sikyatki Polychrome vessels after the inception of that type, absence of Sikyatki Polychrome on the floors suggests these rooms were abandoned by 1375. Even if Sikyatki Polychrome was a rare or special-use type (that is, mortuary or ritual) not used in these rooms, the abundance of Awatovi Black-on-yellow in the floor assemblages together with a smaller amount of Jeddito Black-on-yellow suggests the rooms were last used around 1350 to 1375, and then filled with later trash.

Excavated fill sherds conformed to characteristic assemblages from pueblo trash-filled rooms. Room fill (Tables 3.5-3.7) contained a wide variety of ceramic types, including sherds of Sikyatki Polychrome, datable to after A.D. 1375. Thus, these rooms are likely to have been abandoned while other parts of the pueblo were still occupied. Pond's (1966) kiva, for example, has Sikyatki Polychrome in floor context, suggesting it was not abandoned till after 1375.

### Developmental Sequence
### for Decorated Yellow Ware

Tree-ring dates for Pueblo IV period ceramic types are remarkably scarce, and no tree-ring dates have been obtained from Homol'ovi. Still, it is no longer necessary to follow Colton and Breternitz in assigning types such as Jeddito Black-on-yellow to a period spanning 250 years. Technological and stylistic features that help to refine the Jeddito Yellow Ware chronology are described below. Particularly when whole vessels or at least large bowl rim sherds are available, these features help produce a relative chronology for the 14th-century portion of the Jeddito Yellow Ware sequence.

Pueblo ceramics of the 14th century display the results of a great deal of experimentation in design styles and decorative techniques, and almost any combination of colors and painting techniques could possibly be found during any decade of that century. My general developmental sequence for Jeddito Yellow Ware is based on a series of trends observed in the Homol'ovi sherd material, in Awatovi ceramics (Smith 1971), and in whole vessels from Homol'ovi and the Hopi Mesas, some now in museums (particularly the Field Museum of Natural History and the U.S. National Museum). These trends are: (1) a shift from orange and bright yellow to cream-colored pottery; (2) a shift from bichrome to polychrome; (3) a shift from white outlining, to red outlining, then to massed red areas; (4) changes in the way bowl design fields are framed and defined; (5) changes in design treatment from rigid and geometric to loose and "organic"; and (6) a change from rotational symmetry to asymmetry and bilateral symmetry. The dates presented cannot yet be tied into an absolute chronology with any confidence because of a lack of tree-ring dates for particular types and styles.

Precursors to Jeddito Yellow Ware are Jeddito Black-on-orange, a sherd-tempered, oxidized ware made of an orange-firing yellow clay, and Tusayan Black-on-white, a reduced ware made of a gray clay that fires yellow if oxidized. The successor to Tusayan Black-on-white is Bidahochi Black-on-white, which appears to have been contemporaneous with the early yellow ware types. It has very little temper and a clean, shattering fracture. Smith (1971: 592) sees Jeddito Black-on-orange and Jeddito Polychrome as the "bastard issue of the Northern Polychromes by Tusayan Black-on-white, with some mid-wifely assistance by St. Johns Polychrome..." and suggests that it is the first coal-fired type produced on the Hopi Mesas.

The late Pueblo III to early Pueblo IV period types of Jeddito Black-on-orange and Jeddito Polychrome differ in several ways from the Pueblo III period northern polychrome style. They are the earliest types in the Hopi area to carry a new style, influenced more by St. Johns Polychrome and other types from the south and southeast (Smith 1971: 73). This new style is characterized by paneled designs or three- and four-fold rotational layouts, areas filled with a combination of hatching and corbelling, and a broad, subrim framing line. The broad red bands used in both interior and exterior designs of northern polychrome are not found on Jeddito types. Northern polychromes examined by Smith only rarely had the subrim framing lines characteristic of both Jeddito orange and Jeddito yellow types. Paneled layouts are rare in northern polychrome and common on Jeddito types. There are still some characteristics held in common among northern polychromes, Jeddito Orange types, Bidahochi Black-on-white, and the early yellow ware types; for example, offset-quartered layouts occur frequently on all these types. Both Jeddito Polychrome and the later Bidahochi Polychrome have thin white outlines, in the manner of some of the later northern polychromes, the later White Mountain Red wares, and Homolovi Polychrome.

The earliest Jeddito Yellow Ware types are Huckovi Black-on-orange and Huckovi Polychrome, Awatovi Black-on-yellow, and Bidahochi Polychrome. These have orange and bright yellow paste. Change from Jeddito Black-on-orange to Huckovi Black-on-orange is primarily seen in the loss of visible sherd temper, and secondarily in stylistic change. Change from Tusayan Black-on-white to Awatovi Black-on-yellow is at first only a change of firing atmosphere and fuel, followed by stylistic changes. Bidahochi Black-on-white and Awatovi vessels with virtually the same designs can be found,

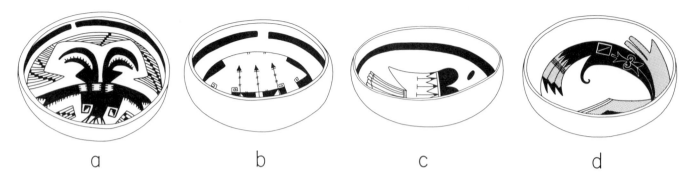

Figure 3.11. Rim design configuration for Jeddito Yellow Ware: *a*, Awatovi Black-on-yellow; *b*, *c*, Jeddito Black-on-yellow; *d*, Awatovi Polychrome (late style Sikyatki Polychrome with engraving). Not to scale. (See Appendix B.)

and the only difference between them is one of firing atmosphere.

Colton gives the beginning date for Jeddito Black-on-yellow as A.D. 1300. Smith divided this type in two on the basis of paste texture, color, and style, and dated them relative to each other on the basis of stratigraphic evidence at Awatovi. Hence, we have Awatovi Black-on-yellow beginning around 1300 and phasing gradually into Jeddito Black-on-yellow, which is the dominant type by 1400. Anything written before 1971, of course, includes the whole range under the term Jeddito. Breternitz (1966: 78) gives a possible range of 1255+ to 1430 for Jeddito Black-on-yellow, with a best fit between 1300 and 1400, and notes the "commonly accepted date of 1300 remains the most plausible beginning date for Jeddito Black-on-yellow." He gives no end date.

Bidahochi Polychrome is dated A.D. 1320 to 1400 by Colton, and Breternitz was unable to find tree-ring evidence to date this type. Collections of whole vessels and sherds suggest this type was not common, and that its stylistic affinity is clearly with Awatovi Black-on-yellow geometric treatment. Smith notes that Bidahochi Polychrome occurred in the Western Mound at Awatovi in levels with Awatovi Black-on-yellow and Bidahochi Black-on-white (about 1300–1350), and also in levels dominated by Jeddito Black-on-yellow (1350–1400). But Bidahochi Polychrome and Sikyatki Polychrome (1375 onward) tend not to co-occur at Homol'ovi II. Hence, an end date of 1375 or thereabouts may be inferred.

Across the continuum of change between Awatovi and Jeddito Black-on-yellow, paste color tends to become lighter. Many Jeddito Black-on-yellow and Sikyatki Polychrome sherds and vessels have a pale, almost ivory, colored paste. Although the white outlining of Bidahochi Polychrome would have been visible on a dark yellow paste, it would have been much less visible on a light yellow paste, and invisible on a creamy or ivory colored ground. This is one possible reason

white outlining was discontinued in favor of red. Red was already being used occasionally as slip on yellow paste, and soon came to be used for outlining (early Sikyatki Polychrome). Massed areas of red had been previously used in the 13th-century Tsegi Polychrome styles.

The lighter paste of yellow ware, particularly the later types, also allowed some yellow color to show through if only a thin layer of paint was applied. Painters could outline these washed areas in dark brown as usual. This is Paayu Polychrome, perhaps a poor man's Sikyatki Polychrome (Sikyatki requires two different pigments). The watery effect of the thin paint may have referred symbolically to water, the way spattered paint is often used to refer to raindrops.

Sometime in the late 1300s, then, the red paint began to be used in massed areas; this is the later style of Sikyatki Polychrome. Lighter paste probably also facilitated visibility of stippling, spattering, and engraving as well as of variable density paint and the addition of orange and red colors. Lighter paste may also reflect a refinement in control over the process of coal firing. All of these techniques are more common in the late 14th-century yellow ware complex.

Toward the end of the 14th century, potters were broadening the subrim framing line and placing it lower on the rim. Then they began to drop the thin line that defines a circular design field in the bottom of a bowl, leaving the design floating below the broad, broken line. Finally, sometime after the abandonment of the Homol'ovi sites, even this line disappeared (Levin 1990), leaving the entire interior surface unbounded and free for decoration (Fig. 3.11).

No vessel or sherd found at the Homol'ovi sites in this excavation or any previous one, judging by museum collections, exhibits the flamboyant zoomorphic style of the Sikyatki Polychrome Fewkes recovered at the site of Sikyatki. It appears that the elaborate polychrome bird and feather designs are a post-1400 phenomenon, possibly even post-1450. This style correlates with an absence of design framing lines, which are present on all the Homol'ovi yellow ware bowls.

## Economic Importance of
## Jeddito Yellow Ware at Homol'ovi

The most striking characteristic of the Homol'ovi II ceramic assemblage is the abundance of Jeddito Yellow Ware relative to other wares. As noted above, vessels of this ware were imported to Homol'ovi from the Hopi Mesas, specifically Awatovi. Jeddito Yellow Ware constitutes 65 percent of the surface sherds (92 percent of the surface decorated ware sherds) and 40 percent of the excavated sherds (87 percent of the excavated decorated ware sherds). If this ceramic ware was a luxury item, a valuable commodity traded throughout the Southwest by a network of elite individuals, as has been suggested (Upham 1982), there were a truly staggering number of elites at Homol'ovi. The sheer quantity of this ware, together with its apparently uniform distribution from room to room and across the entire surface of the site, suggests that it was the most commonly used ceramic ware at Homol'ovi II, accessible to everyone who lived there.

Further evidence of the significance of imported ceramics in the local economy at the household level is the abundance and even distribution of sherds of Awatovi Yellow Ware cooking pots. Although up to 75 percent of utility ware vessels could have been locally made, about 20 percent of the corrugated and plain utility sherds on the site are Awatovi Yellow Ware, almost certainly made on the Hopi Mesas. Mogollon and Alameda Brown wares, also imports, make up another 5 percent.

## Locally Produced Ceramics at Homol'ovi

The small proportion of locally produced Winslow Orange Ware in the assemblage suggests that local production of decorated ware was not an important activity during the major occupation of the pueblo. The few sherds that do appear probably date from the early to mid 1300s. We know from ceramics at Homol'ovi III that Winslow Orange Ware was manufactured from about 1275 to 1300 and possibly persisted until about 1350, with Homolovi Polychrome the most common type at the end of that span. Homolovi Polychrome is the most abundant Winslow Orange Ware type at Homol'ovi II. But the floor assemblages at Homol'ovi II, thought to date to the mid 1300s based on known dates for Jeddito Yellow Ware and radiocarbon dates from hearths, contain very little Winslow Orange Ware. Only one partial Homolovi Polychrome vessel was present, and it is misfired and stylistically aberrant. All the rest

of the decorated vessels are Jeddito Yellow Ware.

Our hypothesis based on the evidence currently available suggests that local manufacture of decorated ceramics was phased out at Homol'ovi by the mid 1300s. Manufacture of utility ware may have persisted somewhat longer, but was certainly supplemented by imported Awatovi Yellow Ware vessels in the later part of the occupation.

That local ceramic manufacture should be phased out in favor of imported wares is not really surprising, considering the local environmental conditions and the evident importance of trade and other forms of interregional interaction in the 14th century. The middle Little Colorado River has probably never offered abundant wood resources. Potters would have competed for scarce brush, driftwood, and the odd cottonwood tree, all of which would also be needed for heating and cooking (Adams 1989b). Corncobs might have supplied some fuel, but by the time Homol'ovi II and the nearby village of Homol'ovi I had reached several hundred rooms each, fuel resources might have been extremely scarce. Further evidence that fuel for firing pots might have been a problem is found in the Winslow Orange Ware sherds themselves. Although some have fairly hard paste and bright orange color, proving that it was possible to make a well-fired pot from local materials, the majority are soft and crumbly, and at least a third of Homolovi Polychrome sherds are muddy colors characteristic of incomplete oxidation.

In addition, population aggregation in the 14th century into large pueblos appears to have been accompanied by a certain amount of economic specialization. Potters at Awatovi were producing ceramics for export as well as local use, and they found a ready market at Homol'ovi. Perhaps Awatovi traders obtained much-needed cotton in exchange for their pots (Adams, Chapter 11). For Homol'ovi people, importing was an alternative to using dwindling local fuel supplies to fire one's own pottery. In addition, the extremely well-fired Jeddito Yellow Ware was much harder and stronger than what could be made locally. It must have traveled well and worn well compared with the softer Winslow Orange Ware. Aesthetics and prestige may also have played important roles in the replacement of local with Hopi-made ceramics, but these factors cannot be evaluated with the evidence now at hand.

Information gleaned from the Homol'ovi II ceramic assemblage from the 1984 research season proves that even materials from vandalized deposits can be interpreted usefully and contribute to regional studies of economic, technological, and social processes. From the site surface collection we have been able to make some inferences about site chronology and trading relationships with other regions and to compare the overall inferences about site chronology and trading relationships with other regions and to compare the overall assemblage at Homol'ovi with ceramics used at other, contemporaneous sites. Excavation provided us with partial floor assemblages that gave us insights into the kinds of ceramics in use at the time these rooms were abandoned.

Questions have been raised here about how and why rapid ceramic change happens, such as the replacement of local with imported ceramics, and some possible answers are suggested. Clearly, further work at Homol'ovi II will lead to refinements of chronology necessary to help study this problem and others. The prognosis for finding ceramics in floor contexts that are only minimally disturbed in future excavations at the site seems good, or at least better than we had anticipated. If parts of the pueblo were indeed two or more stories high, it is possible that deeply buried rooms may be found with complete floor assemblages, which would allow studies of room function, vessel function, and the actual proportions of local and imported vessels in use at the time particular areas of the site were abandoned.

The use of experimental replication and various diagnostic tests to discern local and nonlocal ceramics has been demonstrated. Further studies are needed to assess the performance characteristics of various ceramic wares at Homol'ovi in terms of durability under conditions of use and transport. Answers to such questions will contribute to an understanding of regional craft specialization and trade in the Western Pueblo region.

Stylistic studies summarized here have helped refine the Pueblo IV ceramic chronology, and they also support inferences about ritual organization and changes in iconographic systems (Adams 1989, 1991; Cole 1989). The relatively meager pickings at Homol'ovi II in its current vandalized state were supplemented for this purpose with whole vessels collected in the 1890s and early 1900s. Even though such collections are poorly documented, they were used to address particular problems for which exact proveniences are not necessary.

More work is needed to place artistic change in ceramics in its social context. Some interesting suggestions can be advanced on the basis of available information (Hays 1989; Levin 1990). Change in pottery design structures at about A.D. 1350 and regional patterns in the colors used for pottery and its decoration may be viewed as rules negotiated among groups of potters. These rules may be related to visual communication of information about a vessel's origin and quality and about various aspects of its maker's identity. The breakdown of rules for bounding and framing designs in bowls after the abandonment of Homol'ovi may be related to the final aggregation at the Hopi Mesas, after which long-distance trade in ceramics became less important in the lives of Hopi potters. The increase in depiction of life forms and apparently ritual subjects on pottery at that time, in the mid 1400s, may stem from an intensification of ritual activity and an active negotiation of ritual iconography among the aggregating groups.

Clearly, studies of ceramics from Homol'ovi and experimental work with materials and technology from this place and time have much to contribute to an understanding of late prehistoric economic and ideological interrelationships among Pueblos.

# CHAPTER FOUR

# Manufacture of Gila Polychrome in the Greater American Southwest: An Instrumental Neutron Activation Analysis

Patricia L. Crown and Ronald L. Bishop
Department of Anthropology, Arizona State University
Conservation Analytical Laboratory, Smithsonian Institution

Gila Polychrome was the most widespread abundant polychrome in the Greater American Southwest between A.D. 1300-1450 (Fig. 4.1). At Homol'ovi II a total of 52 Roosevelt Red Ware sherds were recovered, 41 from surface collection and 11 from excavation. The vast majority of these sherds were Gila Polychrome. Ten of these were selected for instrumental neutron activation analysis to help address questions concerning where the type was manufactured and what mechanisms enabled it to become so widespread. A long-standing debate concerns whether or not Gila Polychrome was manufactured by a single culturally unified group. If made by a single group, the widespread distribution of the pottery must be the result of exchange (Doyel 1976: 33; Grebinger 1976: 45; Haury 1945; Lindsay and Jennings 1968) or migration (Franklin and Masse 1976; LeBlanc and Nelson 1976: 77-78; Mayro and others 1976), with the source of pots or people generally attributed to the so-called "heartland" of the Salado culture, the Tonto-Globe area of central Arizona. The alternative explanation argues for manufacture of the pottery on a local basis by indigenous potters (Danson and Wallace 1956; Di Peso 1976; Schroeder 1957). Specific arguments for exchange, migration, or indigenous production hinge on the abundance of the material in regional assemblages and its association with a suite of other "Salado" traits, most notably extended inhumations and compound architecture.

The issue has relevance for addressing a problem of wider significance in the Southwest, that of 14th-century developments and interaction. Exchange of Gila Polychrome pottery over a broad area from a single production source fits the traditional view that each Southwestern culture group had distinct ceramic manufacturing techniques and decorative styles. Alternatively, if Gila Polychrome vessels were manufactured by emigrants from the Tonto-Globe area, the pottery distribution would provide physical evidence for one of the greatest population dispersals yet documented in Southwestern prehistory. Finally, if we posit local manufacture by populations spread throughout the area of Gila Polychrome occurrence, we suggest that macroscopically uniform pottery was manufactured in a geographic area crosscutting the major Southwestern cultural boundaries.

Over the last thirty years, several researchers have conducted small-scale studies to determine the production loci for Gila Polychrome. Petrographic, x-ray diffraction, and x-ray fluorescence analyses of Gila Polychrome produced data interpreted as indicating local manufacture at a number of sites in the Greater Southwest (Crown 1983: 302; Crown and others 1988; Danson and Wallace 1956; Di Peso 1976: 59; LeBlanc and Nelson 1976: 75; Lightfoot and Jewett 1984; Martin and Rinaldo 1960: 186-195; Wallace 1954). Despite these results, the question of exchange versus local production remained unresolved for much of the area in which Gila Polychrome occurs, particularly in those areas where it represents less than 15 percent of the total decorated assemblage at any one site (Doyel and Haury 1976: 130). This issue has particular relevance for Homol'ovi II where the Salado polychromes occur as less than one percent of the decorated assemblage.

## ANALYTICAL PROCEDURE

To resolve this question, we analyzed 184 Gila Polychrome sherds from 21 sites by instrumental neutron activation analysis (Fig. 4.1). The research was designed to amplify the earlier studies by including material from

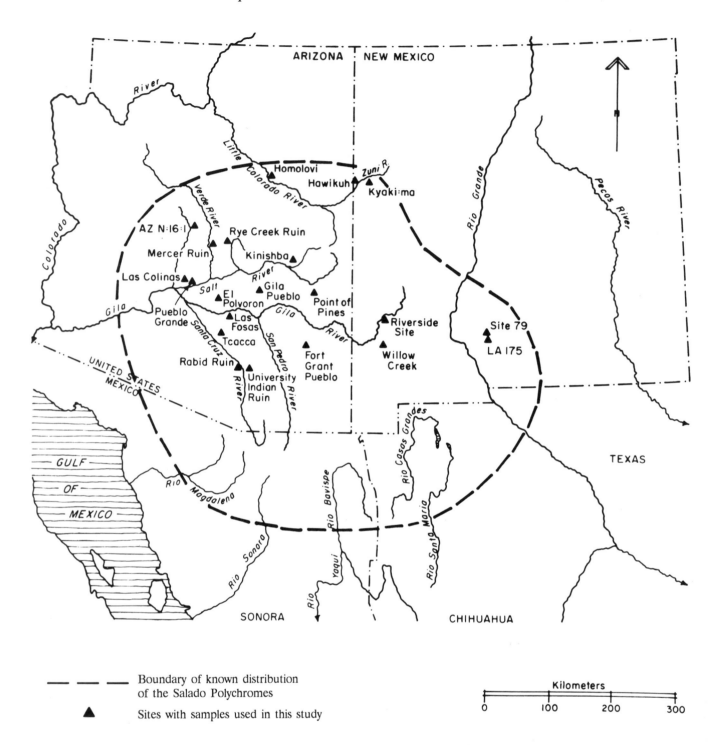

Figure 4.1. Boundary of known distribution of Gila Polychrome
and sites with Gila Polychrome samples used in this study.

more sites and using a technique that would provide more sensitive and precise quantitative data.

The sampling design included a limited number of sherds from each site, because broad patterns of Gila Polychrome compositional variation were sought at the expense of individual site characterization. If significant differences in ceramic pastes covaried with site or subregional provenience, the hypothesis of a single source for the Gila Polychrome in the Southwest could be rejected.

The attempt was made to examine ten bowl sherds from each site, and to include sites from throughout the area of Gila Polychrome distribution. However, problems arose with obtaining even ten sherds from sites in particular geographic areas due to an absence of excavated material. The importance of including these areas for adequate geographic spread resulted in sample sizes of two to ten sherds per site (including two jar sherds in the total sample). Ten bowl sherds from Homol'ovi II were included in the analysis.

Multi-elemental analysis of each sample was carried out using procedures described by Blackman (1986). Seventeen elemental concentrations with an analytical precision of better than five percent (one standard deviation), five of which are determined to better than two percent, were retained for subsequent numerical analysis. These elements extended over several chemical groups: alkalies, rare earths, and transition elements, reflecting a wide range of geochemical processes and enhancing the chances of finding fine divisions within the data.

Initially, the concentrations of Na, K, Sc, Fe, Sb, Cs, La, Ce, Sm, Eu, Yb, Lu, and Th were transformed to log concentration (Harbottle 1976) and submitted to average linkage hierarchical cluster analysis using a matrix of Euclidean distances as the measure of similarity. Concentration data for Ba, Rb, Cr, and Hf were withheld from this initial stage of group formation. The grouping tendencies within the data matrix were summarized in a dendrogram (Sneath and Sokal 1973: 58–60). Clusters of samples formed in this manner are seldom of sufficient refinement for direct archaeological interpretation, so that additional stages of numerical evaluation must be carried out to approximate the potential for archaeologically meaningful structure within a compositional data matrix (Bishop, Rands, and Holley 1982; Bishop and Neff 1989).

Initial inspection of the dendrogram revealed several clusters of samples that shared a common site provenience and the suggestion of high chemical similarity. Using the larger clusters as references, eigenvectors were extracted from a group's variance-covariance matrix and the likelihood of a sample belonging to the reference group was calculated given the generalized distance of that sample from the multivariate group centroid (Bishop, Harbottle, and Sayre 1982; Bishop and Neff 1989).

In evaluating groups with only a few members, we reduced the number of variates using different combinations in turn. In the evaluation and refinement of each group, we sought the smallest group composition that appeared to be internally chemically homogeneous and demonstrably separable from other such formed groups. Samples outside of a stated 95 percent confi-

dence interval enclosing a group were removed and the group's characteristics recalculated. Evaluated one at a time, initially ungrouped samples that fell within a more conservative 80 percent confidence ellipse were added to the group and the group reevaluated. Proceeding iteratively in this manner, some of the initial groups were found to be highly distinctive in their compositional profiles, and several smaller groups were merged into a larger single group.

In an earlier study, twelve trial reference groups were defined (Crown and Bishop 1987). Recent statistical analysis of a larger number of samples has modified our original modeling of the data, reducing the number of groups to eleven and reassigning a few samples; for the most part, however, our recent work has resulted in the expansion of the original groups with fewer samples being "unclassified."

The elemental mean concentrations and standard deviations for each Gila Polychrome reference group are given in Tables 4.1 and 4.2. The correspondence between compositional group and site provenience is listed in Table 4.3. The terms we use to refer to the groups, either implying direction ("East") or site provenience (Fort Grant), are only working labels.

The major distinctions in the compositional data are among a "Core" group, three regional groups to the north, comprised of samples from (1) Homol'ovi and Hawikuh, designated HNORTH, (2) AZ N:16:1, and (3) Kinishba, and two small groups of samples from the Rye Creek and Mercer sites. To illustrate these relationships, the characteristic vectors (eigenvectors) were extracted from the pooled variance-covariance matrix and plotted. The characteristic vectors are linear combinations of the original measurements and provide a convenient set of reference axes against which group relationships can be viewed. Unfortunately, although group separations were obtained in multivariate space, only two dimensions can be shown. In Figure 4.2, the separation of the "Core" group from the more divergent groups is readily apparent. Elemental loadings on the reference axes reflect especially the contributions of La, Ce, Hf, and Th. The present sampling makes it a moot point whether the Rye Creek and Mercer groups represent "outlier" members of the Core unit or not, although all members of the two small Mercer and Rye Creek groups lie outside of a multivariate 95 percent confidence ellipse about the Core group. We illustrate the separation of samples that made up the "Core" group of Figure 4.2 using the first two discriminant axes derived from their pooled variance-covariance matrix (Fig. 4.3); canonical loadings are given in Table 4.4. Groups that plotted close together in Figure 4.3 (for example, the Gila and East groups) are separated on other combinations of axes. With the exception of a

Table 4.1. Gila Polychrome Compositional Reference Units

|       | CORE n = 78 | KINISHBA n = 7 | HNORTH n = 15 | AZ:N:16:1 n = 9 | MERCER n = 7 | RYE n = 6 |
|-------|-------------|----------------|---------------|-----------------|--------------|-----------|
| Na*   | 1.38 ( 13)  | 1.35 (  7)     | 0.436 ( 31)   | 1.24 (  9)      | 0.913 ( 23)  | 1.22 ( 15) |
| K*    | 2.62 ( 11)  | 4.30 ( 14)     | 2.00 ( 19)    | 0.910 ( 30)     | 2.04 ( 15)   | 2.26 ( 11) |
| Sc*   | 13.2 ( 16)  | 13.9 (  7)     | 13.7 ( 14)    | 26.0 (  9)      | 14.6 (  5)   | 13.2 ( 18) |
| Cr*   | 58.6 ( 38)  | 283. ( 11)     | 52.8 ( 10)    | 46.8 ( 19)      | 123. (  7)   | 61.9 ( 44) |
| Fe*   | 4.08 ( 17)  | 3.92 (  8)     | 3.12 ( 24)    | 6.20 (  6)      | 4.43 (  6)   | 4.15 ( 21) |
| Rb    | 120. ( 31)  | 192. ( 27)     | 113.( 29)     | 31.5 ( 31)      | 79.7 ( 35)   | 111. ( 23) |
| Sb*   | 0.841 ( 30) | 1.41 ( 13)     | 1.19 ( 26)    | 0.949 ( 30)     | 1.01 ( 12)   | .889 ( 18) |
| Cs*   | 8.70 ( 33)  | 9.64 ( 38)     | 8.54 ( 19)    | 2.33 ( 20)      | 6.10 (  9)   | 12.0 ( 24) |
| Ba    | 776. ( 28)  | 2090. ( 17)    | 824. ( 38)    | 935. ( 19)      | 950. ( 17)   | 848. ( 27) |
| La*   | 46.0 ( 12)  | 148. ( 16)     | 47.5 ( 15)    | 24.4 ( 11)      | 50.6 ( 13)   | 38.8 ( 10) |
| Ce*   | 80.2 ( 13)  | 228. ( 18)     | 84.2 ( 16)    | 41.0 ( 12)      | 89.0 ( 21)   | 69.2 ( 10) |
| Sm*   | 7.45 ( 12)  | 16.0 ( 13)     | 6.91 ( 14)    | 4.78 (  7)      | 7.46 ( 19)   | 6.29 (  4) |
| Eu*   | 1.35 ( 22)  | 3.17 ( 15)     | 1.33 ( 15)    | 1.03 ( 15)      | 1.25 ( 44)   | 1.33 (  5) |
| Yb*   | 3.77 ( 21)  | 2.45 ( 15)     | 3.48 ( 17)    | 3.13 (  6)      | 3.37 ( 49)   | 3.09 ( 11) |
| Lu*   | 0.522 ( 25) | 0.265 ( 44)    | 0.499 ( 20)   | 0.468 ( 11)     | 0.470 ( 46)  | 0.436 ( 14) |
| Hf*   | 6.46 ( 31)  | 13.0 (  5)     | 5.95 ( 21)    | 4.19 ( 30)      | 6.01 ( 35)   | 5.88 ( 29) |
| Th*   | 12.5 ( 21)  | 72.3 ( 17)     | 16.2 ( 25)    | 5.41 ( 32)      | 10.8 ( 24)   | 11.8 ( 23) |

(Data listed in parts per million except for Na, K, and Fe which are percents.
Numbers in parentheses represent one standard deviation expressed as percent.
* = data used for group refinement.)


Table 4.2. Core Area Compositional Reference Groups

|       | GILA n = 23 | LAS FOSAS n = 7 | IN. RUIN n = 10 | EAST n = 21 | FT. GRANT n = 8 | LAS COLINAS n = 10 |
|-------|-------------|-----------------|-----------------|-------------|-----------------|--------------------|
| Na*   | 1.37 (  6)  | 1.33 (  6)      | 1.35 (  6)      | 1.57 (  8)  | 1.35 ( 14)      | 1.32 (  8) |
| K*    | 2.53 ( 10)  | 2.54 ( 18)      | 2.88 (  4)      | 2.64 (  6)  | 3.01 ( 11)      | 2.52 (  6) |
| Sc*   | 14.6 (  9)  | 14.5 ( 12)      | 10.9 (  5)      | 13.4 ( 11)  | 11.4 ( 14)      | 15.3 ( 11) |
| Cr*   | 56.9 ( 17)  | 53.7 ( 27)      | 40.2 ( 14)      | 67.5 ( 46)  | 43.7 ( 19)      | 86.1 ( 14) |
| Fe*   | 4.21 (  9)  | 4.56 ( 15)      | 3.41 (  6)      | 4.21 ( 18)  | 3.34 ( 13)      | 4.35 (  9) |
| Rb    | 113. ( 29)  | 121. ( 35)      | 154. ( 12)      | 120. ( 30)  | 143. ( 31)      | 103. ( 33) |
| Sb*   | 0.736 ( 19) | 0.975 ( 23)     | 1.05 ( 15)      | 0.681 ( 23) | 0.837 ( 24)     | 1.20 ( 14) |
| Cs*   | 9.91 ( 19)  | 9.03 ( 21)      | 10.3 ( 19)      | 6.70 ( 22)  | 6.36 ( 22)      | 9.96 ( 29) |
| Ba    | 748. ( 20)  | 970. ( 13)      | 821. ( 22)      | 804. ( 25)  | 664. ( 33)      | 677. ( 49) |
| La*   | 41.9 (  7)  | 46.3 (  7)      | 43.7 (  7)      | 48.4 ( 12)  | 52.7 ( 17)      | 46.5 (  5) |
| Ce*   | 74.7 (  8)  | 77.5 ( 11)      | 72.2 (  9)      | 85.2 ( 14)  | 90.7 ( 17)      | 81.4 (  7) |
| Sm*   | 7.04 (  8)  | 8.14 ( 14)      | 7.02 (  5)      | 8.00 ( 14)  | 7.69 ( 12)      | 6.97 (  4) |
| Eu*   | 1.29 ( 21)  | 1.31 ( 34)      | 1.28 (  6)      | 1.49 ( 25)  | 1.21 ( 24)      | 1.37 ( 10) |
| Yb*   | 3.44 ( 10)  | 4.69 ( 31)      | 4.03 ( 11)      | 3.87 ( 17)  | 4.65 ( 15)      | 3.02 (  9) |
| Lu*   | 0.479 ( 10) | 0.699 ( 37)     | 0.574 ( 15)     | 0.516 ( 26) | 0.623 ( 18)     | 0.420 ( 12) |
| Hf*   | 5.46 ( 14)  | 8.81 ( 35)      | 6.29 ( 13)      | 7.99 ( 26)  | 7.42 ( 22)      | 4.71 ( 12) |
| Th*   | 11.4 ( 11)  | 11.1 ( 10)      | 13.3 (  9)      | 13.1 ( 11)  | 17.7 ( 18)      | 9.81 (  5) |

(Data listed in parts per million except for Na, K, and Fe which are percents.
Numbers in parentheses represent one standard deviation expressed as percent
of mean value.  * = data used for group refinement.)

Table 4.3. Provenience Distribution by Compositional Reference Group

| | No.of Sherds | Gila | Las Fosas | Ind. Ruin | East | Las Colinas | Ft. Grant | Mercer | Rye | Kinishba | HNorth | AZ:N:16 | Unclas. |
|---|---|---|---|---|---|---|---|---|---|---|---|---|---|
| Gila Pueblo | 10 | 5 | | | | | | | | | | | 5 |
| El Polvoron | 10 | 8 | 1 | | | | | | | | | | 1 |
| Las Fosas | 10 | 4 | 6 | | | | | | | | | | 0 |
| Tcacca | 10 | 6 | | | | | | | | | | | 4 |
| Pueblo Grande | 10 | | | | | 2 | | | | | | | 8 |
| Las Colinas | 10 | | | | | 8 | | | | | | | 2 |
| Univ. Ind. Ruin | 10 | | | 7 | | | | | | | | | 3 |
| Rabid Ruin | 6 | | | 3 | | | | | | | | | 3 |
| Fort Grant | 9 | | | | | | 8 | | | | | | 1 |
| Riverside | 8 | | | | 6 | | | | | | | | 2 |
| Willow Creek | 10 | | | | 7 | | | | | | | | 3 |
| LA 175 | 5 | | | | 3 | | | | | | | | 2 |
| Site 79 | 5 | | | | 4 | | | | | | | | 1 |
| Kinishba | 10 | | | | 1 | | | | | 5 | | | 4 |
| Point of Pines | 10 | | | | | | | | | 2 | | | 8 |
| Hawikuh | 10 | | | | | | | | | | 10 | | 0 |
| Homol'ovi | 10 | | | | | | | | | | 5 | | 5 |
| Kyakima | 2 | | | | | | | | | | | | 2 |
| Rye Creek | 9 | | | | | | | | 6 | | | | 3 |
| Mercer | 10 | | | | | | | 7 | | | | 1 | 2 |
| AZ N:16:1 | 10 | | | | | | | | | | | 8 | 2 |

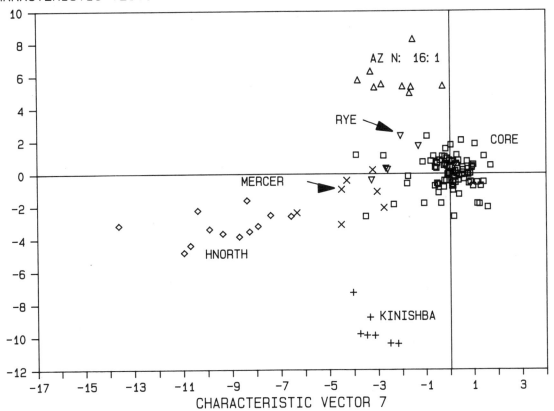

Figure 4.2. Bivariate plot of standardized characteristic Vectors 7 and 10. Vectors derived from the pooled variance-covariance matrix of "Core" Group (Table 4.1) consisting of the compositional reference units of Gila, Las Fosas, University Indian Ruin, East, Ft. Grant, and Las Colinas.

CANONICAL VARIABLE 2

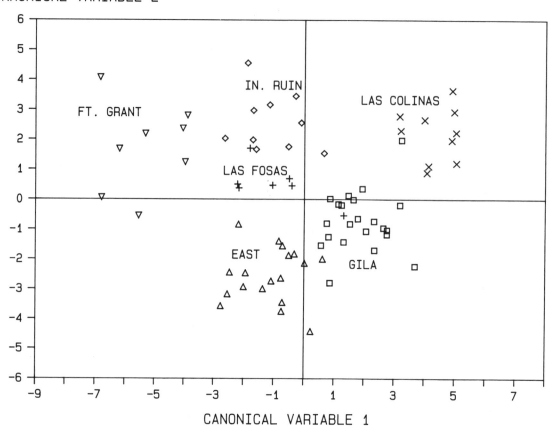

Figure 4.3. Bivariate plot of "Core" Group discriminant axes 1 and 2.

Table 4.4. Coefficients for Canonical Variables
for Core Group Samples

|     | VAR 1  | VAR 2  | VAR 3  | VAR 4  | VAR 5  |
|-----|--------|--------|--------|--------|--------|
| Na  | -3.81  | -19.95 | -3.59  | -1.17  | -2.26  |
| K   | -1.18  | 8.69   | -6.40  | 3.51   | -3.72  |
| Sb  | 4.18   | 8.37   | -4.19  | 4.72   | 6.35   |
| Sc  | 9.35   | -19.95 | 26.94  | -50.03 | 17.56  |
| Cr  | 2.22   | 1.62   | -2.78  | 2.09   | 1.83   |
| Fe  | -2.29  | 22.51  | -15.9  | 44.51  | 2.21   |
| Cs  | 4.38   | -0.10  | 6.47   | -0.46  | -6.90  |
| La  | -11.32 | 22.9   | -23.68 | -2.70  | 11.42  |
| Ce  | -2.51  | -8.48  | -6.80  | -25.07 | -18.66 |
| Eu  | 3.46   | -2.12  | -2.74  | -0.76  | -3.14  |
| Sm  | 21.58  | -30.6  | 8.73   | 21.97  | -3.35  |
| Yb  | -10.4  | 7.82   | -1.20  | -2.78  | -3.55  |
| Lu  | 0.01   | 1.75   | 6.31   | -5.38  | 2.93   |
| Th  | -15.24 | 3.86   | 13.84  | -1.52  | 8.94   |
| Hf  | -3.59  | -7.15  | 1.26   | 1.01   | 2.82   |

single sample from the Las Colinas cluster, all samples were correctly classified by the discriminant analysis program, which illustrates the tendency toward group compositional differentiation in a reduced dimensional space. The majority of ceramic samples from several sites are member reference groups characterized by internal compositional homogeneity. It is not possible to state precisely what these units represent in terms of *real* sources for the vessels, but as *analytic* sources the reference units clearly covary with provenience. Interestingly, samples from sites only 35 km apart came from clearly distinct analytic sources.

Given 21 sites and 11 compositional reference groups, some sites share analytic sources. In all instances where two or more sites share a single analytic source, the sites are in close proximity. These shared analytic sources may represent a single center producing vessels for two sites, a single materials source used by potters from multiple production loci, or simply areas of high geological homogeneity with true ceramic manufacture at multiple loci using multiple compositionally similar materials sources. Larger samples would have permitted more definitive interpretations. By way of example, we can point to the compositional relationships among the ceramics analyzed from the sites of Homol'ovi and Hawikuh. At one level, sherds from these two sites may be considered to constitute a single subregional reference unit notable for the patterned divergence of this group from the other samples analyzed. On a more refined level, however, there are differences in the correlations of certain elements (for example, Na, Fe, Sc, Ce, and Sm) that strongly suggest that a single specific source of raw material was not exploited by potters at the two sites, and that the groups could be compositionally differentiated with more extensive sampling.

Sixty-two samples could not be assigned unambiguously to any of the eleven compositional groups. However, several samples found just outside of the stated confidence interval were of the same site provenience as those constituting the group. Over 50 percent of the sherds from three sites failed to be identified with a single analytic source; these sites are Point of Pines (AZ W:10:50), Kyaki:ma (only two samples), and Pueblo Grande. Clearly vessels from these sites were manufactured from a number of different materials sources, but the broad dispersion of samples analyzed admits three interpretations. The heterogeneity may represent potters working with a wide variety of compositionally distinct materials, geographically disparate sources with the vessels or materials brought into the site from outside, or sampling error. It is also possible that some vessels were "locally" manufactured and others exchanged from different loci of production.

## DISCUSSION

The results obtained in this study demonstrate that the Gila Polychrome bowls found at 21 sites in the Southwest were not all manufactured from the same materials. Instead, eleven distinct but internally homogeneous analytic sources are present in the sample. The most parsimonious interpretation of these data involves equating analytic source with locus of production. If we accept that multiple production loci are present in these data, and note the correlation of production loci with geography, we can conclude that Gila Polychrome bowls were being manufactured throughout their area of distribution within the Southwest. Each manufacturing locus produced vessels apparently distributed primarily within a restricted area. Corroboration of this interpretation would require identification of local clay-nonplastic materials sources for each of the 11 groups, with no guarantee that the proper mix of materials could be recreated in the laboratory for proof of local

manufacture. Alternative procedures for reinforcing the argument for local manufacture would entail comparison of the Gila Polychrome assemblage from each site with types known to have been manufactured at the sites, or examination of much larger samples of Gila Polychrome sherds and evaluation of the compositional variation in accordance with the Criterion of Abundance (Bishop, Rands, and Holley 1982). The scope of the present study precludes enlarging the sample to the size demanded by these procedures. However, the small-scale petrographic studies discussed previously strengthen arguments for local manufacture.

Although the majority of the samples from most sites fell into one group, low numbers of samples from these same sites fell into different groups. Although lacking in statistical robustness, this observation suggests that even though most sites apparently had a single nearby primary source for Gila Polychrome bowls, vessels from distant sources were exchanged into the sites.

Turning specifically to the Homol'ovi II sample, several observations can be made. First, the sherds do not represent a homogeneous sample, but derive from multiple analytic sources. As noted above, although five of the Homol'ovi sherds were grouped with sherds from Hawikuh, sufficient differences exist between the two sets of sherds to suggest that the groups could be compositionally separated given a larger sample. We would not argue that the 15 samples in the HNORTH compositional reference group represent a single raw material source.

Gila Polychrome bowls from Homol'ovi appear to derive from at least two materials sources that are distinct from the materials sources used to produce the Gila Polychrome vessels from other sites in this study. Whether the Homol'ovi II materials sources represent distinct production loci as well is not known. We cannot specify where the vessels were manufactured on the basis of this analysis. All of the bowls analyzed may have been manufactured at Homol'ovi or all may have been produced elsewhere and traded into the site. Although our interpretive abilities are limited at this level, it is clear that the materials used to produce the Homol'ovi bowls are not compositionally identical to the vessels from any other sites analyzed, suggesting distinct production loci, wherever these are located.

Gila Polychrome occurs at many sites and in large portions of the Greater Southwest that were not represented in the study. Further research should fill some of these gaps. However, the basic question has been answered with a minimal data set, that is, Gila Polychrome bowls were manufactured in virtually every portion of the Southwest examined in this study. The results indicate that the pottery was manufactured far outside of the area where any previous research has suggested local manufacture in an area constituting over 130,000 square kilometers. Manufacture apparently occurred "locally," that is, in the absence of empirical evidence for trade, even at sites and in areas where the amount of Salado polychrome pottery represents less than one percent of the total decorated assemblage (Doyel and Haury 1976: 129). This widespread production is particularly intriguing when assessed within the broader confines of Southwestern ceramic manufacturing traditions. Gila Polychrome occurs in sites and areas that are traditionally defined as Anasazi, Mogollon-Western Pueblo, and Hohokam, and was apparently manufactured in these areas characterized by long-standing distinct ceramic manufacturing traditions and decorative styles. Apparently, Gila Polychrome was simply added to these long-standing repertoires, while traditional techniques and decorative styles continued to be used in manufacturing types that were quite distinct from the Gila Polychrome products.

The study leaves unanswered the question of whether the pottery was manufactured by migrants from the Salado "heartland" or by indigenous populations in the areas of its occurrence. Instrumental neutron activation analysis results cannot provide substantiation of arguments for or against migration, but it is difficult to envision migration of people from the Tonto-Globe area resulting in the distribution of ceramic production techniques we see here. Such an exodus should have been accompanied by a corresponding population decline in the Salado "heartland," yet the 14th century was apparently a time of population increase in the Tonto-Globe area (Doyel 1976: 10; LeBlanc and Nelson 1976: 78). Salado "peoples" may have expanded into some portions of the Southwest, but the occurrence of locally manufactured Salado pottery alone cannot be taken to indicate the presence of emigrants from the Tonto-Globe area.

The question remains of how the knowledge to manufacture this pottery spread, as does the reason for its tremendous popularity. It may represent a fad (Di

Peso 1976), an elite exchange network (Wilcox 1987), or a regional cult. Research with whole Salado polychrome vessels investigating decorative styles, iconography, and contexts of recovery for particular designs may provide a means for answering the remaining question of why Gila Polychrome came to be the most widespread pottery manufactured in the Greater Southwest (Crown 1990).

*Note*: Analytical data are curated in the Smithsonian Archaeometric Research Collections and Records (SARCAR) facility of CAL. Details of the analytical procedures, numerical procedures, or copies of the data are available through request to the SARCAR Manager. Tables were provided camera-ready by the authors.

*Acknowledgments*. The neutron activation analysis was carried out by Bishop at the National Bureau of Standards as a Guest Worker in the Nuclear Methods Group, and the authors wish to thank M. James Blackman for facilitating the neutron activation analyses at that facility. Completion of the study was expedited by Crown's appointment as a Research Collaborator in the Conservation Analytical Laboratory (CAL) of the Smithsonian Institution. We are grateful to Lambertus van Zelst, Director of CAL, for permission to use those facilities. A number of institutions generously provided materials for this study: the Arizona State Museum, University of Arizona; the Fort Burgwin Research Center; the Museum of the American Indian; the National Park Service; the Pueblo Grande Museum; and the Zuni Archaeological Program. Crown's study of the Salado polychromes has been funded by the American Philosophical Society and Southern Methodist University. Dr. W. James Judge, Dr. Hector Neff, and two anonymous reviewers provided critical comments on an earlier version of Chapter 4. We are deeply indebted to all of these people, but we must take full responsibility for any errors of fact or logic in our study.

# CHAPTER FIVE

# Ground Stone

Lee Fratt
Arizona State Museum

The 121 ground stone artifacts recovered during the 1984 field season at Homol'ovi II include 70 items from excavation and 51 from the site's surface. The excavated ground stone assemblage includes all of the artifacts found during excavation; however, only a select group of ground stone artifacts observed on the site's surface was recovered. This group includes 14 items found in the collection units and 37 "diagnostic" artifacts from the site's three plazas (Fig. 1.2). "Diagnostic" artifacts collected from the plaza surfaces outside the collection units include complete or nearly complete specimens, artifacts with some morphological integrity that could yield information about ground stone tool use at the site, and items subject to collection by vandals (Chapter 1). Whereas all the ground stone artifacts that were found in the collection units were saved, the nondiagnostic ground stone artifacts observed outside of the plaza collection units were not recorded or recovered.

Although the surface assemblage recovered represents an unknown sample of the ground stone actually observed on the site's surface, these artifacts were analyzed and included with the excavated artifacts because there was no statistically significant difference between the surface assemblage and the excavated assemblage and because they increased the sample's size. The analysis goals were: (1) to obtain information about the kinds of activities that involved using ground stone implements, (2) to determine the degree of reuse of ground stone artifacts and the utilization of local and nonlocal materials for ground stone manufacture, and (3) to examine depositional and postdepositional processes at the site. These goals were constrained by the nature of the subsurface contexts and the surface collection strategy. For example, of the 70 excavated artifacts, 32 (46 percent) were from disturbed deposits (see Table 5.2). Likewise, information about activities involving ground stone tool use in the plazas was limited by the collection strategy. Despite these difficulties, the analyses of morphological characteristics, use-wear, and artifact distribution reveal trends in ground stone manufacture and use at Homol'ovi II that warrant further investigation.

## ANALYSIS METHODS

To obtain information about ground stone artifact use and reuse at Homol'ovi II, various morphological characteristics and evidences of use-wear were recorded for each artifact. Because almost all the ground stone artifacts recovered from Homol'ovi II are made of sandstone, this particular use-wear analysis pertains to sandstone artifacts and does not necessarily apply to artifacts made of other kinds of stone.

## MORPHOLOGICAL CHARACTERISTICS

Macroscopic evidences of manufacture and use that were observed and recorded include grinding, pecking, flaking, and the contour of used surfaces. Other characteristics that were recorded include condition, weathering, material, artifact size, and shape.

Pecking occurs when a stone is struck with the point or edge of another hand-held stone of equal or greater hardness. The resulting surface displays numerous small, usually closely placed depressions (Fig. 5.1c, d). Microscopically, pecking leaves impact scars, cones, and dimples on the sand grains and cement (J. Adams 1986).

Pecking can occur during manufacture or use. Pecking that appears on a ground use-surface, especially on manos or metates, is generally attributable to resharpening. Because grinding surfaces are generally not sharpened until needed, the presence or absence of pecking on manos and metates, together with other features such as differences in thickness and use-surface contour, can suggest differences in use-life for individual artifacts. Pecked areas on nonused surfaces usually result from manufacture, but they may indicate an artifact has been reshaped or reused.

Figure 5.1. Evidences of manufacture or use on ground stone artifacts: *a,* flaked edges on a mano; *b,* ground surface on a mano; *c,* pecked surface on a grinding slab; *d,* pecked surface on a mano. (Top edge of *b* is 5.34 cm.)

Flaking occurs when pieces of stone are struck from the artifact (Fig. 5.1*a*), leaving visible flake scars with relatively sharp edges (J. Adams 1986). Flaking is easiest to recognize macroscopically and on artifacts made of relatively fine-grained material. Whether artifacts made of medium- to coarse-grained material had been flaked usually could not be determined because the presence and placement of flake scars were difficult to distinguish from fortuitous breakage. Flaking generally is associated with manufacture, but may indicate that an artifact has been reshaped for secondary use.

The contour of used surfaces was recorded for all artifacts. The used surface contour refers to the general shape in profile and relative to a flat object, such as a ruler, laid across the surface. Contours were recorded as flat, concave, convex, and, in the case of manos, concave with rounded ends, a contour that distinguishes manos used with trough metates. Additionally, the shape of longitudinal cross sections was recorded for metates, and transverse (lateral) cross-section shape was recorded for manos.

The contour of an artifact's use-surfaces, its size, and other attributes of shape indicate how the artifact was used and the length or intensity of use. The use-surface contour of a mano is complementary to the use-surface contour of the metate in which it was used. Thus, manos having convex use-surfaces with rounded ends were used on trough metates, whereas manos with flat or convex use-surface contours with unrounded ends were used on slab metates. Woodbury (1954: 54) notes that metates that were used relatively little are uniform in thickness and those that were well used are thinner at one end. Bartlett's (1933: 13) observation that small, thin manos represent exhausted tools seems reasonably well accepted (Cameron 1985). Although exhausted manos were found (see Fig. 5.5*c, d*), no exhausted

metate remains were recovered from Homol'ovi II during the 1984 field season.

Trying to infer the degree of wear from the shape of artifacts and use-surfaces is a frustrating exercise in the perils of isolating form, function, and use. For example, although slope and concavity of metate use-surfaces have been offered as indices of the degree of wear (Woodbury 1954: 54), other researchers (Bartlett 1933; Boyer 1986; Wiseman 1970) have pointed out that the shape of metate grinding surfaces results from the interaction of several factors, including manufacture, the granularity of the material, and the length of the mano relative to the width of the metate. It is clear that the relationship between form and use or function is complex and depends on several different interacting processes that are difficult to isolate (Woodbury 1954: 80–81).

Identification of local materials was accomplished through comparisons to raw material samples collected from several locations in the study area. Both the artifacts and the raw materials were identified and characterized by a geologist.

Size measurements include length (measured from end to end), width (measured from side to side), thickness (measured from surface to surface), and weight. Measurements were taken to the nearest tenth of a centimeter with a ruler or electronic digital calipers. A digital scale was used to weigh small artifacts and a mechanical scale was used for large artifacts.

The condition of each ground stone artifact was recorded as complete, incomplete, or fragmentary and was used to estimate the number of artifacts represented by the assemblage. The number of artifacts represented by fragments of manos and metates could usually be determined because there is a lot of variability between individual artifacts and fragments are distinctive. But the number of piki stones, griddles, and miscellaneous unidentified artifacts represented by fragments could not be determined because the burned condition of some erased distinctive characteristics, the distinguishing attributes of these artifacts were unknown, and the fragments were generally small and similar (J. Adams 1979: 27).

Weathering, or exposure to extreme heat as in a fire, may cause even well-cemented sandstone to become friable. An artifact was classified as friable if it crumbled when touched. As a result of these problems, functional identification of many of the surface artifacts and excavated artifacts that were badly weathered depended primarily on morphological characteristics rather than on traces of use-wear.

Besides weathering, other factors reflecting processes of discard and deposition, such as artifact condition and burning, were examined. Whether an artifact had been burned was usually easy to identify, but it was difficult to determine whether the burning occurred during use (piki stones, griddles, and some abraders), after discard, or when an activity area or room burned. It was also often difficult to distinguish burning from patination, especially on artifacts collected from the site's surface.

## MICROSCOPIC USE-WEAR

Ground surfaces on lithic artifacts result when the stone is rubbed against some other material. This material can be another stone, with or without an intermediary material between the two surfaces (stone against stone contact, J. Adams 1989a: 263), or it can be another substance such as wood, bone, shell, or hide wherein processing involves the use of only one stone. During grinding, elevated areas of an artifact's unmodified, uneven surface are worn down so that the ground surface becomes progressively more even (Fig. 5.1b). Some ground surfaces may even develop a sheen or glassy appearance from tribochemical wear due to heavy, continuous use (J. Adams 1986: 69–70, 106).

If an artifact could not be identified as having been ground from macroscopic evidence alone, it was examined with a 20x binocular light microscope. Microscopic traces of grinding or abrasion include scratches, frosting, chipping, rounding, polishing, impact scars, and leveling of sand grains relative to interstices (the spaces between individual grains) or filling of interstices with debris, cement, or patination (J. Adams 1989b).

Whether or not differences in microscopic use-wear can be detected depends on the type of material processed and the granularity of the sandstone used to make the tools. Traces of use-wear give clues as to how the artifact was manufactured and used, what substances were ground or abraded, the length or intensity of use, and whether the artifact was reused (J. Adams 1986, 1989a, 1989b). Determining this information for ground stone artifacts requires considering the interaction of several different factors. For example, whether a surface was ground by use (termed the use-surface) or ground to shape during manufacture is often difficult to determine, especially when the artifacts are fragmentary, made of fine-grained material, or well shaped, such as manos. Identifying surfaces ground by use was based on the presence of microscopic use-wear and on characteristics of the wear of sand grains relative to interstices. These patterns contrast to stone-on-stone wear with no intermediary material, which would characterize grinding for shaping. The presence of sheen also distinguished ground use-surfaces from shaped surfaces. This distinction is important because the number of use-surfaces may reflect how intensely ground stone artifacts were used at a site.

Microscopic traces of use-wear not only aid in identifying manufacturing techniques and distinguishing used from unused surfaces, but also yield information about the kinds of materials that were processed (J. Adams 1986, 1989a, 1989b). During the 1987–1989 field seasons at Homol'ovi III, volunteers from Earthwatch and the University of Arizona made tools out of locally obtained sandstone and then used these tools to process a variety of materials, including corn, bone, shell, wood, hide, clay, sherds, sunflower and amaranth seeds, and other pieces of sandstone. These experimental artifacts were then brought back to the Arizona State Museum in Tucson and the microscopic traces of use-wear on the different artifacts were compared (J. Adams 1989a).

This study, reported in detail by J. Adams (1989b), showed that different patterns of microscopic use-wear were associated with processing different materials. Thus, wear produced by stone-on-stone contact, like that produced by grinding corn, seeds, sherds, or clay between two ground stone tools, is readily distinguishable from wear produced by one stone abrading more resilient material like wood or bone. By using these experimental artifacts for reference it has been possible to distinguish the microscopic traces of wear resulting from using sandstone artifacts to grind or abrade different kinds of material.

The following patterns of microscopic use-wear and the materials with which they are associated were discerned on the Homol'ovi II ground stone assemblage. These groups are less specific than those discussed by J. Adams (1989b) because of differences in raw materials (especially granularity) between the experimental and prehistoric artifacts, patination, burning, and the possibility that the prehistoric artifacts were used to process more than one kind of material.

1. Grain grinding (Fig. 5.2): attributable to grinding corn or amaranth. Sand grains are worn level to interstices. Entire sand grains are plucked out in some areas, leaving pits on the surface. Tops of sand grains are frosted, scratched, and chipped but this wear does not extend down the sides of individual sand grains or appear on sand grains in pits or depressions on the surface. A lustrous sheen appears across the leveled grains and interstices disappear as grinding debris accumulates and as sand grains are worn down. The entire surface may develop a bright, glassy sheen from continuous use.

2. Other hard material (Fig. 5.3): attributable to stone-on-stone grinding with no intermediary material or to grinding sherds or clay or to abrading shell. The pattern of wear is similar to corn grinding in that sand grains are worn level to interstices and individual grains may be plucked out leaving pits on the surface. However, the leveled tops of the sand grains are more

Figure 5.2. Photomicrograph (40x) of use-wear on a Homol'ovi III mano attributed to grain grinding. The surface has been uniformly leveled as sand grains are worn to the interstices. (Photograph by Lee Fratt.)

Figure 5.3. Photomicrograph (40x) of use-wear on a Homol'ovi III handstone that is similar to the wear on the experimental artifacts used to grind clay or sherds. There are deep gouges on the surfaces of the sand grains and the surface topography is slightly uneven, as indicated by the presence of interstices. (Photograph by Lee Fratt.)

severely damaged and show deep gouges and scratches or they appear to be crushed. Wear does not extend down the sides of individual sand grains or appear on grains in the pits. No lustrous sheen appears on the leveled grains. Distinguishing stone-on-stone grinding due to use rather than shaping depended primarily on the relative degree to which the surface was worn, as indicated by how much sand grains had been leveled to interstices.

3. Hide processing: some leveling of sand grains to interstices and some chipping and rounding of sand grains occurs. The most distinctive characteristic is the polish that covers the entire contact surface (not just the tops of the leveled sand grains) and that appears, along with chipping and rounding of individual grains, in pits and depressions on the used surface.

4. Resilient material (Fig. 5.4): attributable to abrading material such as wood or bone with no upper stone. Instead of being leveled to interstices, sand grains remain elevated but their tops and sides are chipped and rounded. These characteristics, especially the appearance of wear extending down the sides of sand grains, are present across most of the used surface. The wear produced by abrading wood is not yet distinguishable from that produced by abrading bone (J. Adams 1989b: 271). Consequently, no attempt was made to identify this use-wear in the Homol'ovi II assemblage.

The greater variety in material texture, or granularity, of the stone used to make the prehistoric artifacts was the major factor constraining the use-wear analysis. In order to determine an artifact's granularity, its grain size was compared to the scales in Wentworth (1922: 33).

Figure 5.4. Photomicrograph (40x) of use-wear on a Homol'ovi III grinding slab that is similar to the wear on the experimental artifacts used to grind resilient material such as wood or bone. Chipping and polishing extend from the top and down the sides of the elevated sand grains and the surface topography is extremely uneven. (Photograph by Lee Fratt.)

Granularity was classified as conglomerate, coarse, medium, fine, or variable. Whenever possible, granularity was determined by examining unaltered surfaces. Generally, the finer the texture of the stone, the more difficult it is to detect traces of use-wear due to grinding or abrasion, because identifying microscopic use-wear relies on detecting differences between wear on the tops and sides of individual sand grains as well as in pits, depressions, and interstices (J. Adams 1989b).

Relatively coarse surfaces on manos and metates may indicate either pecking to resharpen a well-used artifact or the presence of unworn patches on the use-surface. The latter suggests that the artifact was relatively little used. Resharpened areas are characterized by the presence of impact scars, cones, and dimples. These traces of wear may not be easy to detect on fine-grained stone artifacts and in such cases, resharpening may be identi-

fied by the relative regularity of the pecked areas. On coarse-grained artifacts, the microscopic traces of resharpening are easier to detect, as is the degree to which individual grains are worn to a single plane. Conversely, macroscopic traces of wear from use or manufacture, such as flake scars or pecking, are often easier to identify on fine-grained objects than on coarse-grained objects.

Identifying the use of the Homol'ovi II artifacts was further complicated by the possibility of reuse, which can alter traces of earlier manufacture and use (Holmes 1896), the possibility of multiple use (Woodbury 1954; J. Adams 1986), and relative degree of weathering. The effects of weathering differ according to the length of time an artifact was exposed on the ground surface, the environment of deposition, and the nature of the stone used to make the artifact.

At Homol'ovi II, some traces of use-wear that are typically present on excavated artifacts were often lacking on artifacts collected from the site's surface. For example, the direction of scratches on excavated ground stone that was exposed on the surface before being buried may be indistinct or nonexistent. Therefore, artifacts on which the direction of scratches can be determined may have been buried relatively quickly following their loss or discard. On 69 percent of the surface artifacts, scratches on sand grains were absent or their direction (indicating direction of use) could not be determined, regardless of granularity, because patination partially or wholly covered the used surface. In contrast, the direction of scratches could be determined for 67 percent of the excavated artifacts. Also, there were relatively few small particles on the use-surfaces of exposed artifacts, a use-wear feature typical of manos and metates (J. Adams 1986).

## MATERIAL

Of the 121 ground stone artifacts recovered, 117 (97 percent) were sandstone, three (2 percent) were vesicular basalt, and one (1 percent) was an unknown rock, perhaps a siltstone or volcanic tuff (Table 5.1). If the composition of an artifact was not readily identifiable, the standard guide by Hamilton and others (1974) was used.

Locally available material was used for 85 percent of the ground stone artifacts and 15 percent of them, including the artifact made of unknown material, were made from rock presumably obtained from nonlocal sources. Locally available stone can be obtained from outcrops located within 5 km of Homol'ovi II, including Shinarump and Moenkopi sandstone and vesicular basalt from the Owl Rock member of the Chinle Formation.

Table 5.1. Material of Homol'ovi II Ground Stone Artifacts

| Artifact | Material | | | | | |
| --- | --- | --- | --- | --- | --- | --- |
| | Shinarump Sandstone | Moenkopi Sandstone | Vesicular Basalt | Nonlocal(?) Sandstone | Other | Total |
| Manos | 38 | 2 | 1 | 12 | | 53 |
| Metates | 7 | 1 | | 2 | | 10 |
| Piki Stones or Griddles | 1 | 1 | | | 1[a] | 3 |
| Manos or Metates | | | | 2 | | 2 |
| Abraders | 6 | 2 | | 1 | | 9 |
| Grinding Slabs | 2 | | | | | 2 |
| Paint Palette | | 1 | | | | 1 |
| Handstone | 1 | | | | | 1 |
| Hoes | 1 | 1 | | | | 2 |
| Architectural Fragments | 1 | 10 | | | 1[a] | 12 |
| Miscellaneous Unidentified | 12 | 10 | | | 1[b] | 23 |
| Other | | 1 | 2 | | | 3 |
| Total | 69 | 29 | 3 | 17 | 3 | 121 |
| (Percent) | (57.0) | (24.0) | (2.5) | (14.0) | (2.5) | |

a. Burned sandstone.    b. Unknown, not sandstone and nonlocal(?)

Of the 117 sandstone artifacts recovered, 84 percent were made of locally available materials and 15 percent were made of rock obtained from apparently nonlocal sources. Two artifacts were severely burned, which precluded identifying their material as local or nonlocal sandstone (Table 5.1). The dominance of the locally available sandstone in the assemblage directly reflects its abundance in the Homol'ovi II area. The village was built atop the Shinarump Conglomerate, the basal member of the Chinle Formation, and another outcrop of Shinarump Conglomerate that was used for resource procurement is 3 km southeast of Homol'ovi II. The material of some ground stone artifacts made of Shinarump Conglomerate appears identical to that at the procurement site. The Shinarump overlies the Moenkopi Formation that outcrops on numerous buttes near Homol'ovi II.

The ground stone artifacts made from the locally available Shinarump and Moenkopi sandstones were readily distinguishable from those made of other, presumably nonlocal, types of sandstone. Artifacts were identified as being made of Shinarump or Moenkopi based on color, texture, and bedding. Shinarump is highly variable, ranging from dark purplish to light tan or buff and from conglomerate to fine-grained. The sand grains tend to be poorly sorted and range from angular to rounded. Shinarump also ranges from well cemented, approaching a true quartzite, to very poorly cemented and friable.

Moenkopi sandstone exhibits varying shades of red or green depending on the amount of hematite in its illite clay cement and on the environment of formation. Moenkopi ranges from medium- to fine-grained and the sand grains are better sorted. Specimens range from well cemented to very poorly cemented and friable, but they never exhibit the quartzite-like qualities characterizing some of the Shinarump material. Moenkopi sandstone often exhibits relatively thin, parallel, horizontal beds along which it readily spalls.

The vesicular basalt used for three artifacts was probably procured locally. Similar material appears in the Owl Rock member of the Chinle Formation, and an outcrop was found 5 km east of Homol'ovi II. An alternative source for this material is the streambed of the Little Colorado River or one of its tributaries, many of which flow through volcanic formations along the Mogollon Rim and in the Hopi Buttes. Two of the vesicular basalt artifacts recovered may be pieces of water-worn cobbles because, though rounded, they show no purposeful shaping or use-wear.

Although the type of sandstone used to make 17 artifacts could not be identified, they are presumed to have been obtained from nonlocal sources, that is, sources located more than 5 km from Homol'ovi II (according to Richard Lange). Possible candidates include Clear Creek and Chevelon Canyon, both of which are south of Homol'ovi II. One of the nonlocal types of sandstone may be from the upper member of the Chinle Formation, judging from the bluish purple color of the sand grains, and another type may be Coconino sandstone, based on the cross bedding of its well-sorted and well-rounded grains.

## ASSEMBLAGE DESCRIPTION

The Homol'ovi II ground stone artifacts were sorted into the conventional morphologically based categories. These categories were then modified according to the information obtained from the use-wear studies. The traces of microscopic use-wear were particularly informative and in several cases they belied the classification of a particular artifact based on morphological evidence alone. One artifact originally classified as a mano was reclassified as a handstone because microscopic use-wear indicated it had not been part of a grinding kit and had not been used to grind grain. Examination of microscopic use-wear also helped identify several artifacts as flagstone fragments that originally had been placed in the miscellaneous unidentified category.

The classifications used here are modified from Woodbury (1954) and J. Adams (1979). The assemblage was divided into four general descriptive categories based on whether the inferred primary use was (1) food processing (grinding grain, cooking), (2) nonfood processing (including tools used to shape other artifacts and apparent utilitarian artifacts that were ground to shape), (3) other, or (4) miscellaneous unidentified. The third category refers to artifacts that were shaped by grinding but apparently were not used for utilitarian tasks. They may have been used in ceremonies or kept for their unique or aesthetic qualities. The fourth category includes implements that may have been multi-purpose tools and fragments of artifacts whose use could not be identified. Recovery contexts, measurements, and other details of the ground stone artifacts are presented in Tables 5.2 through 5.5. Additional descriptive information is given in Fratt (1991).

### Food Processing Implements

Ground stone food processing implements include manos, metates, and piki stones. The stone mano and metate comprise the pueblo grinding kit that was used to process whole grains like corn into meal. The material to be processed was placed on the large, stationary metate and the smaller, hand-held mano was rubbed over the surface of the metate in a back-and-forth motion, thereby crushing the corn or other material (Reinhart 1965). Although manos and metates could have been used to grind many different kinds of material, J. Adams (1979: 5) reports that Hopi informants from Walpi Village consistently identified them as corn-grinding tools. Another artifact whose modern counterpart is still used at Hopi and other pueblos is the piki stone. It is used to cook a thin corn gruel into a wafer bread called piki. The stone is cured by successively oiling and heating it until the surface is smooth and slick, thereby preventing the thin corn gruel from sticking while it cooks (O'Kane 1950: 42-44). Piki bread is used as a daily food item as well as an item distributed and eaten on ceremonial occasions (J. Adams 1979: 5, 27).

### Manos

Only 3 of the 53 manos recovered from Homol'ovi II were complete (Table 5.3). Most of the manos were made of Shinarump or Moenkopi sandstone (Tables 5.1, 5.2). The predominance of Shinarump sandstone in the mano assemblage (72%) suggests that it had qualities that made it especially suitable for grinding grain. One such quality may have been its wide range of granularity. Bartlett (1933: 4) reports that among the Pueblo Indians, milling stones of different granularity were used to grind corn meal to various degrees of fineness. Moenkopi sandstone exhibits only medium- and fine-grained textures that presumably limit its use to the final stages of grinding, when finely ground meal is produced. In contrast, the wider range of granularity exhibited by Shinarump sandstone would make it suitable for use during all grinding stages. The differences in cement or in mineral composition between these two local types of sandstone also may have affected their use-life or grinding efficiency.

Granularity ranged as follows: 9 artifacts (17%) were made of conglomerate sandstone, 10 (19%) were coarse, 16 (30%) were medium, 17 (32%) were fine, and 1 (2%) had variable texture. If the conglomerate and coarse-grained categories are combined, then the number of manos in the three major categories is relatively even. These data indicate that all stages of grain grinding had equal importance at Homol'ovi II.

The number of grinding surfaces may reflect the relative intensity of grain grinding, according to the hypothesis that the more grinding surfaces a mano has, the more surface area is available for grinding. At Homol'ovi II, 18 manos (34%) had one grinding surface, 26 manos (49%) had either two adjacent or two opposed grinding surfaces, 8 manos (15%) had three grinding surfaces (one surface opposed to two adjacent grinding surfaces), and 1 mano (2%) had four grinding surfaces (two opposing sides each with two adjacent use-surfaces).

Differences in cross section have been attributed to the degree of use and the variation in type of stroke used with the mano (Bartlett 1933; Cameron 1985). Manos whose transverse cross sections could be determined (74% of the assemblage) were grouped into three categories following conventions established by Bartlett (1933) and Woodbury (1954) and continued by J. Adams (1979). Manos with one grinding surface or two opposite grinding surfaces were classified as loaf-shaped

**Table 5.2. Recovery Contexts of Ground Stone Artifacts**

| | Floor Fill or Contact | Undisturbed Fill | Disturbed Fill | Surface | Unknown* | Total |
|---|---|---|---|---|---|---|
| *Artifact type* | | | | | | |
| Manos | 4 | 9 | 19 | 20 | 1 | 53 |
| Metates | 1 | 4 | 1 | 3 | 1 | 10 |
| Piki Stones or Griddles | 1 | 1 | 1 | | | 3 |
| Manos or metates | | | | 2 | | 2 |
| Abraders | | 4 | 1 | 4 | | 9 |
| Grinding Slabs | 1 | | 1 | | | 2 |
| Paint Palette | | 1 | | | | 1 |
| Handstone | | | | 1 | | 1 |
| Hoes | | | | 1 | 1 | 2 |
| Architectural fragments | | 4 | 4 | 4 | | 12 |
| Miscellaneous Unidentified | | 5 | 5 | 13 | 0 | 23 |
| Other | | | | 3 | | 3 |
| Total | 7 | 28 | 32 | 51 | 3 | 121 |
| (Percent) | (6) | (23) | (26) | (42) | (3) | |
| *Artifact condition* | | | | | | |
| Whole | 3 | 5 | 4 | 5 | 3 | 20 |
| Incomplete | 1 | | | 3 | | 4 |
| Fragmentary | 3 | 21 | 27 | 37 | | 88 |
| Unknown | | 2 | 1 | 6 | | 9 |
| Total | 7 | 28 | 32 | 51 | 3 | 121 |
| (Percent) | (6) | (23) | (26) | (42) | (3) | |

*These artifacts were recovered from excavated proveniences but the nature of the proveniences is unknown.

manos (10, 19% of the mano assemblage) and included artifacts with rectangular, oval, or square cross sections (Fig. 5.5). Faceted manos with at least two adjoining use-surfaces (23, 44% of the mano assemblage) included specimens with triangular, truncated, or diamond-shaped transverse cross sections. Wedge-shaped manos with one or two grinding surfaces that converged at one end (6, 11% of the mano assemblage) had wedge-shaped transverse cross sections. Longitudinal cross section indicates on what type of metate the mano was used. Of the 39 manos (74% of the assemblage) whose transverse cross section could be determined, all had been used with slab metates.

Finger grooves, which may have provided a more secure hold during use, had been pecked into the edges of eight manos (15%) that were relatively thick, had loaf-shaped transverse cross sections with two opposing grinding surfaces, and had rectangular plan views. Finger grooves appear most often on apparently similar manos in assemblages recovered from Awatovi (Woodbury 1954: 74–75). The telltale pits, dimples, cones, and impact scars on sand grains of the grinding surfaces indicate that 21 manos (40%) were resharpened.

Detectable scratches on individual grains of at least one grinding surface appeared on 44 manos, and on 36 of them the direction of the scratches was perpendicular to the long axis, the expected direction according to descriptions of use (especially in Bartlett 1933). Three manos differed from this norm. The scratches on the flat grinding surface of one were oriented in the direction of two corners rather than edge to edge, suggesting it may have been a one-handed mano (J. Adams 1979, 1986). Plan view, cross sections, and original size could not be determined for this fragment. Scratches on the convex surface of the second mano fragment were both perpendicular and parallel to the longitudinal axis. Its other flat grinding surface had perpendicular scratches. One of the flat grinding surfaces on the third mano had scratches that were parallel to the longitudinal axis. The direction of scratches on use-surfaces of 5 of the 44 manos could not be determined due to weathering or to the fine texture of the material.

Sooting and heat-altered color indicate exposure to fire and 22 manos (42%) seem to have these characteristics. However, distinguishing sooting or heat-altered color from patination caused by weathering is difficult

Figure 5.5. Manos: *a*, complete, loaf-shaped, with finger grooves; *b*, incomplete, loaf-shaped; *c*, *d*, exhausted, faceted; *e*, exhausted fragment used with a trough-shaped metate; *f*, exhausted, incomplete. (Length of *a* is 21.0 cm.)

when the effects of these processes on the raw materials used are unknown.

Four manos (8% of the assemblage) had been re-shaped and reused as pecking stones, including one of conglomerate, two coarse-grained, and one medium-grained Shinarump sandstone. Two other manos had a concave area on one use-surface. Concave use-surfaces are not typical of grinding on a metate. Microscopic examination showed that the wear in these areas was not due to grain grinding and these two manos were classified as reused. One was medium-grained Shinarump and the other was medium-grained unidentified sandstone.

On 14 manos, including the five previously discussed on which the direction of scratches could not be determined, scratches resulting from use had been completely or partially obliterated. Eight were recovered from the site's surface, representing 40 percent of the surface manos, and six from excavation, representing 18 percent of the excavated manos. These proportions suggest that weathering does affect characteristics on surface artifacts.

*Metates*

Of the 10 slab metates recovered from Homol'ovi II, 3 were whole. As with the manos, most of the metates were made of Shinarump sandstone (Tables 5.1, 5.2). Three metates were conglomerate, one was coarse-grained, one was medium-grained, and five were fine-grained (including the one of Moenkopi sandstone and the two of presumably nonlocal sandstone). All of the metates had one grinding surface, nine were concave, and one flat.

Measurements of whole metates are listed in Table 5.3. The longitudinal concavity of these metates was

### Table 5.3. Measurements of Whole Ground Stone Artifacts

| Artifact | Length (cm) | Width (cm) | Thickness (cm) | Weight (kg) |
|---|---|---|---|---|
| Mano, exhausted | 5.4 | 8.5 | 2.6 | 0.20 |
| Mano | 13.5 | 6.6 | 2.4 | 0.20 |
| Mano | 21.0 | 10.4 | 4.3 | 1.30 |
| Metate | 33.0 | 27.0 | 10.7 | 11.80 |
| Metate | 34.0 | 24.0 | 13.5 | 13.20 |
| Metate | 36.4 | 29.0 | 8.5 | 15.70 |
| Abraders, tabular flat | 7.3 | 10.8 | 1.2 | 0.20 |
| irregular grooved | 9.7 | 7.3 | 3.9 | 0.30 |
| flat | 10.1 | 5.8 | 0.9 | 0.06 |
| flat | 6.6 | 3.8 | 1.3 | 0.04 |
| flat | 5.3 | 4.6 | 2.0 | 0.07 |
| flat | 5.4 | 5.0 | 3.1 | 0.10 |
| flat | 7.4 | 6.2 | 2.5 | 0.20 |
| flat | 8.7 | 5.4 | 3.2 | 0.20 |
| Grinding slab | 33.0 | 17.3 | 3.1 | 2.50 |
| Grinding slab | 26.0 | 15.6 | 5.0 | 2.50 |
| Handstone | 12.8 | 9.4 | 5.8 | 1.10 |
| Hoe | 17.0 | 10.2 | 4.6 | 1.20 |
| Hoe | 13.2 | 12.4 | 3.0 | 0.60 |
| Misc. unidentified, #1 | 3.8 | 2.2 | 2.2 | 0.01 |
| #2 | 5.5 | 4.4 | 4.4 | 0.20 |
| #3 | 5.6 | 5.0 | 1.4 | 0.06 |
| #4 | 5.0 | 5.0 | 5.0 | 0.09 |

*Note*: Miscellaneous unidentified artifacts #1, #3, and #4 may or may not be whole; measurements are provided because they are unusual.

measured by placing a flat ruler lengthwise across both ends of the metate and recording the distance between the bottom of the ruler and the lowest point on the metate's grinding surface in millimeters.

The grinding surfaces of all three whole metates had been resharpened by pecking. On the oval metate the entire grinding surface had been pecked (Fig. 5.6*b*). On the two rectangular metates pecking was concentrated in the middle of the grinding surface with the perimeters remaining unpecked and smooth (Fig. 5.6*a*). The resharpening pattern of the rectangular metates suggests that grinding was most intense in the middle of the use-surface, whereas the pattern on the oval metate suggests that grinding was equally intense across the whole surface. This indicates that the area of most intense grinding is not the same on all slab metates, which may be caused by the grinding stroke used or the differently shaped use-surfaces.

Figure 5.6. Metates: *a*, rectangular, medium-grained, complete, flat; *b*, oval, coarse-grained, complete, flat. (Length of *a* is 33.0 cm.)

Figure 5.7. Piki stone and possible griddle fragments: *a*, *c*, possible griddle fragments; *b*, piki stone fragment with oily surface. (Top edge of *b* is 18.2 cm.)

The sides, ends, and bottoms of the three whole metates were shaped by pecking and flaking. On two of the metates (Fig. 5.6), the shaping appears to have evened out the bottom surface. The bottom of the third metate had a ridge down the center; the resulting instability during grinding suggests that this artifact may have been set in a bin. Besides bearing impact scars from flaking and pecking, the tops of sand grains on the bottoms of the whole metates appear to have been crushed, presumably due to pressure applied to the implement during use. If this trait is a distinctive feature of metate use, it may help identify fragments that are difficult to classify as either manos or metates (Boyer 1986).

All of the metates bore microscopic evidence of grinding grain, but none had developed a sheen on the use-surface. The direction of grinding, which could be identified on five artifacts, was parallel to the longitudinal axis.

None of the whole artifacts were exhausted. If the depth of a metate's longitudinal concavity is a rough measure of relative wear, as has been suggested (Woodbury 1954: 60–61), then the similar measurements of the whole metates (10.0 mm, 10.3 mm, 9.2 mm) suggest that all three were about equally worn. Only the whole, rectangular, medium-grained metate may have been re-used because the use-surface is covered with a black deposit that may be patination or black pigment.

## Mano or Metate Fragments

Two artifacts that were recovered from the surface of Homol'ovi II could not be identified as either manos or metates because of their small size and fragmentary condition. These artifacts were classified as food-processing implements because their used surfaces indi-

cated that they were part of a grinding kit consisting of a top and bottom stone and showed evidence of grinding grain. One of the artifacts had one used surface but whether the other stone had one or two could not be determined.

## Piki Stone and Griddle Fragments

Piki stones are carefully selected and prepared sandstone slabs on which piki is cooked over a hearth. Piki stones are made from well-cemented, fine-grained sandstone that produces tabular slabs of suitable thickness. The stones are shaped and the cooking surface ground and rubbed with oil (historically, cottonseed, watermelon seed, or corn oil; O'Kane 1950: 40–46). There are few deposits of sandstone suitable for piki stones, and Hopi women often obtain their material from sources that are distant from their homes (O'Kane 1950: 42–43). Because obtaining the proper raw material, manufacture, and preparation of piki stones is time-consuming, they are valued possessions of Hopi households (J. Adams 1979: 23).

One partial piki stone and two fragments that may be from piki stones or griddles were recovered, all of fine-grained sandstone (Table 5.1). Piki stones have an extremely smooth cooking surface that is alternately rubbed with oil and heated until it develops an oily feel. The piki stone fragment has this distinctive smooth and oily surface, although any evidence of oil penetration could not be detected because of the fragment's burned condition. This piece consists of one corner of a square or rectangular stone (Fig. 5.7*b*). The other two fragments were classified as possibly from piki stones or griddles because, despite having other characteristics of piki stones like a finely finished surface, they show no clear oil penetration and their surfaces lack an oily feel (Fig. 5.7*a*, *c*).

It is difficult to detect traces of microscopic use-wear on the surfaces of these artifacts because of their fine-grained texture and the accumulation of carbon or oil on their surfaces. Scratches visible on the surface of the piki stone fragment indicate that the direction of grinding, presumably during manufacture, was parallel to the short side. All three fragments had cracked or spalled surfaces and the stone of the two possible piki stone or griddle fragments was friable, probably because of heating.

The piki stone fragment was on top of the hearth that was near the northwest wall in Room 211 (Fig. 2.2), and one possible griddle or piki stone fragment was in that room's north corner. The other fragment was recovered from disturbed fill outside Room 206.

### Nonfood Processing Implements

Nonfood processing implements include grooved and ungrooved abraders, paint palettes, grinding slabs, handstones, and flagstones or other artifacts associated with the pueblo's architecture. This group includes multiple-purpose or use-specific tools used to process materials such as bone, wood, stone, clay, and paint pigments (J. Adams 1979: 29). Multiple-purpose ground stone artifacts (ungrooved abraders and grinding slabs) have generalized shapes and may have been used for several different tasks. In contrast, use-specific artifacts have distinctive attributes that help identify how they were used (J. Adams 1979: 29). Whole artifact measurements are shown in Table 5.3.

*Abraders*

The nine abraders (artifacts used to shape other artifacts) were subdivided into ungrooved and grooved types based on descriptions in J. Adams (1979: 40) and Woodbury (1954). The latter cites several problems that he encountered while identifying the Awatovi abraders that also apply to the Homol'ovi II artifacts, especially the general absence of distinctive morphological characteristics on all but the grooved abraders and shaftsmoothers (Woodbury 1954: 98–111). The lack of use-wear studies also hinders identifying these artifacts (J. Adams 1979: 40). For example, despite basing identifications on both morphology and use-wear, no fragments of flat abraders could be identified because too little is known about the traces of microscopic use-wear that are distinctive of flat abraders as opposed to other artifacts, such as grinding slabs.

Distribution of abraders by material is in Table 5.1. All seven flat abraders are whole, including the rectangular tabular flat abrader (Fig. 5.8a). The irregular grooved abrader is whole (Fig. 5.8c) and the shaftsmoother is incomplete (Fig. 5.8b). Tabular flat abraders were intentionally shaped into a rectangle or square, and opposing grinding surfaces were used for abrasion.

Figure 5.8. Abraders: *a*, whole tabular flat; *b*, rectangular shaftsmoother fragment; *c*, whole irregular grooved abrader. (Longest side of *a* is 10.8 cm.)

Grooved abraders have one or more narrow grooves on the abrading surface and may or may not have been intentionally shaped. If shaped, they are classified as shaftsmoothers, although intentional shaping may not have been required for the tool's use (J. Adams 1979: 40).

According to J. Adams (1979: 41), flat and grooved abraders were probably used to shape wooden artifacts. The microscopic use-wear on both of the grooved abraders and five of the flat abraders suggests that these artifacts were used to abrade material with resilient surfaces, such as wood or bone. The use-wear on the other two flat abraders, including the tabular flat abrader, could not be identified because the Moenkopi sandstone is too fine-grained. Whether particular artifacts were used to abrade one specific kind of material or different materials could not be determined. One flat abrader appeared to have two used surfaces and each may have been used to abrade a different kind of material.

The tabular flat abrader recovered is of fine-grained Moenkopi sandstone. The edges and ends were shaped by pecking. The two opposing grinding surfaces are slightly concave and show no evidence of resharpening. The direction of scratches on the sand grains of one grinding surface are perpendicular to the longitudinal axis whereas the scratches on the other grinding surface, which itself was severely spalled, were multidirectional. The fact that individual grains on the intact grinding surface were worn level to the interstices, and the absence of sheen and polish on the interior of pits, indicate that the artifact was used to process relatively hard materials such as stone or hard wood (J. Adams 1989b).

The irregular grooved abrader is of fine-grained Shinarump sandstone (Fig. 5.8c). The single U-shaped groove is oriented diagonally across the surface. The sandstone's friability and patina may account for the relative absence of use-wear in the groove. The rectangular shaftsmoother fragment, collected from the

Central Plaza surface, is made of medium-grained Shinarump sandstone (Fig. 5.8*b*). The artifact's edges were pecked and ground to shape. The sand grains on the surface of the groove are scratched parallel to the length of the groove, indicating direction of use. Traces of use-wear in the groove include impact scars, abrasion, and sheen, but the material being abraded could not be identified. The stone is friable and has a single, shallow U-shaped groove parallel to the longitudinal axis of the artifact.

The six irregular flat abraders are most notable for their consistent appearance. All are made of medium- or fine-grained sandstone, four of Shinarump, one of Moenkopi, and one of presumably nonlocal material. None was intentionally shaped or pecked to sharpen. The abrader of nonlocal material was originally part of a mano, as indicated by the microscopic use-wear on one of its surfaces.

*Grinding Slabs*

J. Adams (1979: 32) described grinding slabs as irregularly shaped stones that lack the distinguishing attributes of metates and palettes, such as a grinding area that covers the entire surface on the former and the carefully shaped borders of the latter. As a result, analysts have posited that they are multipurpose tools used to grind or crush both food and nonfood items (J. Adams 1979: 64; Woodbury 1954: 116). The two complete grinding slabs from Homol'ovi II are shown in Figure 5.9*a*, *b*; measurements are in Table 5.3. Both were shaped into rough ovals and the bottoms left unmodified.

The two artifacts each have one used surface, but the surface on one of the slabs is concave and exhibits more wear than the other, which is flat. The used surface of the flat grinding slab is relatively uneven and largely unworn, with the high areas exhibiting the most wear (Fig. 5.9*a*). The microscopic use-wear present seems attributable to grinding some relatively hard substance. In contrast, the use-wear on the concave grinding slab is heaviest on the outside edges of the use-surface. Microscopic examination shows that the use-wear in this area is attributable to grinding grain and that it differs from the use-wear in the center, indicating that the slab was used to grind more than one material. This evidence and the slab's concave surface probably mean it was originally a metate, but was reused to grind a non-grain material. The microscopic use-wear in the slab's center was most similar to the wear on an experimental tool used to grind sherds.

The concave grinding slab has a small amount of red and yellow pigment on the top and bottom surfaces.

Figure 5.9. Grinding slabs and paint palette fragment: *a*, *b*, complete grinding slabs; *c*, paint palette fragment. (Length of *a* is 33 cm.)

Whether the presence of the pigment reflects the artifact's use or is fortuitous is uncertain; however, studies of ground stone artifacts with pigment from Homol'ovi III show that even ephemeral use of an artifact for grinding or mixing pigment produces a stained surface (Logan 1990).

The flat grinding slab was in the disturbed fill of Room 216. The slab with the pigment came from intact prehistoric deposits in Activity Area 221, associated with a sherd concentration on the area's occupation surface. J. Adams (1979: 64) notes that grinding slabs may have been used to process a variety of substances, including seeds, paint pigments, and pottery clay. Possibly the grinding slab from Area 221 was used to grind sherds for pottery temper, as suggested by the slab's microscopic use-wear, or to grind or mix pigment for ceramic decoration, as suggested by the pigments. Either of these hypothesized uses could have involved the use of a top stone that would have produced a concave use-surface.

*Paint Palette Fragment*

According to Woodbury (1954: 112) and J. Adams (1979: 45-46), palettes have concave grinding surfaces surrounded by a raised border and were specifically used to grind and mix pigments. A corner of a grinding slab was identified as a palette despite the absence of a raised border, because much of the single, slightly concave use-surface is covered with granules of ground blue-green pigment (Fig. 5.9*c*). The fragment is made of fine-grained Moenkopi sandstone. The edges were shaped by flaking and pecking. Sand grains on the use-surface are scratched perpendicular to the longitudinal axis.

## Handstone

The term handstone applies to a variety of hand-held tools that differ in the degree to which they were shaped and in their use. J. Adams (1979: 48) and Woodbury (1954: 85–86) refer to this group as "polishing, rubbing, pecking, and pounding tools."

The one handstone recovered is made of coarse-grained Shinarump. The artifact is complete and rectangular; measurements are in Table 5.3. Its wedge-shaped transverse cross section suggests that it may be a reused mano, although there is no other evidence supporting this possibility.

The artifact's single, concave use-surface appears to have been pecked in the center, a characteristic often exhibited by ground stone tools that Hopi informants identified as floor polishers (J. Adams 1979: 51–52). The microscopic use-wear indicates that the handstone was used to process some relatively hard material; however, the wear could not be identified more specifically because there were no floor polishers, experimental or artifactual, available for comparison. The scratches on the sand grains indicate that the direction of use was perpendicular to the longitudinal axis.

## Hoes

Hoes are broad-bladed tools with at least one and usually two side notches and a relatively sharp, pointed end (Woodbury 1954: 166). These characteristics suggest that they may have been used for digging, but attempts to confirm this by examining traces of use-wear have been inconclusive (Woodbury 1954: 166; Lange and others 1987: 126–147).

Two sandstone hoes, characterized by the notches in their sides, were recovered. One hoe, made of conglomerate Shinarump, was originally a rectangular mano with two opposing use-surfaces and a loaf-shaped transverse cross section. It had been used on a flat metate. It was reshaped by flaking and pecking notches into the sides and roughly shaping one end to a blunt point. The other hoe is square and made of fine-grained Moenkopi sandstone. The bit broke off, a common occurrence in hoes recovered from the Homol'ovi area (Lange and others 1987: 126–147).

How the 2 hoes recovered from Homol'ovi II and the 89 from survey in the Homolovi Ruins State Park were used is difficult to determine because they have diverse shapes and sizes but lack use-wear (Lange and others 1987: 126–147). For example, the presence of side notches suggest that the hoes were hafted but the lack of use-wear in the notches makes this questionable. Woodbury (1954: 169) notes that even if the hoes were hafted, they may have been suitable only for working sandy rather than clayey soils. That both small and large hoes from Homol'ovi II and the surrounding area have side notches suggests that they were intended to be hafted even if they actually were used without hafts. Most of the 89 hoes found during survey were recovered from small, presumably agricultural sites (Lange and others 1987: 126–147) and they were probably important agricultural tools. Similar implements have been recovered from Awatovi and other sites (Woodbury 1954: 165).

## Architectural Remains

Eleven ground stone fragments were tentatively identified as pieces of flagstones and one artifact was classified as a possible hearthstone; however, none of these artifacts were found in situ. They are similar to the hearthstones and flagstones found in place on room and pit structure floors at Homol'ovi III.

Flagstones are relatively thin, tabular slabs of stone with flat or slightly uneven used surfaces and well-shaped sides. The sides are often shaped by pecking and some flagstones have beveled sides that were ground to shape. The bottom surfaces are generally more uneven than the used surfaces and may be patinated due to contact with the soil. The most distinctive characteristic of flagstones is their consistent thickness. The Homol'ovi II artifacts ranged from 1.4 cm to 1.9 cm thick and had a mean thickness of 1.6 cm. Like the flagstones and hearthstones at Homol'ovi III, almost all those from Homol'ovi II were of fine-grained Moenkopi sandstone (Table 5.1).

The macroscopic use-wear on these artifacts is similar to that on the Homol'ovi III assemblage. The upper surfaces are worn smooth and, except for a slight concavity in the center of some, are quite flat. Bottom surfaces are either unmodified or slightly shaped. Moenkopi sandstone tends to spall along its naturally horizontal bedding planes, producing relatively flat surfaces that do not need a lot of shaping. The advantages of this characteristic undoubtedly contributed to its selection for making flagstones. The use-surface of the possible hearthstone is concave rather than flat, suggesting that exposure to high heat may have warped the stone.

Because of their fine granularity, microscopic traces of use-wear could be observed on only two artifacts and it was similar to that on known flagstones from Homol'ovi III. Sand grains were leveled to the matrix but the resulting flattened surface is uneven because the grains were not worn to the same horizontal plane, as is typical of stone-on-stone wear (J. Adams 1989b: 263–264). The tops of the sand grains appear to have some abrasive wear. The surface also has a relatively high density of pits and depressions, and the sand grains in these low areas are chipped and polished.

Figure 5.10. Miscellaneous Unidentified (*a, b, d, f*) and Other (*c, e*) artifacts: *a*, fragment of a circular beveled artifact; *b*, whole cylindrical artifact; *c*, fragment of a red painted artifact; *d*, handled(?) abrader fragment; *e*, unworked cylindrical vesicular basalt artifact, condition unknown; *f*, white pigment(?). (Length of *e* is 6.9 cm.)

## Other Implements

Based on their appearance or lack of wear, three artifacts were apparently not used to process food or nonfood substances but had some other, unknown function. All these artifacts seem to be fragments of larger objects, which further constrains determining their function.

The crescent-shaped artifact shown in Figure 5.10*c* is made of fine-grained Moenkopi sandstone that was shaped by pecking and grinding. The object was originally circular or semicircular. Its striking feature is the painted decoration on the ground surfaces. Although the hematite paint has flaked off in several places, two or three red lines are still visible where the flat and beveled surfaces meet, and there are patches of paint on the flat surface indicating that this part of the stone may have been completely painted. The artifact's bottom surface is heavily patinated and appears to be ground, but whether the grinding reflects use or shaping is uncertain. The black patination may have contributed to the aesthetics of the object by providing an interesting contrast to the light red of the stone and the darker red of the hematite paint on the opposite surface.

The other two artifacts, which may have been used for display or ceremonial purposes, are cylindrical pieces of vesicular basalt. Both have one rounded and one jagged end, suggesting they are pieces of larger objects; however, the lack of shaping or wear on the artifacts indicates they actually may be complete (Fig. 5.10*e*).

## Miscellaneous Unidentified Ground Stone

Most of the 23 unidentified artifacts are fragments of larger objects, some of which may have been use-specific tools and others multipurpose tools. Four of these fragments had distinctive morphological characteristics or use-wear and are described in more detail. Over half of the miscellaneous unidentified ground stone came from the site's surface (Table 5.2).

Of the 19 undistinctive artifacts, 6 are made of medium-grained Shinarump, 4 are made of fine-grained Shinarump, and 9 are made of fine-grained Moenkopi sandstone. All of these fragments have only one used surface. Three fragments had microscopic use-wear attributable to stone-on-stone grinding or grinding some other hard substance and four fragments had microscopic use-wear attributable to grinding substances that had resilient surfaces. The variations in the microscopic use-wear, together with differences in size and shape, indicate these fragments represent a diverse group of ground stone implements.

Miscellaneous Unidentified Artifact 1 (Table 5.3) is of an unknown, non-sandstone material that is light buff, fine-grained, and relatively soft (Fig. 5.10*f*). It could be a nonlocal siltstone or a volcanic tuff. It has several small, juxtaposed use-surfaces with numerous multidirectional scratches that appear to be from use. These features are similar to the wear on pigments from Homol'ovi III, raising the possibility that this artifact was used as white pigment.

Miscellaneous Unidentified Artifact 2 (Table 5.3) is complete, cylindrical, and made of fine-grained Shinarump sandstone (Fig. 5.10*b*). Both ends have convex use-surfaces that appear to have been used for grinding as well as pecking or pounding. The microscopic use-wear on one end is similar to stone-on-stone wear, whereas that on the other end suggests a relatively soft material was ground. The artifact may have been used like a pestle to crush and grind.

Miscellaneous Unidentified Artifact 3 (Table 5.3), of fine-grained Moenkopi sandstone, has a flat, circular ground surface surrounded by flat, ground, beveled sides (Fig. 5.10*a*). Although the grinding on the circular, flat surface may reflect wear, the beveled sides were probably shaped. The sand grains are worn to the interstices, suggesting it was ground against a fairly hard material.

Miscellaneous Unidentified Artifact 4 (Table 5.3) is of conglomerate Shinarump sandstone (Fig. 5.10*d*). The edges are uneven; the thick edge has been ground flat and seems to be the only part of the artifact that was used. The sand grains are worn to the interstices and are scratched and abraded, suggesting it was used on a hard material. The scratches are perpendicular to the longitudinal axis, indicating the object was rubbed against surfaces that were larger than its used surface.

## DISCUSSION

### Recovery Contexts

Table 5.2 summarizes proveniences of the ground stone artifacts recovered from Homol'ovi II and Table 5.4 shows the specific proveniences of the surface artifacts.

Most of the ground stone artifacts collected from the surface were from the pueblo's three plazas and almost half were recovered from the East Plaza. All of the plazas had manos and miscellaneous unidentified fragments; however, manos comprise proportionately more of the excavated assemblage than of the surface assemblage, whereas the opposite is true of the miscellaneous unidentified artifacts. This and the fact that over twice as many whole artifacts were recovered from the subsurface deposits than from the surface is undoubtedly due to vandalism.

The proveniences of the 70 excavated ground stone artifacts are shown in Table 5.5. The intact prehistoric deposits that yielded ground stone artifacts are Rooms 211, 212, 216, and Activity Area 221. Although the west half of Room 211 was disturbed, the floor in the east half of the room was intact and three hearths were found in this area. A piki stone fragment was on top of one of the room's four-sided hearths and a possible piki stone or griddle fragment was in the room's north corner. Whether the fragments are from the same or different stones is uncertain. It is also difficult to determine whether the piki stone fragment over the hearth was reused after the original stone broke or was simply left in place. Excavators found stones inside the hearth that may have served to support the piki stone. The hearths and piki stones suggest that piki was prepared in this room. If the fragments represent two different stones they may indicate that Room 211 was specialized for making piki (J. Adams 1979: 23).

Room 212 was severely vandalized and only a small portion of the floor was intact. The floor of Room 216 was moderately damaged. One whole metate came from the floor in Room 212 and three manos, including one that was reused as a pecking stone, were recovered from the intact floor in Room 216. The presence of these artifacts suggests that grain grinding took place in both rooms.

The fill of Activity Area 221 was largely undisturbed. The deposits have been interpreted as probably secondary trash consisting of fill that was cleaned out of a burned storage room, and the ground stone assemblage supports this interpretation. This assemblage, 61 percent

**Table 5.4. Provenience of Ground Stone Artifacts from the Surface**

| Artifact | West Plaza | Central Plaza | East Plaza | South of Pueblo | Total |
|---|---|---|---|---|---|
| Manos | 7 | 2 | 9 | 2 | 20 |
| Metates | 3 | | | | 3 |
| Manos or Metates | | 1 | 1 | | 2 |
| Abraders | | 2 | 2 | | 4 |
| Handstone | 1 | | | | 1 |
| Hoe | | 1 | | | 1 |
| Architectural | | 1 | 3 | | 4 |
| Misc. unidentified | 2 | 2 | 9 | | 13 |
| Other | 1 | | | 2 | 3 |
| Total | 14 | 9 | 24 | 4 | 51 |

**Table 5.5. Provenience of Excavated Ground Stone Artifacts**

| Artifact | Room 206 | 211 | 212 | 215 | 216 | 217 | Area 221 | Total |
|---|---|---|---|---|---|---|---|---|
| Manos | 7 | 3 | 7 | 1 | 4 | | 11 | 33 |
| Metates | | | 2 | | 1 | | 4 | 7 |
| Piki stones, griddles | 1 | 2 | | | | | | 3 |
| Abraders | 1 | | | | | | 4 | 5 |
| Grinding slabs | | | | | 1 | | 1 | 2 |
| Paint palette | | | | | | | 1 | 1 |
| Hoe | | | | | | 1 | | 1 |
| Architectural | 1 | | 3 | | | | 4 | 8 |
| Misc. unident. | | | 1 | | 1 | 2 | 6 | 10 |
| Total | 10 | 5 | 13 | 1 | 7 | 3 | 31 | 70 |

of which was burned, includes whole and fragmentary manos, metate fragments, one grooved and three flat abraders, the paint palette, a grinding slab, fragments of architectural debris, and miscellaneous unidentified artifacts. The single grinding slab recovered is interesting because it was found on the occupation surface south of the ramada, along with a concentration of pottery sherds. The slab's use-wear indicates it may have been used to grind sherds for pottery temper, suggesting that pottery manufacture may have occurred in this part of Activity Area 221.

## Ground Stone Reuse

Seven artifacts (6 percent of the total ground stone assemblage) had definite evidence of secondary use, including six manos and one grinding slab. The grinding slab was probably not used to grind pigments, but the two small spots of pigment on the top and bottom surfaces presumably represent some kind of reuse involving pigment. Although it is possible that the presence of pigment is fortuitous, this is considered unlikely because the pigment appears on both surfaces. The reused manos include four reshaped and used as pecking stones, one reshaped and used as a hoe, and one reshaped and used as an irregular flat abrader. Two other manos with concave use-surfaces may also have been reused.

Only eight whole ground stone artifacts were recovered from intact proveniences at Homol'ovi II and in all, 20 artifacts, representing 16.5 percent of the entire ground stone assemblage, were complete (Table 5.3). None of the whole manos recovered fit any of the whole metates.

The relative paucity of whole artifacts suggests that ground stone implements were well used. Most of the manos were used until they broke or were exhausted. Exhausted manos are worn so that the top and bottom surfaces converge at the edges (Fig. 5.5), making the implement too thin to hold during use (Bartlett 1933; Woodbury 1954: 81-82). The inhabitants appear to have used their manos as much as possible, despite the abundance of locally available material. The small number of reused manos supports the presumption that raw materials were obtained locally, based on the expectation that as the availability and accessibility of raw materials increases, the number of reused artifacts decreases. Because the paucity of whole ground stone artifacts is partly a factor of the severe vandalism in the excavated area, these trends suggest interesting avenues for further research when excavations continue at Homol'ovi II.

## Use of Nonlocal Stone

Locally available Shinarump and Moenkopi sandstone was used for 81.0 percent of the ground stone recovered from Homol'ovi II (Table 5.1). Vesicular basalt that was probably obtained from the Owl Rock member of the Chinle Formation comprised 2.5 percent, and 14.0 percent of the artifacts were made of sandstone presumably obtained from nonlocal sources. One artifact was made of an unidentified material that is presumably nonlocal. These figures indicate that the local Shinarump and Moenkopi sources met almost all of the inhabitant's needs for manufacturing ground stone tools.

Over half of the artifacts recovered were of Shinarump sandstone (Table 5.1). This sandstone apparently was especially suited for food grinding implements, because almost all the manos and metates were made of it. Moenkopi sandstone was used for the piki stone, one possible griddle fragment, and all but one of the architectural remains. Moenkopi has a clay cement and fine-grained texture suitable for piki stones or griddles, and it has a tendency to spall in horizontal slabs that make it ideal for hearth slabs and flagstones. Seventy-eight percent of the artifacts made of presumably nonlocal material were manos and metates. This distribution reflects either the dominance of these artifact types in the assemblage or selective procurement for particular grinding qualities.

## Ground Stone Technology

This part of the discussion focuses on the food-processing implements recovered from Homol'ovi II because more is known about their manufacture and use than about nonfood processing artifacts (J. Adams 1979).

The one piki stone fragment and two possible piki stone or griddle fragments are temporal markers as well as indicators of social and cultural change in the Pueblo area (Woodbury 1954: 176-177). Piki stones are relatively recent additions to the Plateau pueblo ground stone tool kit, first appearing during the Pueblo III transition period (A.D. 1250-1300). They seem to have been introduced from other cultures to the south and represent a new technique for preparing food (Adams 1991). Whether or not the preparation and distribution of piki was associated with ceremonial occasions during the prehistoric period is unknown. At present, piki bread is prepared on piki stones in conjunction with ceremonies held at the Hopi villages (J. Adams 1979: 26; Woodbury 1954: 176-177). The stones are similar to those found at Homol'ovi II and other contemporary prehistoric sites (Burton 1990: 192-193).

Slab metates are another temporal technological marker of social and cultural change. They appeared during the Pueblo II and early Pueblo III periods (A.D. 1000-1150) in the Plateau region and gradually replaced the trough form (Woodbury 1954: 58-59), apparently in association with changes in architecture and specialization of activities (Woodbury 1954: 61-65). In contrast to the portable trough metate, most slab metates were permanently plastered into position in bins that were built in rooms used for domestic activities (Woodbury 1954: 59-65).

The presence of manos, metates, and piki stones, along with the floral remains (Miksicek, Chapter 8) and the chipped stone assemblage (Sullivan and Madsen, Chapter 6), reflects the importance of domestic crops at Homol'ovi II. The increasing variety of ground stone tools in contrast to the diminishing variety of chipped stone tools has been noted in late "Anasazi" assemblages throughout the Plateau region (J. Adams 1979; Woodbury 1954). Although manos and metates were probably also used to process wild foods like nuts and seeds (Woodbury 1954: 60), their primary importance as corn-grinding implements is reinforced by information obtained from 20th-century Hopi residents at Walpi Village (J. Adams 1979: 5) and by the fact that all the manos and metates from Homol'ovi II with identifiable use-wear showed microscopic traces of grinding corn or amaranth.

The significance of the variety of mano physical attributes, especially in assemblages dating to the Pueblo III period and later, has intrigued researchers since at least the 1930s (Bartlett 1933; Cameron 1985). One topic that has received much attention is the relationship between the various forms of transverse cross section and mano use. Bartlett (1933: 13) associates differences in mano transverse cross section with a new grinding stroke necessitated by the introduction and eventual replacement of trough metates by slab metates. This new stroke may have reduced the amount of corn that spilled over the edges of the slab metate during grinding, a problem previously solved by the trough metate's raised sides. Manos used with the new stroke have triangular, truncated, or diamond-shaped transverse cross sections that are here referred to as faceted. Although Bartlett's association of faceted transverse cross sections with the introduction of slab metates is intriguing, a recent study of manos and metates recovered from various occupation periods at Chaco Canyon suggests that the grinding stroke producing manos with faceted cross sections may have been developed on trough rather than slab metates (Cameron 1985).

Woodbury (1954: 67–71) suggests an alternative explanation for manos with faceted transverse cross sections that still predicates their appearance on the development of a new grinding stroke, but associates the new stroke with stages of corn-grinding rather than with the introduction of a new metate form. Noting that manos with faceted transverse cross sections represent an addition to the Pueblo grinding kit rather than a replacement of the earlier loaf-shaped (including rectangular, square, and oval) and wedge-shaped forms, Woodbury speculates that the manos with faceted transverse cross sections were used during the final stages of corn-grinding to produce finely textured meal, whereas the manos with loaf- and wedge-shaped cross

sections were used during the earlier stages of corn-grinding when the meal was still relatively coarse. Woodbury's hypothesis that using different strokes to grind corn to different textures produces manos with different transverse cross sections combined with Bartlett's observation that manos and metates of different textures were used to grind corn during different stages of processing suggests that there may be an association between transverse cross section and material granularity (Woodbury 1954: 81–92; Bartlett 1933). According to Bartlett, coarse-grained manos and metates are used during the early stages of grinding to reduce the corn kernels to a coarse meal. If the grinding stroke used during this initial processing produces manos with loaf- or wedge-shaped cross sections, then a majority of manos with these kinds of cross sections should be made of coarse-grained material. Concurrently, fine-grained manos and metates are used during the final stages of grinding to pulverize the meal to a fine texture. If the grinding stroke used during this last stage of grinding produces manos with faceted transverse cross sections, then a majority of manos with such cross sections should be made of fine-grained material.

The distribution of the Homol'ovi II manos by transverse cross section and material granularity is shown on Table 5.6, along with the results of related studies by Wiseman (1970), Woodbury (1954), and J. Adams (1979). Only data for loaf-shaped transverse

**Table 5.6. Association of Mano Transverse Cross Section and Material Granularity at Four Sites**

| Transverse Cross Section | Material Granularity | | |
|---|---|---|---|
| | Coarse (%) | Fine (%) | N |
| Loaf shaped[1] | | | |
| Sapawi'i | 61 (79.0) | 16 (21.0) | 77 |
| Awatovi[2] | 20 (67.0) | 10 (33.0) | 30 |
| Homol'ovi II | 5 (62.5) | 3 (37.5) | 8 |
| | 86 (75.0) | 29 (25.0) | 115 |
| Faceted[1] | | | |
| Sapawi'i | 20 (34.0) | 39 (66.0) | 59 |
| Awatovi[3] | 55 (32.0) | 116 (68.0) | 171 |
| Homol'ovi II | 6 (40.0) | 9 (60.0) | 15 |
| Walpi | 1 ( 2.0) | 54 (98.0) | 55 |
| | 82 (27.0) | 218 (73.0) | 300 |

1. Loaf-shaped includes rectangular, square, and oval forms. Faceted includes truncated, triangular, and diamond-shaped forms.
2. These percentages are for manos used with trough metates only.
3. The material texture for 4 percent of the manos was not recorded (Woodbury 1954: 77).
*Sources*: Sapawi'i (Wiseman 1970), Awatovi (Woodbury 1954), Walpi (Adams 1979).

cross sections with two parallel opposing surfaces and for faceted transverse cross sections are given. The information on manos with wedge-shaped transverse cross sections is not included because Woodbury and Adams did not provide separate data for them.

The data summarized on Table 5.6 show association between loaf-shaped transverse cross sections and coarse material and between faceted transverse cross sections and fine material. In all the assemblages, over half the manos with loaf-shaped transverse cross sections are made of coarse-grained material and over half the manos with faceted transverse cross sections are made of fine-grained material. A chi-square test of association was calculated to determine the significance of the association between the two variables, and the results (df = 1, chi square = 78.0) show the association to be statistically significant (p < .001).

Woodbury (1954: 71) and Wiseman (1970) attribute the association between transverse cross section and material granularity to differences in the stroke used during the early grinding stages, when coarse-grained material is used, and later grinding stages, when fine-grained material is used. The data examined support their hypothesis. Additionally, the strength of the association suggests that the basic techniques of grinding were relatively standardized.

## SUMMARY

The ground stone assemblage recovered from surface and subsurface contexts during the 1984 field season at Homol'ovi II provides information about ground stone use and technology. The assemblage indicates that ground stone tools were used for a variety of tasks at Homol'ovi II. Some tools, such as the grooved abraders and piki stone, were probably highly specialized, whereas other tools, such as the irregular flat abraders and grinding slabs, probably had multiple uses. The prevalance of implements to grind grains like corn and amaranth into flour, and to then prepare the flour for consumption, emphasizes the importance of corn and other grains at the site.

The study of this assemblage suggests several directions for future research. Most important is the systematic recovery of additional ground stone artifacts from intact prehistoric contexts at Homol'ovi II so that comparisons can be made with ground stone assemblages from other sites. More detailed inferences could then be drawn about the use of ground stone artifacts by Homol'ovi II inhabitants. Further investigation of the development of slab metates and the apparent changes in corn grinding technology that accompany changes in metate type and mano form would lend insight into processes of cultural change. The continued investigation of microscopic and macroscopic traces of use-wear on ground stone also promises to increase our understanding of how ground stone tools were used, the relationship between technology and demographics, and how form and function articulate.

# CHAPTER SIX

# Chipped Stone

Alan P. Sullivan and John H. Madsen
University of Cincinnati
Arizona State Museum

Lithic artifacts were recovered from all excavated rooms, an activity area, and surface collection units at Homol'ovi II. The most striking aspect of the lithic assemblage from the pueblo is its abundance. The analysis of artifactual remains from Rooms 211, 212, 215, 216, 217, Activity Area 221, and 23 surface collection units indicates that chipped stone makes up 40 percent of the recovered remains at Homol'ovi II. This chapter presents an overview of chipped stone technological activities at the site. Emphasis is placed on documenting variation among chipped stone artifacts from various intrasite contexts and exploring the implications of this variation with respect to the spatial distribution of activities involving lithic reduction, tool use, and discard.

## METHOD OF ANALYSIS

The chipped stone assemblage was sorted into three basic groups: debitage, tools (including cores), and miscellaneous artifacts (for example, hammers and polishing stones).

### Debitage Analysis

The basic units of analysis used to investigate the debitage recovered from Homol'ovi II have been developed on the basis of several well-established relationships between lithic technological variability and its resultant byproducts (Newcomer 1971; Henry and others 1976). For example, relatively high percentages of complete flakes and debris dominate debitage assemblages resulting from flake production (Jelinek 1976; Sullivan and Rozen 1985). On the other hand, high percentages of broken flakes and flake fragments typically are produced during tool manufacture (Rozen 1979, 1981; see also Sullivan and Rozen 1985).

Complete flakes are pieces of stone detached from parent material that show a striking platform, an interior surface with a bulb of percussion, concentric force rings or ripple marks that originate at the impact point and, occasionally, a hinge on the terminal end. Complete flakes have intact lateral and terminal edges.

A broken flake is defined as any piece of stone detached from parent material that shows all or portions of the striking platform and at least some portions of the bulb of percussion and concentric force rings. Broken flakes are missing either the lateral or terminal edge and in most cases portions of both.

Flake fragments are medial-distal fragments of flakes that have one, all, or portions of each of the following attributes: concentric force rings, ripple marks, and a hinge fracture. The striking platform and bulb of percussion are missing in all instances.

Debris consists of nonorientable fragments and is synonymous with what Rozen (1984) calls "chunks and splatter." The pieces are removed from parent material but often have no definable interior or exterior attributes.

In addition, because lithic production (flake production or tool manufacture) and the logistics associated with raw material procurement are often reflected in the occurrence of cortex (Doelle 1980; Sullivan 1984), cortical and noncortical attributes were added to each of the four primary units of analysis, thereby yielding the eight debitage categories employed in this analysis (see Sullivan 1980, 1984b).

### Edge Damage

The use of a flake as a cutting or scraping implement often results in unintentional removal of small chips from the edge of the tool. The pattern of utilization on the tool will vary depending on the hardness and texture of the tool, the hardness and texture of the material being worked, and the amount of applied pressure. The presence of uniform and continuous microflakes or abrasion along a working edge is likely the result of utilization. On the other hand, the occurrence of discontinuous microflaking or isolated large nicks along a single edge is difficult to attribute exclusively to either human utilization or to natural causes.

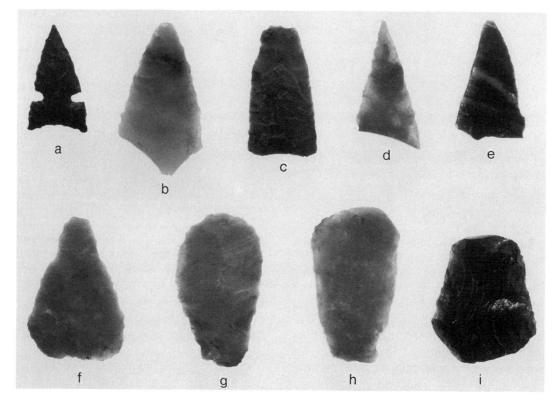

Figure 6.1. Facially retouched tools: *a, b, d, e,* projectile points; *c, f-i,* bifaces. (Length of *c* is 3.4 cm.)

In this study, a 10-power handlens was used to examine all debitage for edge damage. All of the debitage had edge damage of one form or another; however, those flakes with at least 1 cm of continuous edge damage were considered to be the product of utilization, whereas pieces with nicks or discontinuous microflaking were placed into an undamaged category.

### Tool Analysis

Facially retouched pieces (Fig.6.1) were sorted into the following categories: biface tips and bases, complete projectile points, point midsections, and single and multiple platform cores.

Marginally retouched unifacial and bifacial pieces were analyzed as well. Any flaking that extended continuously along an edge for at least 1 cm was considered retouch. Retouch scars are at least 2.5 mm long.

### RAW MATERIAL

The Little Colorado River Valley from its upper reaches near St. Johns, west to the Grand Canyon, is composed mainly of sedimentary deposits. The major geological complex of this valley consists of exposed layers of both Moenkopi and Chinle Formations. Both formations are of Triassic age, the Moenkopi being older and lying south of the river and the Chinle lying mainly on the north side of the river. Of particular interest is a cross-bedded lenticular basal conglomerate and sandstone known as the Shinarump member of the Chinle Formation (Breed and Breed 1972). The conglomerate is composed of pebbles as much as 3 to 7 inches (about 7–18 cm) in diameter. The low bluffs along both sides of the Little Colorado River contain exposed Shinarump beds of subangular to rounded siliceous materials of great variety and color. Although quartz and quartzite are dominant within the conglomerate, there are sizable quantities of cherty limestone, chalcedony, and occasional fragments of petrified wood. All of this stone is excellent raw material for the manufacture of stone tools.

The use of this material for stone tools by people living along the Little Colorado River may extend as far back as the hypothesized Pre-Projectile Point stage, known locally as the Tolchaco complex (Bartlett 1943); however, Keller and Wilson (1975), Sullivan (1987), and Young and Harry (1989) have convincingly shown that the Tolchaco is merely part of an extended use of these terraces. The procurement of stone from the Shinarump conglomerate for the manufacture of tools is clearly evident on most pre-Homol'ovi and Homol'ovi Period sites along the river. The ancestral Hopi village of Homol'ovi II was constructed on an eroding Shinarump sandstone and conglomerate bluff. The surface immediately around the village is literally paved with broken and unbroken siliceous pebbles in numerous stages of reduction. Although many pebbles are split in what appears to have been an attempt to test the quality of the local stone (see Keller and Wilson 1976), the overwhelming majority of material has been reduced into cores, tools, flakes, and debris.

The study collection was sorted into six raw material categories. Ninety percent of the lithic assemblage from Homol'ovi II is probably derived from the Shinarump Conglomerate. The local clastic sedimentary rock includes chert, jasper, and petrified wood. A small amount of the chert and a majority of the jasper are probably tumbled cobbles of petrified wood but were sorted as separate rock types. Within the identifiable metamorphic series is quartzite. Obsidian falls within the igneous series and is intrusive. A sixth category is a catchall for either unidentifiable materials or rock too low in frequency to justify a separate category. Such materials include various porphyritic igneous rocks, basalt, gypsum, and chalcedony. All data pertaining to raw material types are expressed, therefore, in terms of (1) Chert, (2) Obsidian, (3) Jasper, (4) Petrified wood, (5) Quartzite, or (6) Other.

## SAMPLING

Of the 63 surface collection units, chipped stone artifacts from 16 collection units (2 m in diameter) from the exterior of the pueblo (9 units from the north side and 7 from the south side) were selected for analysis. Within the interior plazas of Homol'ovi II, collections from 3 units (5 m in diameter) were examined from the West Plaza and 2 each from the Central and East plazas. These were selected as part of a stratified random sample to ensure representation from all plaza areas and the north and south exteriors.

All chipped stone from excavated rooms was initially analyzed by the following proveniences: surface, room fill, floor contact, floor fill (within 20 cm of floor), and feature fill. With the exception of artifacts lying on intact portions of floors, within floor fill, and from within undisturbed floor features, artifacts were in proveniences that, although stratigraphically layered, were disturbed to varying degrees by vandalism. Although artifact counts from floor and fill contexts were tabulated separately, chipped stone from intact floors and from within feature fill were combined, and all stone artifacts from disturbed fill deposits were merged together for discussion.

Because the artifact frequencies from the various proveniences represent different recovery contexts (that is, surface collected and excavated samples) and recovery unit sizes, interpretations and comparisons about prehistoric technological activities necessarily must be based on percentage (relative frequency) data. This simple data transformation controls for any assemblage size effects that may have been introduced into collections recovered from collection units of different sizes. Also, because variation in recovery unit size clearly affects lithic artifact density values, artifact density has been standardized according to the number of objects per square meter. This was accomplished by simply dividing the number of artifacts recovered from a particular unit by the area (in square meters) of that unit.

Artifact yields from identically sized and adjacent collection units and from floor contexts of excavated rooms are often quite variable. To offset the possibility that small samples might introduce uncontrollable and uninterpretable biases into our analyses, artifacts recovered from the various collection units were aggregated into three major spatial groups that served essentially as primary units of analysis.

1. Exterior Open Space has two major subdivisions: North (Collection Units 24, 27, 30, 51, 53, 56, 59, 61, 63) and South (Collection Units 3, 5, 7, 10, 14, 17, 20).

2. Interior Open Space consists of the West Plaza (Collection Units 32, 33, 35), Central Plaza (Collection Units 39, 40), and the East Plaza (Collection Units 46, 48).

3. Enclosed Space, which consists of Rooms 211, 212, 215, 216, 217, and an outdoor activity area referred to as Activity Area 221.

## RESULTS AND INTERPRETATION

### Exterior Open Space

Lithic assemblages from the north and south sides of Homol'ovi II differ in a number of important ways. With respect to nonassemblage variability, the average lithic artifact density for the south units (33.9 artifacts per square meter) is 4.6 times greater than the average for the north units (7.4 artifacts per square meter). This difference in artifact density indicates that activities involving the reduction of chipped stone materials may have been more "intensive" on the south side of the pueblo than on the north. We suspect that this is related to the greater availability of chert raw material to the south of the mesa on which Homol'ovi II rests.

Turning now to a consideration of assemblage variation examination, Figure 6.2 shows that broken flakes

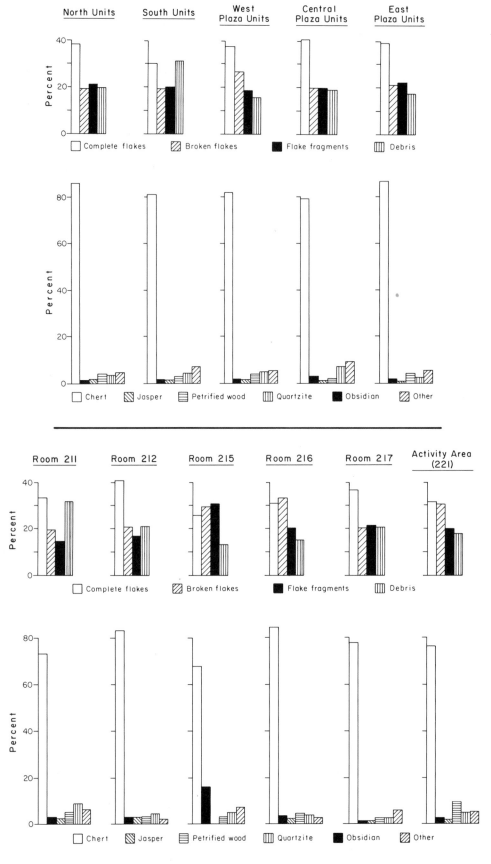

Figure 6.2. Distribution of debitage and raw material by percent.

and flake fragments constitute a minor component of the debitage assemblages recovered from both the north and south sides of Homol'ovi II. Complete flakes dominate all of the exterior and south sides. However, in comparison to the north side, the south side debitage assemblage is notable for its substantially higher percentage of debris and comparatively lower percentage of complete flakes. In addition, only nine tools (five unifacially retouched pieces and four cores) were recovered from only five of the nine north side collection units (that is, four north side collection units, 44.4% disclosed no tools). In contrast, chipped stone tools and other artifacts were recovered from all but one of the south side collection units (14.3% with no tools). With the exception of Collection Unit 20, all south units produced a substantial number of retouched pieces (50), cores (14), and hammerstones (4). Interestingly, these differences in percentages of complete flakes and debris, and in the occurrences of tool types between north and south side collection units have no differences in raw material types (Fig. 6.2).

Based on these assemblage and nonassemblage data, several conclusions appear warranted. The same range and proportions of raw material types were undergoing reduction on both the north and south sides of Homol'ovi II. Chert dominates the chipped stone assemblage, a result, undoubtedly, of its immediate availability just south of the pueblo. By and large, technological activities on both the north and south sides were dominated by flake production, although our data suggest that unifacial tool manufacture was an important aspect of lithic reduction on the south side of the pueblo and not on the north side. Also, the south side was evidently the scene of more intensive lithic reduction than the north as indicated by greater lithic artifact density, a lower debitage-to-tool ratio, and a comparatively high percentage of tools (8.6%) in the chipped stone assemblage (Table 6.1). In fact, the proportion of tools in the south side assemblage is exactly twice as great as that of north side assemblages (4.3%). Thus, in comparison to the south exterior areas, technological activity along the north side was limited almost exclusively to unintensive flake production. This conclusion is warranted because 44.4 percent of the tools from the north side collection units are cores (4 of 9) whereas cores comprise only 21.9 percent of the tools (14 of 64) recovered from south side units.

Additional inferences about factors responsible for variation between the north and south side assemblages are possible. As noted above, although the relatively high percentages of complete flakes and debris, and correspondingly low percentages of broken flakes and flake fragments, indicate an almost exclusive focus on flake production in Homol'ovi II exterior areas (Sullivan

### Table 6.1. Summary Data and Indices on Chipped Stone Assemblages

| Provenience | Debitage | Tools (Cores and retouched pieces) | Debitage to tool ratio | Tool percentage |
|---|---|---|---|---|
| *Exterior and plaza locations* | | | | |
| North units | 199 | 9 | 22.1 | 4.3 |
| South units | 677 | 64 | 10.6 | 8.6 |
| West Plaza | 519 | 29 | 17.9 | 5.3 |
| Central Plaza | 303 | 17 | 17.8 | 5.3 |
| East Plaza | 198 | 18 | 11.0 | 8.3 |
| Total | 1896 | 137 | 13.8 | 6.7 |
| *Excavated Room and Activity Area locations* | | | | |
| Room 211 | 125 | 15 | 8.3 | 10.7 |
| Room 212 | 135 | 19 | 7.1 | 12.3 |
| Room 215 | 81 | 8 | 10.1 | 9.0 |
| Room 216 | 208 | 19 | 10.9 | 8.4 |
| Room 217 | 261 | 36 | 7.2 | 12.1 |
| Area 221 | 1038 | 99 | 10.5 | 8.7 |
| Total | 1848 | 196 | 9.4 | 9.6 |

and Rozen 1985), differences in the percentages of complete flakes and debris between the north and south sides suggest that factors in addition to reduction intensity may have affected proportional differences between the debitage categories. For example, it appears quite likely that postproduction selection of complete flakes for use in household activities conducted elsewhere throughout the pueblo may have occurred. The effect of this selection would have been to decrease the proportional representation of complete flakes in south side assemblages and increase it elsewhere (see below). Also, variation in debitage-to-tool ratios and percentage of tools in the chipped stone assemblage (Table 6.1) suggest that unifacial tool manufacture was a significant aspect of lithic production on the south side. Because many of these unifaces were manufactured from complete flakes, the representation of complete flakes there would be depressed accordingly. The combination of selection of complete flakes for use in nonlithic production activities and in unifacial tool manufacture explains the substantial differences in the occurrence of this debitage category on the north and south sides of Homol'ovi II.

## Interior Open Space

In contrast to the lithic assemblages from exterior spaces of Homol'ovi II, those from the three plazas differ little from one another with respect to debitage category variation. Examination of Figure 6.2 shows that the debitage assemblages from all three plazas have comparatively high percentages of complete flakes. Also similar to the exterior space assemblages, all plaza assemblages are dominated by chert with little variation among the five other raw material types.

Based on average lithic artifact density, the West and Central plazas are denser and more similar to one another (9.3 and 8.2 artifacts per square meter respectively) than either is to the East Plaza (5.6 artifacts per square meter). Although there is, in general, a west-to-east trend of decreasing lithic artifact density in the plazas, it should be noted that the overall density of lithic artifacts in the East Plaza is the lowest of any area investigated during the 1984 field season. Along these lines, the West and Central plazas have greater lithic artifact densities than the north side of Homol'ovi II, whereas all plazas have densities far lower than that of its south side. The overall profile of plaza debitage category variation (Fig. 6.2) is similar to that for the north side and dissimilar to that of the south side units.

The West Plaza differs from all other major spatial areas investigated at Homol'ovi II because the only two bifaces recovered during the 1984 field season came from there. With this exception, the composition of the tool assemblages of the West and Central plazas are quite similar to that of the north units based on similar values of debitage-to-tool ratios and percentage of tools within the chipped stone assemblage (Table 6.1). The East Plaza differs substantially from the others and from the north units in that it has a comparatively low debitage-to-tool ratio (11.0:1) and a relatively high percentage of tools (8.3%). Based on these data, the East Plaza assemblage is most similar to the south side assemblage. This is perhaps a significant pattern because, unlike the West and Central plazas, the East Plaza is not completely enclosed by roomblocks and it opens onto the south side of the pueblo. Thus, the architectural setting of the East Plaza may have "framed" a cultural space in which activities involving chipped stone artifacts were more closely linked to those occurring in open spaces, such as the southern exterior of the pueblo, than those performed in the other two plazas.

On the basis of these data, we offer the following conclusions regarding lithic production activities in the three plazas of Homol'ovi II. Although the intensity of lithic production was similar in the West and Central plazas, there seems to have been a subtle difference in emphasis. That is, in the Central Plaza (where no cores were recovered) unifacial tool manufacture was a more prevalent technological activity (Table 6.1) than in the West Plaza where cores equaled 17.2 percent of all tools. In the East Plaza, lithic production was not as intensive; however, when it occurred there was a strong

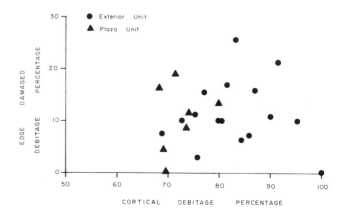

Figure 6.3. Scattergram showing the relation between the percentage of edge-damaged debitage to the percentage of cortical debitage for surface collection units within and outside plaza areas.

emphasis on the manufacture of unifacially retouched pieces, most likely from retouching complete flakes produced there.

It is noteworthy that, overall, debitage from the plazas is considerably less cortical (average equals 72.2%) than debitage from the exterior units (average equals 82.8%). There is, however, only an insubstantial difference in percentages of edge-damaged debitage between these two major spatial subdivisions of Homol'ovi II (averages equal 10.5 % and 11.4% respectively; Fig. 6.3). These aggregated data suggest that a greater proportion of technological activity in the plazas was geared to unifacial tool manufacture and that debitage produced elsewhere (most likely on the south side of the pueblo) may have been partially "decortified" and transported to the plazas for manufacture into tools. At the very least, processes of this sort would explain the absence of cores in the Central Plaza.

### Excavated Rooms and Activity Area

An additional set of limitations constrains the analysis of lithic artifacts recovered from Rooms 211, 212, 215, 216, 217, and outdoor Activity Area 221. With the exception of Room 215, all others were disturbed, to varying degrees, by excavations that resulted in the destruction of directly interpretable stratigraphic relationships and, therefore, the depositional history of each room. Conclusions about whether chipped stone artifacts found in room fill or on room floors were actually deposited there prehistorically, for example, could not be substantiated with any reliability. Artifacts could have followed many different paths in the recent past to eventually be deposited in the locations where we found them. Also, the sample of lithic artifacts from floor contexts is often small and varies considerably between rooms. For these reasons, all artifacts from the fill and floor of each room were combined into a single collection for analytical and interpretive purposes. The major objective of aggregating these samples was to determine if the technology of lithic artifacts from enclosed cultural spaces differed from that of interior and exterior cultural spaces.

Inspection of Figure 6.2 reveals considerable variation between the rooms and the activity area with respect to percentage occurrences of debitage categories and raw material types. These differences may be discussed conveniently as follows: (1) Rooms 212 and 217 are distinctive as they have noticeably high percentages of complete flakes and negligible variation between the remaining debitage categories; (2) Room 216 and Activity Area 221 exhibit comparatively low complete flake percentages and relatively high percentages of broken flakes; (3) Room 215 also has a fairly low percentage of complete flakes but is noteworthy in that its debitage assemblage has unusually high and almost equal percentages of broken flakes and flake fragments; and (4) Room 211 is quite distinctive given its comparatively high and equal percentages of complete flakes and debris. The debitage from all rooms and the activity area is dominated by chert. With the exception of Room 215, there is insubstantial variation among the five other major raw material types. Room 215 is notable for the high percentage of obsidian debitage recovered from its undisturbed deposits.

Interestingly, Table 6.1 shows that excavated units that are similar in terms of debitage category percentages are also similar with respect to debitage-to-tool ratios and tool percentages. Thus, Rooms 212 and 217, Room 216 and Activity Area 221, Room 215, and Room 211 form small sets that contrast with one another in terms of the variables mentioned above. Furthermore, the projectile points and projectile point fragments recovered from Rooms 212 and 217 and Activity Area 221 are the only contexts investigated during the 1984 field season that disclosed these artifact types.

Unfortunately, it is difficult to interpret these data and presumed relationships in a straightforward fashion. For example, are the similarities of the members of the room sets noted above (for example, Rooms 212 and 217, Room 216 and Area 221) attributable to similar technological and depositional processes or to the effects of pothunting? A few simple examples will illustrate how the entropic effects of unsystematic excavation could easily produce some provocative yet misleading data patterns. For example, if the depositional and use histories of these rooms and the activity

area were similar, a rather unlikely scenario, then only selective excavation and disposal of room contents by the pothunters (an equally unlikely set of events) could have created these interroom set differences. However, if the use and depositional histories of these rooms and the activity area were originally dissimilar (most likely reconstruction), then repeated moving and mixing of deposits from different levels and rooms would tend to enhance or depress originally robust aspects of prehistoric assemblage variability in an unpredictable fashion. In line with these arguments, the most heavily disturbed rooms (Rooms 211 and 212) are quite dissimilar in terms of debitage category percentages, whereas rooms that are only moderately disturbed (Rooms 216 and 217) or undisturbed (Room 215) are also dissimilar with respect to debitage category variation, raw material variation, debitage-to-tool ratios, and tool percentages (see Table 6.1). Clearly, lithic artifact variability crosscuts or is uncorrelated with disturbance variability. Although it is likely that the content of these excavated areas was originally dissimilar, it is unlikely that the activities of the pothunters would have preserved those original relationships. We conclude, therefore, that much of the lithic assemblage variation and patterning among the rooms and the activity area are the result of random variability introduced through illegal digging.

Under the assumption, then, that much of the assemblage variability of the excavated units is due to pothunting, with the possible exception of Room 215, the following interpretations are advanced. The assemblage from Room 211 (heavily disturbed) appears to represent the byproducts of flake production with an emphasis on unifacial tool manufacture. The profile of debitage category variation is strikingly similar to that for the south side of Homol'ovi II (Fig. 6.2) where similar interpretations were developed. Debitage from Rooms 212 (heavily disturbed) and 217 (moderately disturbed) exhibits the classic profile of technological activity devoted almost exclusively to flake production (compare the north side debitage category variation). However, the comparatively low debitage-to-tool ratio and high tool percentage suggest that tools made elsewhere were transported and discarded in or near Rooms 212 and 217. The debitage category profiles, debitage-to-tool ratios, and tool percentages for Room 216 and Activity Area 221 suggest relatively equal emphasis on flake production and unifacial tool manufacture. The tools produced in or near these areas were evidently removed to other locations, some perhaps within Homol'ovi II itself. The assemblage from Room 215 (undisturbed) evidently represents byproducts from the manufacture of obsidian tools, which were then probably transported to other locations, and minimal flake production.

It is clear that despite the interpretive limitations discussed above, the lithic material excavated from the rooms and the activity area contrasts with all other major areas of Homol'ovi II in terms of the presence of projectile points, a high average tool percentage, and a low debitage-to-tool ratio. These data suggest that unifacial and bifacial tool production were important aspects of lithic production activities conducted in and around pueblo rooms.

## SUMMARY AND CONCLUSIONS

Despite the tremendous amount and extent of damage sustained by Homol'ovi II, analysis of lithic artifacts recovered from a variety of contexts during 1984 has produced some intriguing findings regarding the factors that may have influenced prehistoric technological activity. Not only do we have new data concerning how lithic raw materials were processed at a large and late prehistoric site in the central Little Colorado River Valley, but we also have a demonstration that general conclusions about sedentary agriculturalist lithic technology can be salvaged from even the most severely disturbed archaeological site. Apparently, pothunters are not interested in collecting chipped stone debitage or tools.

Our major findings are that technological activities at Homol'ovi II were dominated by flake production from locally available cherts and that a not inconsequential aspect of lithic production focused on the manufacture of unifacially retouched pieces. The manufacture of bifacially retouched tools, including both bifaces and projectile points, appears to have been drastically suppressed by late prehistoric times. Interestingly, a similar pattern has been described for ceramic period habitation (Jeter 1980; Rozen 1981) and rockshelter sites (Sullivan 1984a) in the upper Little Colorado River drainage (see also Sullivan and Rozen 1985). Also, it appears that certain areas of Homol'ovi II, such as the West and Central plazas and the pueblo's south side, were the scenes of relatively intensive multiple lithic production activities, whereas other areas, such as the pueblo's north side, were not.

In addition, our results suggest that considerable circulation of debitage, primarily complete flakes, may have been fairly routine. For example, some areas of the pueblo, such as its south side, were apparently donors of flakes and tool preforms. Other areas, such as the Central and East plazas, may have been receivers of lithic artifacts (flakes and preforms) produced elsewhere. It is quite likely that many "reclamation" processes such as scavenging, reuse, and recycling of previously produced and discarded flakes (Schiffer 1985) may have distributed lithic artifacts to areas within

Homol'ovi II where they were required for different kinds of activities. The discontinuities between areas of lithic production and use are not unexpected at sites like Homol'ovi II that are characterized by long and intensive occupation histories.

Perhaps the biggest return from our analysis has been the emergence of and an appreciation for the considerable variation in lithic assemblages collected from different areas of Homol'ovi II. In fact, it appears that one of the major factors influencing assemblage variability is the location where lithic production occurred. For example, areas close to raw material sources such as the pueblo's south side, and those completely bounded by architecture such as the West and Central plazas, were evidently scenes of multiple lithic production activities that were conducted at greater intensities than in those areas located farther away from raw material sources or not enclosed by masonry, such as the East Plaza. One of the clearest examples of how space may influence lithic artifact form surfaced when we compared the percentages of cortical debitage from all exterior units and all plaza units. We discovered that debitage produced in the plaza or arriving there after "preprocessing" elsewhere (the pueblo's south exterior seems most likely) was substantially less cortical than debitage from exterior spaces. It is not unreasonable to suggest that a simple practical consideration such as reducing some of the extremely sharp waste associated with lithic production in high density pedestrian traffic areas, such as the enclosed plazas, may lie behind patterns of this sort.

In addition to data based on artifact density, debitage category variation, and cortical variation, it has been noted that bifacial tools and tool fragments were found in only a few types of spaces rather than being scattered throughout the pueblo. Bifaces (and not projectile points) were found only in the West Plaza, whereas projectile points (and not bifaces) came from rooms and the activity area exclusively. Furthermore, one of the strongest pieces of evidence we have regarding the spatial determinants of lithic artifact production is that exterior units and plaza units have relatively high average debitage-to-tool ratios (16.4:1 and 15.6:1 respectively) and lower average tool percentages (6.5% and 6.3% respectively). On the other hand, the excavated rooms and activity area have substantially lower average debitage-to-tool ratios (9.2:1) and higher tool percentages (10.1%). Two possible interpretations, which highlight the technological distinctiveness of enclosed versus exterior cultural spaces, can be supported with these data: (1) lithic activities located near or in rooms were, in general, oriented more toward tool production than lithic activities conducted in nonenclosed spaces; or (2) pueblo rooms were areas at Homol'ovi II where tools were most likely to have been used and discarded regardless of their locations of manufacture.

Lastly, we have shown that large samples of lithic artifacts collected from a variety of different kinds of "cultural spaces" provide a strong empirical base from which to infer the nature of prehistoric technological activities and the factors, such as spatial variation, that tend to introduce subtle yet interpretable variation into chipped stone assemblages. Most importantly, we have demonstrated that this can be accomplished with varying degrees of success and inferential resolution at severely disturbed archaeological sites like Homol'ovi II.

# CHAPTER SEVEN

# Pollen

Suzanne K. Fish
Arizona State Museum

The pollen samples analyzed from Homol'ovi II room proveniences yielded plentiful pollen in an unexpectedly good state of preservation. Of three samples lacking sufficient pollen for tabulation, destruction in two firebox samples was probably the result of burning. A third sample came from a posthole in Activity Area 221, where burning of the post may also have been a factor. Sample proveniences are listed in Table 7.1. Multiple floor samples were emphasized in order to document the range of plant resources utilized in each room and to compare room functions on the basis of distributions of economic pollen types. Pollen incorporated directly into floor sediments should represent deposition during room occupation, barring undetected stratigraphic disturbance.

## EXTRACTION AND TABULATION METHODS

Approximately 60 cc of sediment was processed per sample. *Lycopodium* tracers were added to monitor extraction results. Following deflocculation in dilute hydrochloric acid, a mechanical swirl method as described by Mehringer (1967: 136-137) was employed to separate the heavier sediment fraction. Heavy liquid flotation in 2.0 zinc bromide further reduced extraneous matrix material. Rinses with hydrofluoric acid, hydrochloric acid, water, and absolute alcohol completed the extraction process. The extract was mounted in a glycerol medium and stained for microscope viewing.

A standard sum of 200 noncultigen grains was tabulated for each sample containing pollen. This sum was used to calculate percentages of the various types presented in Table 7.1. Cultigen pollen was tabulated outside the 200 grain sum in order to avoid numerical constraint of percentages of types that might provide information on environmental conditions. Therefore, the value given for cultigens is not a percent, but represents the number of grains encountered in the course of completing the standard sum. The two cultigen categories in this analysis are corn, *Zea*, and cucurbits, *Cucurbita*. Wild species of the genus *Cucurbita* are a possibility in the latter case, but recovery of cultigen remains in flotation demonstrates the probability that cultivated cucurbits produced this pollen.

## MODERN ENVIRONMENT

Homol'ovi pollen spectra indicate an open environment in the site vicinity, probably a sparse desert grassland dominated by shrubby members of the Compositae Family. Pollen types and frequencies are consistent with surface spectra in northern Arizona today from zones classified by Hevly (1968: 121) as either desert or low, xeric grassland. An exception is less abundant windblown juniper in Homol'ovi samples than in modern ones from similar situations. Pollen frequencies also fall within the general range found by Scott (1980) near modern Walpi. The prehistoric environment appears to have paralleled that in the area today, although the absence of domestic grazing herds should have meant a denser and grassier ground cover and fewer shrubs.

Cheno-Am is a palynological category encompassing chenopods and amaranths. Pollen of this type often dominates spectra of Southwestern archaeological sites, because these species respond as weedy volunteers in culturally disturbed habitats. At Homol'ovi II, Cheno-Am frequencies tend to be moderate; even the higher values do not exceed ones reported for natural vegetation communities in the desert and grassland of northern Arizona (Hevly 1968). On the other hand, values for *Ambrosia*-type are relatively high at Homol'ovi II. Although much of this pollen type is probably contributed by perennial shrubs such as bursage, weedy annual species producing similar pollen may have been prominent about the pueblo.

A well-developed riparian community along the river is attested by occasional windblown arboreal pollen types. Willow (*Salix*), alder (*Alnus*), and hackberry (*Celtis*) were identified in more than one instance. It is doubtful that the source trees were distant by many miles, whether or not they occurred along the nearest part of the river. The ready availability of resource plants from permanently damp habitats is demonstrated by the occurrence of cattail (*Typha*) pollen in Rooms 211, 212, 216, and 217. Sedge (Cyperaceae) pollen in Room 216 accords with sedge seeds recovered from the site, identifying a second resource plant requiring comparatively moist conditions.

## ROOM FUNCTION AND CHRONOLOGY

Pollen spectra offer little evidence for specialized room functions with regard to food preparation or storage. Corn, the most common cultigen type, occurs in samples from Rooms 212, 215, 216, and 217. Abundance does not vary importantly among these rooms. Three floor samples from Room 211 without corn may indicate a room less associated with foodstuffs or with a more restricted range of resources than the others. Economic pollen types (types for which presence or abundance can be associated with a resource plant) other than corn occur in several rooms (Table 7.2). However, some types such as *Curcurbita* are naturally dispersed in such small quantities that their presence is significant information, but absence of the pollen cannot be taken as a reliable indication that the resource was not used.

*Ambrosia*-type frequencies are relatively consistent within most rooms, suggesting that this pollen originated in a generalized pollen rain at the time of deposition rather than from localized human activity within the site. Rooms 211 and 212 are marked by higher frequencies and Rooms 215, 216 (with the exception of one sample), and 217 are marked by lower frequencies of *Ambrosia*-type. It is possible that the *Ambrosia* differences reflect temporal changes in vegetation linked to climate, but just as likely to cultural modification of nearby natural plant communities. Temporal differences, if valid, would pertain to the occupational span associated with specific sampled floors. Since multiple refloorings occurred in some rooms, the date of any particular floor might not be correlated precisely with the sequence of room wall construction. Such palynological suggestions of chronologically similar rooms offer an additional line of potential evidence for assessing occupational contemporaneity.

## RESOURCE USE

The distribution of corn pollen by room has been noted. It was undoubtedly a major resource at Homol'ovi II. Cucurbits are represented by a single instance of this rare pollen type in Room 215. Occurrence here parallels macrofossil evidence, but does not imply absence in the other proveniences.

A common weed of historic Hopi fields is *Cleome* or beeweed. Used as an edible green as well as a material for paint-making, beeweed is encouraged to grow in fields (Whiting 1939: 76–77) and is of sufficient economic importance at Hano to be named in songs along with the three major cultigens (Robbins and others 1916: 59). Beeweed pollen is found in every room, at frequencies less than 10 percent. Some of this pollen was likely introduced on resource plants. In a modern surface pollen transect at Walpi, *Cleome* pollen was found only in samples from agricultural contexts, and at values lower than 5 percent (Scott 1980: 5). The ubiquity of the type also suggests that the plants were an important and widespread component of the agricultural landscape farmed by pueblo occupants.

Cattail pollen (*Typha*) is also well distributed in all five sampled rooms. Intentional introduction is almost certain for a pollen type such as cattail that tends to be localized near its source. Almost all parts of the plant were used by Southwestern groups. The small amounts present in Homol'ovi rooms could result from craft uses, matting, or roofing as well as from edible use of shoots or roots. By a similar argument, sedge pollen in Room 216 is also the probable result of resource use.

Economic presence cannot be inferred without additional evidence for several other pollen types. Cheno-Am pollen, for instance, could be expected in frequencies found at Homol'ovi from natural vegetation or from disturbance plants in residential precincts. Irregular percentages across a single floor or aggregates of grains that would travel poorly by air are clues to resource use of cultivated or gathered chenopod or amaranth species. This kind of evidence was present in Rooms 215, 216, and 217 and accords with recovery of charred seeds of these species. Similarly, anomalously elevated percentages of grass (Gramineae) pollen in one Room 217 sample indicate the likelihood of grass use. Aggregates of wild buckwheat, *Eriogonum*, may be an economic record in Room 216.

Three types of pollen are sufficiently rare that even small amounts in room samples are probably economic. Scott (1980) encountered none of these three types in modern samples collected near Walpi. Pollen of an undetermined species in the Liliaceae or Lily Family occurs in Rooms 211, 215, and 217. Cholla (Cylindropuntia) and prickly pear (Platyopuntia) pollen are present in small amounts in several rooms (Table 7.2). Cholla use is also confirmed by flotation evidence.

## CONCLUSIONS

Pollen results from Homol'ovi II are commensurate with expectations for occupational strata undisturbed since the time of deposition. There is little indication of

**Table 7.1. Percentages of Pollen Types from Homol'ovi II Rooms   (N = 200)**

| Provenience | Ambrosia-type | Other Low Spine Compositae | High Spine Compositae | Artemisia | Liguliflorae | Cheno-Am | Sarcobatus | Gramineae | Cleome | Eriogonum | Sphaeralcea | Cruciferae | Liliaceae | Boerhaavia-type | Labiatae | Onagraceae | Acacia |
|---|---|---|---|---|---|---|---|---|---|---|---|---|---|---|---|---|---|
| **Room** | | | | | | | | | | | | | | | | | |
| 211 floor | 57.5 | 0.5 | 1.0 | 3.0 | | 9.0 | | 3.5 | 2.0 | 0.5 | 0.5 | 1.0 | | | | | |
| 211 floor | 44.5 | | 3.5 | 2.0 | | 18.0 | | 5.0 | 5.0 | 1.5 | | 1.0 | | | | | |
| 211 floor | 52.0 | | 1.5 | 4.5 | | 18.5 | | 5.0 | 4.0 | 2.0 | | | 1.0 | | | | |
| 212 floor | 53.0 | | 3.0 | 1.5 | | 21.5 | | 2.5 | 2.5 | | | | | | | | |
| 212 floor | 50.5 | | 2.5 | 4.0 | | 16.5 | 1.0 | 5.5 | 3.5 | 1.0 | | | | * | | 0.5 | |
| 212 slab firebox | 49.5 | | 3.5 | 1.0 | | 19.0 | | 1.0 | 5.5 | 4.0 | | | | | | | |
| 212 slab firebox | Insufficient pollen | | | | | | | | | | | | | | | | |
| 212 slab firebox | Insufficient pollen | | | | | | | | | | | | | | | | |
| 215 floor | 36.0 | | | 2.5 | | 10.0 | | 8.5 | 4.0 | 3.0 | * | | 1.5 | | | | * |
| 215 15 cm above floor | 29.5 | | | 3.0 | | 26.5 | 0.5 | 5.0 | 5.5 | 4.0 | | | | * | | | |
| 216 floor | 31.5 | | 1.0 | 4.0 | | 27.0 | | 7.0 | 0.5 | 0.5 | 1.0 | * | | | | | |
| 216 floor | 31.0 | 1.0 | 3.0 | 6.5 | 0.5 | 18.5 | | 2.5 | 0.5 | 9.5 | 0.5 | | | | | | |
| 216 floor | 61.0 | | 0.5 | 2.5 | | 19.0 | | 2.0 | 1.0 | 1.0 | * | | | | | | |
| 216 10 cm above floor | 42.0 | | 4.0 | 6.5 | | 26.0 | | | 0.5 | 6.0 | | 0.5 | | | | 0.5 | 1.0 |
| 217 floor | 20.5 | | 12.0 | | | 7.5 | | 51.0 | 2.5 | | | | | | | | |
| 217 floor | 22.0 | | * | * | | 39.5 | | 9.0 | 1.0 | 3.5 | 5.5 | | 1.0 | | | | |
| 217 floor | 23.0 | | 3.5 | 3.0 | | 40.0 | 0.5 | 1.0 | 4.5 | | 1.0 | | | | | | |
| 217 floor | 32.5 | | 7.5 | 4.0 | | 12.0 | | 10.5 | 8.5 | 4.5 | 1.5 | | | | | | |
| **Area** | | | | | | | | | | | | | | | | | |
| 221 posthole | Insufficient pollen | | | | | | | | | | | | | | | | |

**Table 7.2. Occurrence of Economic Pollen in Homol'ovi II Rooms**

| Room | No. of samples | Zea, corn | Curcurbita, curcurbits | Typha, cattail | Cyperaceae, sedge | Cheno-Am, chenopods, amaranths | Gramineae, grasses | Erigonum, wild buckwheat | Cleome, beeweed | Liliaceae, Lily Family | Cylindropuntia, cholla | Platyopuntia, prickly pear |
|---|---|---|---|---|---|---|---|---|---|---|---|---|
| 211 | 3 | | | x | | | | | x | x | | |
| 212 | 3 | x | | x | | | | | x | | x | x |
| 215 | 2 | x | x | x | | x | | | x | x | | x |
| 216 | 4 | x | | x | x | x | | x | x | | x | x |
| 217 | 4 | x | | | | x | x | | x | | x | x |

an environment different from that of today, with the exception of a more varied, permanent riparian community along nearby stretches of the Little Colorado River. At the same time, the consistency and level of beeweed pollen in all samples suggests substantial agricultural land in the general vicinity of the pueblo.

Corn stands out as the prominent cultigen detected by pollen, being identified in all proveniences sampled. These results leave little doubt that corn was a staple in Homol'ovi II subsistence. Cucurbits were also encountered. Prickly pear, cholla, and cattail are the three gathered resources emphasized by pollen. Beeweed and chenopods or amaranths fit a category of annuals that can include gathered plants, encouraged field weeds, semicultivated plants, and true cultigens. Together with several other occasional resources identified palynologically and the added list of non-overlapping charred remains, these elements indicate a broad spectrum of

**Table 7.1 (continued)**

| Provenience | Leguminosae | Rosaceae | Cylindropuntia | Platyopuntia | Ephedra | Abies | Pinus | Quercus | Juniperus | Salix | Alnus | Celtis | Typha | Cyperaceae | Unidentifiable | Zea (No. of grains) | Cucurbita |
|---|---|---|---|---|---|---|---|---|---|---|---|---|---|---|---|---|---|
| Room |  |  |  |  |  |  |  |  |  |  |  |  |  |  |  |  |  |
| 211 floor |  |  |  |  | 1.5 |  | 14.0 | * | 0.5 | 0.5 |  |  |  |  | 5.0 |  |  |
| 211 floor |  |  |  |  | 3.0 |  | 9.5 |  | 1.0 |  |  |  | 3.0 |  | 3.0 |  |  |
| 211 floor |  |  |  |  | 2.0 |  | 3.0 | 1.5 | 2.0 |  |  |  | * |  | 3.0 |  |  |
| 212 floor |  | 0.5 |  | 1.0 | 0.5 |  | 7.0 |  | 1.0 | 0.5 |  |  | 1.0 |  | 4.5 | 5 |  |
| 212 floor |  |  | 1.5 |  | 1.5 |  | 9.5 |  |  |  |  |  |  |  | 2.5 | 3 |  |
| 212 slab firebox | 0.5 |  |  |  | 1.0 |  | 9.5 | 1.0 |  |  |  | 1.0 |  |  | 3.5 |  |  |
| 212 slab firebox |  |  |  | Insufficient pollen |  |  |  |  |  |  |  |  |  |  |  |  |  |
| 212 slab firebox |  |  |  | Insufficient pollen |  |  |  |  |  |  |  |  |  |  |  |  |  |
| 215 floor |  |  |  |  | 2.0 |  | 25.0 | 2.0 | 0.5 | 0.5 |  |  |  |  | 4.5 | 2 | * |
| 215 15 cm above floor |  |  |  | 0.5 | 0.5 |  | 17.5 | 0.5 |  |  |  |  | * |  | 7.0 | * |  |
| 216 floor |  |  |  | * | 0.5 |  | 20.5 | 1.0 |  |  |  |  | * | 2.0 | 3.5 | 1 |  |
| 216 floor |  |  |  |  | 1.5 |  | 13.5 | 2.0 | 1.0 | 1.0 |  |  | 2.0 |  | 4.5 |  |  |
| 216 floor | 1.0 |  |  |  | 0.5 |  | 3.0 | 1.0 | 1.0 |  |  | 0.5 |  |  | 6.0 |  |  |
| 216 10 cm above floor | 0.5 |  | 0.5 | 1.5 | 1.0 |  | 5.0 | 1.0 | 0.5 |  |  |  |  |  |  |  |  |
| 217 floor |  |  |  |  |  |  | 5.5 |  |  |  |  |  |  |  | 1.0 | 6 |  |
| 217 floor |  |  | * | * | 0.5 |  | 11.5 | 3.0 | 0.5 |  |  |  | 1.0 |  | 2.5 | 2 |  |
| 217 floor |  |  |  |  | 7.0 | 0.5 | 6.5 | 2.0 | 1.5 | * |  |  |  |  | 6.0 | 5 |  |
| 217 floor |  | 0.5 |  |  | 3.0 |  | 9.0 | 0.5 | 2.0 | 0.5 |  |  |  |  | 3.5 | 1 |  |
| Area |  |  |  |  |  |  |  |  |  |  |  |  |  |  |  |  |  |
| 221 posthole |  |  |  | Insufficient pollen |  |  |  |  |  |  |  |  |  |  |  |  |  |

\* Indicates a type identified in scanning of additional sample material after completion of a 200 grain standard sum for the purpose of percentage calculation.

environmental exploitation and a strong core of agricultural production.

The tendency of individual rooms to register one of two frequency levels for a pollen type originating in natural vegetation (*Ambrosia* pollen) suggests that there is some temporal differentiation among sampled proveniences. Such potential patterning should be examined further in any future work at the site. No specialization in resource use or storage was apparent among the rooms investigated.

# CHAPTER EIGHT

# Paleoethnobotany

Charles H. Miksicek

Although only five rooms and an outside activity area were tested at Homol'ovi II, over 21.8 kg of plant remains were recovered (both charred and uncarbonized). The constraints of time and money necessitated the development of a careful sampling strategy for dealing with this quantity of material. Macro-remains from Activity Area 221 accounted for over 62 percent (by weight) of this material.

## SAMPLING STRATEGY AND METHODOLOGY

To remove potentially fragile uncharred material, all of the Homol'ovi flotation samples were first screened through 10-mm and 5-mm mesh before flotation. These uncarbonized remains were much more durable than expected so this step could be eliminated from future analyses. Large fragments of cultigens to be used for radiocarbon dating were also selected, and bones, sherds, and lithics were collected for the appropriate specialists. The part of each sample that passed through the 5-mm mesh was recombined with the fraction retained in the screens, material that had been removed was recorded, and the entire sample was floated in a washtub with a 3-mm screen.

After drying, each floated sample was passed through a nested series of geological sieves with mesh sizes of 4 mm, 2 mm, and 0.5 mm. This size sorting produces faster and more accurate analysis. Each fraction was examined under a dissecting microscope at 10 magnifications. Seeds and wood charcoal were identified with the aid of modern comparative material collected in northern Arizona. A grab sample of 20 fragments of charcoal was selected from each flotation sample; it was increased to 30 or more fragments when the charcoal assemblage was especially diverse. Each fragment was fractured to give fresh transverse and radial sections and then identified at 25 power. Raw data from the flotation, charcoal, and macrobotanical analyses are presented in Tables 8.7 to 8.10.

The vast majority of the macrofossils from Activity Area 221 (94.8% by weight) were charred and partially fused ears of corn. Wood charcoal comprised 5.1 percent of the total, and beans and smaller seeds accounted for less than 0.1 percent of the total. Most of the plant remains recovered from Activity Area 221 probably represent redeposited material cleaned from a burned storage room. Relatively intact ears were first sorted from the 221 collection. No ears were complete from shank to tip, so it was impossible to determine an average length for Homol'ovi maize types. Some ears were severely fused in the charring process, but it was still possible to carefully pry apart individual cobs or take measurements from ears exposed on the surface of separate masses of charred corn. This amount of fusion suggests that the ears still had a relatively high moisture content before they were burned, and that they may have been drying on the roof or within the storage room that was destroyed by fire.

At least two visually distinct types of maize are present in the Homol'ovi collection. One type has smaller ears, cigar-shaped cobs (tapered toward both ends), thicker glumes, and small kernels with a high frequency of flinty endosperm. This type compares most favorably to modern representatives of the Pima-Papago suprarace of corn. The second group has larger, straighter cobs, longer glumes, and larger kernels all with floury endosperm. Many of the cobs of this second type are markedly flattened in cross section (fasciated). These larger ears are quite similar to Pueblo Flour varieties still grown by the Hopi today.

The collection from Area 221 was first sorted into these visually distinct groups, then each category was further sorted according to row number. A random sample of ears or cobs from each row number was then measured using variables described in Nickerson (1953). A total of 300 ears from Area 221 was sorted to type and row number and then 110 ears were measured in detail. Ears recovered from Rooms 211 (1), 212 (6), 215 (4), and 216 (7) were also analyzed. The results of this analysis are reported in Table 8.1 and summarized in Figure 8.1. Representative ears are shown in Figure 8.2. Several uncharred ears were included in this collection.

**Table 8.1. Metric Data for A Sample of All Carbonized Whole Cobs from Homol'ovi II**

| | Pueblo Flour | | | | Pima-Papago | | |
|---|---|---|---|---|---|---|---|
| | Mean | SD | Range | | Mean | SD | Range |
| Number of Measured Cobs | 47 | | | | 81 | | |
| Mean # of Rows of Grains[1] | 11.8 | | | | 10.4 | | |
| % 8 Rowed Cobs | 0 | | | | 23 | | |
| % 10 Rowed Cobs | 32 | | | | 38 | | |
| % 12 Rowed Cobs | 49 | | | | 34 | | |
| % 14 Rowed Cobs | 17 | | | | 4 | | |
| % 16 Rowed Cobs | 2 | | | | 0 | | |
| Mean Cupule Width (mm)[1] | | 6.8 | 0.86 | 5.0–9.3 | | 5.5 | 0.84 | 3.7–7.3 |
| Mean Cupule Height (mm)[2] | | 3.4 | 0.38 | 2.6–4.3 | | 3.2 | 0.37 | 2.1–4.5 |
| Mean Rachis Diameter (mm)[1] | | 12.5 | 1.66 | 9.5–15.7 | | 9.0 | 1.12 | 6.6–11.6 |
| Mean Cob Diameter (mm)[1] | | 16.4 | 1.89 | 13.0–21.9 | | 12.6 | 1.82 | 8.9–17.5 |
| Mean Ear Diameter (mm)[1] | | 28.6 | 2.48 | 24.6–32.8 | | 25.9 | 2.30 | 21.4–30.3 |
| Mean Kernel Width (mm)[2] | | 7.1 | 0.92 | 5.9–9.6 | | 6.6 | 0.78 | 5.1–7.7 |
| Cob-Rachis Index[2] | | 1.3 | 0.13 | 1.1–1.6 | | 1.4 | 0.19 | 1.1–2.1% |
| % Fasciated Cobs | 56 | | | | 23 | | |
| % Ears with Flint Kernels | 0 | | | | 21 | | |

Significance levels for Student's T-test:  1 = Highly significant ($p < 0.001$);  2 = Significant ($p < 0.05$).
*Note*: Sample includes 110 cobs from Area 221, 1 from Room 211, 6 from Room 212, 4 from Room 215, 7 from Room 216.

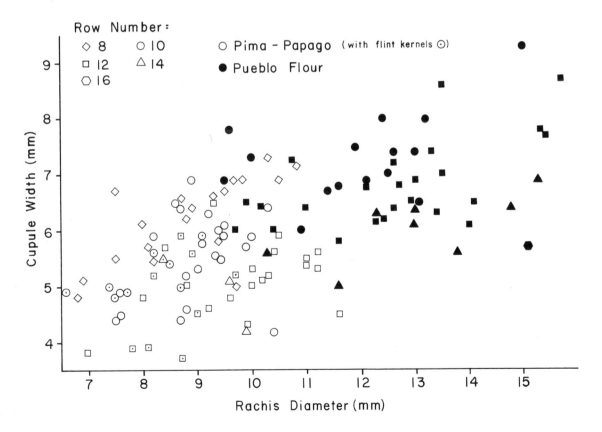

Figure 8.1. Relation of cupule width to rachis diameter by row number and corn variety.

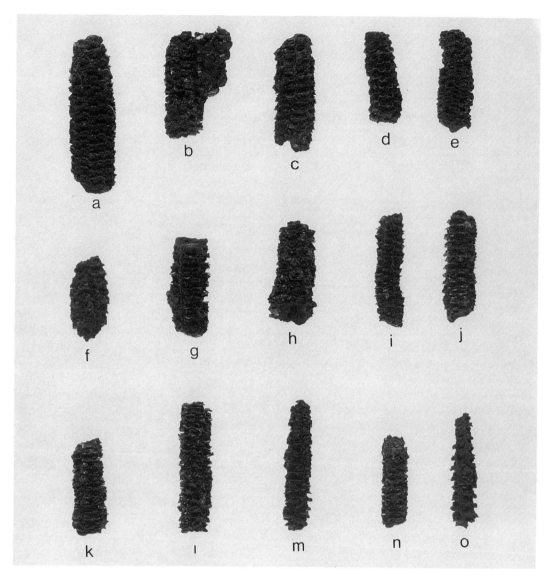

Figure 8.2. Corn cobs: *a-c*, 14 row, large cob; *d, e*, 14 row, small cob; *f-h*, 10 row, large cob; *i, j*, 10 row, small cob; *k-m*, 8 row, small cob; *n, o*, underdeveloped. (Length of *h* is 5 cm.)

As a result, 20 percent was subtracted from each measurement on the uncarbonized ears to compensate for shrinkage during burning and to make the measurements more comparable.

Flotation samples from Activity Area 221 were also subsampled. Each complete lot was first weighed and then several 100 gm subsamples were selected for analysis. These subsamples were collected from the top, middle, and bottom of each sample bag to avoid biases introduced by differential settling (small seeds will filter down to the bottom of a pile). The 100-gm subsamples were analyzed according to the standard procedure outlined above, averaged together, and then the seed con-

tent of the whole lot was estimated by proportional methods (if 5 seeds were identified in 100 gm then 1000 gm should have produced 10 times as many or 50 seeds).

## ROOM 215 AND COMMENTS ON PRESERVATION

The contents of the firebox in Room 215 (Feature 2) had been sealed by sandstone slabs while the room was still in use. This unusual situation caused the preservation of a large quantity of uncarbonized plant remains (Tables 8.2, 8.3). Under normal circumstances, uncharred plant remains from an open site are considered

**Table 8.2. Proportion of Plant Remains Preserved by Charring from Room 215 Flotation Samples**

| Common Name | Scientific Name | Total | Percent Charred |
|---|---|---|---|
| **Present only as charred remains:** | | | |
| Maize Kernels | *Zea mays* | 181 | 100 |
| Pigweed Seeds | *Amaranthus* spp. | 1 | 100 |
| Greasewood Seeds | *Sarcobatus vermiculatus* | 14 | 100 |
| Cholla Buds | *Opuntia whipplei* | 1 | 100 |
| Grass Stems | Gramineae | ++ | 100 |
| **Partially preserved by carbonization:** | | | |
| Maize Cobs Fragments | *Zea mays* | 124 | 33 |
| Lambsquarters Seeds | *Chenopodium* spp. | 4 | 25 |
| Squawbush Seeds | *Rhus trilobata* | 27 | 4 |
| Indian Ricegrass Seeds | *Oryzopsis hymenoides* | 1941 | 2 |
| **Present only as uncharred material:** | | | |
| Common Bean | *Phaseolus vulgaris* | 2 | |
| Summer Squash Seeds | *Cucurbita pepo* | 44 | |
| Cushaw Squash Seeds | *Cucurbita mixta* | 2 | |
| Squash Rind Fragments | *Cucurbita* spp. | 57 | |
| Bottle Gourd Rind | *Lagenaria siceraria* | 2 | |
| Cotton Seeds | *Gossypium hirsutum* | 30 | |
| Dropseed Grass Seeds | *Sporobolus* | 805 | |
| Purslane Seeds | *Portulaca oleracea* | 1 | |
| Sunflower Seeds | *Helianthus annuus* | 1 | |
| Banana Yucca Seeds | *Yucca baccata* | 78 | |
| Narrow-leaf Yucca Leaves | *Yucca* spp. | 1 | |
| Utah Juniper Seeds | *Juniperus osteosperma* | 21 | |
| One-seed Juniper Seeds | *Juniperus monosperma* | 8 | |
| Juniper Leaf Scales | *Juniperus* spp. | ++ | |
| Piñon Nut Fragments | *Pinus edulis* | 34 | |
| Piñon Needles | *Pinus edulis* | 14 | |
| Sedge Seeds | *Scirpus* sp. | 9 | |
| Horsetail Stems | *Equisetum* sp. | ++ | |

++ = Remains numerous

suspect, likely to have been introduced by later people, burrowing animals, or disturbances. The cultivated plants (maize, squash, gourd, and cotton) could only have been deposited by humans and are consistent with other types of remains recovered from Homol'ovi. Piñon and juniper do not occur near the site today and could not have been introduced by animals in the recent past. They were probably deliberately imported to the pueblo by the inhabitants of Homol'ovi II from small canyons along streams that drain the Mogollon Rim or from higher elevations northeast or south of Homol'ovi. The distance to either source is between 20 and 40 km. In all likelihood, Feature 2 represents a sealed and undisturbed deposit that provides a unique opportunity to examine what would be missing from an archaeobotanical study if only charred plant remains were recovered.

Generally, starchy seeds such as maize, ricegrass, or dropseed are only preserved if they are charred during parching for consumption or storage. The high starch content makes these grains very vulnerable to insect or rodent damage. Flinty types of corn are often parched because it makes the kernels easier to grind and digest. Even today, the Hopi parch some floury varieties to make a toasted corn that is consumed like "corn nuts" or popcorn. The presence of both fresh and charred ricegrass seeds in Feature 2 suggests that someone had been processing these grains near the hearth before it was abandoned. The uncharred dropseed grains may have been deposited after the hearth was no longer being used for cooking. The carbonized plant remains from Feature 2 are listed in Table 8.4.

Evidence for fleshy fruits or vegetables, such as squash, cholla buds, *quelites* (spinachlike greens such as

#### Table 8.3. Uncarbonized Plant Remains from Room 215, Feature 2
(Contents of Flotation Samples)

|  | A | B | C | D | E | F | G |
|---|---|---|---|---|---|---|---|
| Weight (gms) | 493 | 97 | 62 | 215 | 32 | 135 | 424 |
| **Crops** | | | | | | | |
| Maize Cob Fragments | 24 | 3 | 21 | 33 | 1 | | |
| Beans | | 1 | 1 | | | | |
| Squash Seeds (C. pepo) | 3 | 11 | 4 | 12 | 2 | | |
| C. mixta Seeds | | 2 | | | | | |
| Squash Rind Fragments | 6 | 20 | 27 | 2 | 2 | | |
| Bottle Gourd Rind | 1 | | | 1 | | | |
| Cotton Seeds | 4 | 5 | 13 | 6 | 2 | | |
| **Edible Seeds** | | | | | | | |
| Indian Ricegrass Seeds | 292 | 578 | 280 | 752 | | 1 | |
| Dropseed Grass | | | | 769 | 36 | | |
| Lambsquarters Seeds | | | 1 | 1 | 1 | | |
| Purslane Seeds | | | | 1 | | | |
| Sunflower Seeds | | | 1 | | | | |
| **Fruits or Nuts** | | | | | | | |
| Yucca Seeds | 2 | | 65 | | 11 | | |
| Squawbush (Rhus) Seeds | 2 | | 16 | 7 | 1 | | |
| Utah Juniper Seeds | 6 | 7 | 3 | 4 | 1 | | |
| One-seed Juniper | | | 4 | 3 | 1 | | |
| Piñon Nuts | 1 | 10 | 11 | 11 | 1 | | |
| **Aquatic Plants** | | | | | | | |
| Sedge Seeds | | | 1 | 7 | | 1 | |
| Horsetail Stems | ++ | 5 | | ++ | | | |
| **Miscellaneous Remains** | | | | | | | |
| Narrow-leaf Yucca Leaf | 1 | | | | | | |
| Piñon Needles | 14 | | | | | | |
| Juniper Leaf Scales | 8 | 13 | ++ | | 10 | 1 | |

++ = Remains numerous.
*Note*: A–G are subsamples from the Feature.

#### Table 8.4. Carbonized Plant Remains from Room 215, Feature 2
(Contents of Flotation Samples)

|  | A | B | C | D | E | F | G |
|---|---|---|---|---|---|---|---|
| **Seeds** | | | | | | | |
| Maize Kernels | 83 | 30 | 15 | 45 | 4 | 3 | 3 |
| Cob Fragments | 1 | 6 | 17 | 14 | 3 | | |
| Ricegrass Seeds | 16 | 17 | | 4 | | 1 | 1 |
| Pigweed Seeds | | | | | 1 | | |
| Lambsquarter Seeds | 1 | | | | | | 1 |
| Greasewood Seeds | | | | | | 14 | 12 |
| Squawbush Seeds | | 1 | | | | | |
| Piñon Nuts | | 2 | 10 | | | | |
| Cholla Bud | | | 1 | | | | |
| Grass Stems | ++ | ++ | ++ | * | | ++ | * |
| Unidentified Gruel | | | 1 | | | | 11 |
| **Wood Charcoal** | | | | | | | |
| Willow | 2 | 1 | 1 | | 2 | | 4 |
| Cottonwood | 7 | 9 | 7 | 5 | 7 | 21 | 13 |
| Saltbush | 12 | 5 | 12 | 9 | | 9 | 13 |
| Greasewood | 3 | | 3 | 13 | 9 | | |
| Rabbitbrush | 3 | 1 | 5 | | 2 | | |
| Sagebrush | 1 | | 2 | | | | |
| Mormon Tea | 2 | | | 9 | | | |
| Squawbush | 1 | 12 | 1 | 4 | | | |
| Rose Family | | 1 | | | | | 1 |
| Oak (cf. Gambel's) | 1 | | | | | | |
| Unidentified Charcoal | 3 | 2 | | 1 | | | 1 |

++ = Remains numerous.     * = Present.
*Note*: A–G are subsamples from the Feature. A grab sample of 20 to 30 charcoal fragments was identified from each lot.

pigweed, lambsquarters, purslane, or beeweed), banana yucca fruits, squawbush berries, cactus fruits, or juniper berries, is usually not recovered from open sites unless a waste pit is discarded into a hearth (as may have been the case with the squawbush seeds), the mature seeds are parched for food (lambsquarters or pigweed), or a cooking accident occurs (the cholla bud). In some rare instances uncharred squash seeds have been recovered from open sites but exactly how these are preserved is not understood (one uncharred squash seed was recovered from the hearth in Room 216).

The other plant remains may have been present in Room 215 for a multitude of other purposes. The maize cobs may have been tossed into the hearth as supplemental fuel. The cotton seeds could be waste from fiber processing. The narrow-leaf yucca may reflect basket weaving. Juniper boughs and saltbush branches were often burned by the Hopi to make an edible ash used to enhance the color of blue cornmeal products (Whiting 1939). Whiting (1939: 99) reports that horsetail stems were used by the Hopi for making a sacred bread. Sedges may have been used for bedding, mats, or ceremonies as the Hopi associate them with water (Whiting 1939: 70). The Hopi use conifer boughs for various ritual purposes: Douglas fir is associated with katsinas, whereas Ponderosa pine needles were used in "cloud tobacco" or tied to pahos to bring cold weather and snow (Whiting 1939: 63). It is possible piñon needles may have been substituted in the past when Douglas fir or Ponderosa was not readily available. Piñon gum and needles have also been used as a medicinal incense (Whiting 1939: 63). Altogether, Feature 2 is a small time capsule of the plant materials present in Room 215 before the hearth was covered and abandoned.

## PLANT REMAINS FROM OTHER ROOMS

### Room 211

Flotation samples collected from the hearth (Feature 1), a firepit (Feature 2), and the floor near Feature 1 yielded numerous charred plant remains, including maize cobs and kernels, ricegrass and dropseed grains, and banana yucca seeds (Table 8.5). Although the floor sample contained relatively few corn remains (only 14 compared to 22 and 160), it produced over ten times as many grass seeds as the other samples. This may be an example of the McKellar Hypothesis (Rathje and Schiffer 1982) as it relates to botanical remains. This hypothesis states that in areas that are regularly cleaned (Homol'ovi floors were probably swept periodically), small objects (tiny grass grains) are likely to remain behind as "primary refuse." Larger plant remains (cobs, yucca seeds) were probably swept up and discarded or burned, leaving behind a high proportion of seeds smaller than 2 mm in diameter. These small seeds were probably "escapees" from material that was processed near the hearths. Other potential food remains recovered from Room 211 include beeweed (the young plants may be used as a *quelite* or for organic pottery paints), hedgehog cactus (edible fruits), banana yucca (edible fruits), greasewood, tansy mustard, lambsquarters, and pigweed (these last plants have edible seeds). Feature 1 was the only context sample in which saltbush charcoal was significantly more abundant than cottonwood.

### Room 212

Both the circular firepit (Feature 1) and the slab-lined hearth (Feature 2) yielded an abundance of charred plant remains, including maize cobs and kernels, beans, cotton, ricegrass, dropseed, tansy mustard, juniper, banana yucca, piñon, and squawbush (Table 8.5). Feature 1 contained the highest number of globemallow (*Sphaeralcea*) seeds of any context at Homol'ovi II. Globemallow is a common weed in agricultural fields that was used as a medicinal plant by the Hopi (Whiting 1939) and many other Southwestern groups.

### Room 216

Although only a single flotation sample was analyzed from the hearth of this room (Feature 1), it still produced a diverse assemblage of food plants, including maize, squash, ricegrass, dropseed, lambsquarters, annual saltbush, and tansy mustard (Table 8.5). The locoweed (*Astragalus*) and knotweed (*Polygonum*) seeds probably represent agricultural weeds and incidental inclusions.

### Room 217

A single sample from the badly vandalized firepit of this room was not as productive as the above sample from Room 216. Only maize, beans, pigweed, and beeweed were identified from Room 217 (Table 8.5).

### Exterior Activity Area 221

It is often difficult to envision just how much food one individual consumes within a year. It is also rare that enough charred plant material is recovered from a site to provide dietary estimates for a prehistoric population. A few simple calculations will illustrate the magnitude of the problem. The 20 to 25 liters of plant remains recovered from Area 221 may seem like a vast quantity of material, but they would have fed one person for only about a month and a half. Based on the sampling strategy outlined previously, the 19.5 kg of charred plant remains recovered from Activity Area 221 contained an estimated 213,000 maize kernels. Before carbonization, these would have provided 33.88 kg of food (100 Hopi corn kernels similar to the ones in this collection weigh 15.9 gm). With an average caloric content of 36 Calories per 100 gm (FAO 1961), this would amount to 122,330 Calories or 48.9 person days of food (figuring an average of 2500 Calories per person per day; FAO 1961). The same amount of corn would contain 3726 gm of protein or 62.1 person days (11 gm protein per 100 gm maize, 60 gm protein per person per day; FAO 1961). The Area 221 collection also contained an estimated 939 beans that would have yielded 197 gm of food (100 uncharred beans of a similar mixture of varieties weigh about 21 gm). These beans would have provided 0.26 person days of calories (333 Calories per 100 gm; FAO 1961) or 0.67 person days of protein (20.3 gm protein per 100 gm beans; FAO 1961). Clearly, with a known sample and legitimate assumptions about preservation, an estimate of total required storage for various assumed populations could be generated. The data from Area 221 offer hope but no firm information on which to base such estimates.

If the plant remains from Area 221 are representative, then cultivated plants accounted for the major proportion of the vegetable component of the prehistoric diet at Homol'ovi. Faunal remains from this and other rooms at Homol'ovi II suggest that jackrabbits, cottontails, and other game also made an important contribution to the diet (Szuter, Chapter 9). Crops amounted to 99.7 percent of the nonwoody plants from the flotation samples by weight, and maize cobs and kernels alone totaled 91.2 percent. Gathered wild plants such as yucca fruits, wild greens, cheno-am seeds, grass seeds, juniper berries, and cactus fruits undoubtedly

# Table 8.5. Carbonized Plant Remains from Homol'ovi II Flotation Samples

| Plants | Room 211 | | | | Room 212 | | | | Room 216, Feature 1 | Room 217, Feature 1 | Area 221 | | | |
|---|---|---|---|---|---|---|---|---|---|---|---|---|---|---|
| | Feature 1 | Feature 1 | Floor | Feature 2 | Feature 1 | Feature 2 | Feature 2 | Feature 2 | | | A | B | C | D |
| Sample Weight (gms) | 82 | 358 | 81 | 154 | 56 | 32 | 79 | 12 | 148 | 67 | 1,680 | 2,532 | 14 | 1,708 |
| Maize Kernels | 6 | 64 | 8 | 95 | 47 | 70 | 37 | 7 | 15 | 14 | 8,266 | 20,712 | 10 | 17,866 |
| Cob Fragments | 16 | 36 | 6 | 65 | 171 | 23 | 3 | 32 | 21 | 7 | 3,024 | 7,216 | 12 | 1,196 |
| Beans | | | | | 1 | | 1 | 2 | | 5 | 151 | 658 | 2 | 120 |
| Squash Rind | | | | | | | | | | | 7 | 101 | | 17 |
| Squash Seed | | | | | | | | | 1* | | | | | |
| Cotton Seeds | 1 | 2 | | 4 | 1 | | 1 | | | | | 127 | 1 | |
| Ricegrass Seeds | 105 | 11 | 201 | 73 | | | | 86 | 1 | | 202 | 202 | 6 | 85 |
| Dropseed Grass | 2 | 1 | 888 | | 429 | | | 2 | 6 | | 202 | | 335 | 51 |
| Tansy Mustard | | | 2 | 13 | 14 | | | | 5 | | 218 | 202 | | 68 |
| Pigweed Seeds | | 1 | | 2 | | | 3 | 1 | | 3 | | | 13 | |
| Lambsquarters Seeds | 2 | 1 | 16 | 17 | 2 | | | | 5 | | | | | |
| Greasewood Seeds | 2 | | 1 | 1 | | | | 2 | 45 | | | | | |
| Locoweed Seed | | | | | | | | | 1 | | | | | |
| Indian Buckwheat | | | | 2 | | | | | | | | | | |
| Purslane | | | | | 57 | | | 1 | | | | | | |
| Rocky Mountain Beeweed Seeds | | 2 | | 8 | 1 | | | | | 1 | | | 1 | |
| Globemallow Seeds | | 1 | | | 135 | | | 1 | | | | | | |
| Cholla Buds | | | | | | | | | | | 17 | | | 17 |
| Yucca Seeds | 54 | 4 | 27 | 29 | | | 1 | 58 | | | | | 13 | |
| Knotweed Seeds | | | | | | | | | 3 | | | | | |
| Squawbush Seeds | | | | | 6 | | | | | | | | | |
| Utah Juniper Seeds | | | | | 2* | | | | | | | 25 | 2 | |
| Piñon Nuts | | | 1 | 1 | 8 | | | | | | | | | |
| Oregon Grape Seeds | | | | 1 | | | | | | | | 25 | | |
| Hedgehog Cactus Seeds | 3 | 15 | 2 | | | | | | | | | | | 68 |
| Fishhook Cactus Seed | | | | 1 | | | | | | | | | | |
| Juniper Scale Leaves | | | 11 | 8 | | | | | | | | | | ++ |
| Grama Grass Seed | | | | 1 | | | | | | | | | | |
| Unidentified Gruel | | | | | | | 3 | | | | | | | |
| Grass Stems | ++ | ++ | ++ | ++ | ++ | ++ | ++ | ++ | | | | | | |
| **Wood Charcoal** | | | | | | | | | | | | | | |
| Douglas Fir | | | | | | | | | | | | 2 | | |
| Ponderosa Pine | | | | | | | | | | | 1 | | | 1 |
| Oak | | | | | | | | | | | | | | 1 |
| Reed | | | 1 | | | | | 1 | | | 1 | 1 | | 1 |
| Willow | 1 | 7 | 1 | 3 | 4 | 2 | 1 | 5 | 1 | 2 | 3 | 7 | 7 | 1 |
| Cottonwood | 3 | 5 | 2 | 35 | | 21 | 30 | 6 | 9 | 21 | 21 | 14 | 8 | 26 |
| Saltbush | 22 | 36 | 12 | 6 | 13 | | 2 | 12 | 2 | 2 | 2 | 2 | 14 | |
| Greasewood | | | 1 | 1 | 7 | | | 1 | | | | | | |
| Rabbitbrush | 4 | 19 | 13 | 4 | 6 | | | 5 | 6 | 5 | 3 | 2 | 1 | 2 |
| Sagebrush | | | 1 | 3 | | | | | 3 | | | | | |
| Mormon Tea | | 2 | | | 3 | | | | | | | | | |
| Squawbush | | | 1 | | 3 | | | | | | 1 | 3 | | |
| Yucca | | | | | 1 | | | 1 | | | | | | |
| Rose Family | | | | | | | | | 1 | 1 | 1 | | | |
| Juniper | | | | | | | | | 1 | | | 2 | | 1 |
| Unidentified | | | | 8 | 3 | | | | | | | | | |

*Uncarbonized seed.   ++ = Remains numerous.

*Note*: Seed content was estimated from several 100 gm subsamples for Area 221 A, B, C, D.

added variety and important key nutrients (vitamins and minerals) to the diet. Wild plants or game would also have been available when crops were still in the field or stored reserves were low.

These other food plants may have been stored or processed in a nearby room before it was destroyed by fire. Storage seems likely as plants available at different seasons were recovered together. The tansy mustard seeds would have been gathered in late spring or early summer. Grass seeds and cactus buds could have been collected in late summer. The crops, juniper berries, and yucca fruits would have been harvested or gathered in early fall.

## COMPARISON WITH OTHER SITES IN THE AREA

The Homol'ovi II archaeobotanical assemblage fills in some important gaps in our understanding of the lifeways of indigenous people living in the Little Colorado River drainage. To date, few botanical data have been published for Pueblo IV groups. Table 8.6 contains comparative data for sites near Homol'ovi that bracket it in time. The Coronado Project data come from sites located southeast of Homol'ovi, ranging in age from Basketmaker III to early Pueblo II (Gasser 1982). The El Morro Valley is located east of Ramah, New Mexico and contains late Pueblo III, proto-Zuni sites (Miksicek, unpublished data cited in Gasser 1982). The Walpi data illustrate historic Hopi plant use (Gasser 1981).

All six data sets are remarkably similar if one takes into account differences in preservation through time. The Coronado and El Morro assemblages consist entirely of charred plant remains from flotation samples. Homol'ovi contains a mixture of both carbonized and uncarbonized remains. The Walpi data set includes mostly uncharred remains from bulk, macrobotanical samples. Throughout the period covered in Table 8.6, maize was the most abundant plant food. Beans, squash, gourds, and cotton appear to increase in importance through time but this increase may be due to better preservation (that is, more uncharred specimens in more recent sites). Wild plants such as cheno-ams, grass seeds, beeweed, yucca, squawbush, and cacti seem to decrease in importance in the more recent samples. The use of piñon nuts and juniper berries seems to remain fairly constant (the apparent increase is probably once again due to preservation). The most obvious difference, of course, is the suite of crops introduced after European Contact. The only plant that seems conspicuously absent from Homol'ovi is prickly pear, but this may be a reflection of the vagaries of sampling and

recovery. Several of the pollen samples analyzed by Suzanne Fish (Chapter 7) yielded evidence of prickly pear.

## CULTIVATED CROPS

### Maize

In maize classification, the term "race" refers to a group of similar maize types that share a number of inherited characteristics. With each race, there may be several distinct "varieties" or "cultivars" that differ by only a few traits such as kernel color, for example Hopi blue and white flour corn. Several closely related races may be grouped together into a "suprarace" such as Pima-Papago, which includes Onaveño (a 10 to 12 row flint corn), Mais Blando (a 10 to 12 row flour corn), Mexican Flint (an 8 row flint), Harinoso de Ocho (a large kernel, 8 row flour corn). In folk classifications of maize types kernel color and texture are often the most common traits used for naming varieties. In charred collections of corn, color cannot be determined so the archaeobotanist has to rely on texture and cob morphology.

As discussed previously, the Homol'ovi collection contains at least two different types that are statistically distinct for all measurements studied (Table 8.1, Fig. 8.1). The Pima-Papago group could probably be subdivided. The smaller ears with mostly flinty kernels may represent Onaveño flint. The ears with floury kernels and cupule widths around 7 mm could be classified as Harinoso de Ocho. As with metric traits on any biological population, there is some degree of overlap among these types. This is not unexpected because Pueblo Flour was probably derived from the Pima-Papago group, with the addition of a few genes from Fremont Dent or some of the larger Mexican Dents or flour varieties. Also some modern Hopi varieties, for example purple (*kokoma*) and red (*palaqa*) flour corn, are intermediate between the Pima-Papago and Pueblo races. The Pima-Papago races were the most common types of corn grown in the Southwest between A.D. 700 and 1300. They are still cultivated by Piman-speaking peoples and in northern Mexico. Pueblo Flour types begin to appear in Southwestern maize collections by Pueblo II times, usually accounting for less than 20 percent of the total. Because almost 40 percent of the Homol'ovi corn falls into the Pueblo Flour range, it appears to have been well established by the middle of the 14th century. The modern Eastern and Western Pueblo groups grow predominately Pueblo Flour varieties. Whiting (1939) describes over twenty named types of maize grown by the Hopi in the early part of this century. Gasser (1981) found ten different color classes of kernels in the historic Walpi collection. Unfortu-

**Table 8.6. Comparative Botanical Data for Sites Near Homol'ovi**

| Plant | (No. of samples) | Coronado A.D. 650–1225 (272) | El Morro 1200–1325 (147) | Homol'ovi ca. 1350 (21) | Walpi 1690–1800 (6) | Walpi 1800–1915 (18) | Walpi 1915–1975 (17) |
|---|---|---|---|---|---|---|---|
| | | | | Percent of samples with: | | | |
| Maize Kernels | | * | * | 100 | 100 | 83 | 70 |
| Maize Cob Fragments | | 75 | 92 | 90 | 100 | 89 | 88 |
| Beans | | 3 | 12 | 48 | 83 | 22 | 35 |
| *Cucurbita pepo* | | 1 | 1 | 28 | 33 | 33 | 47 |
| *C. mixta* | | * | * | 5 | 100 | 89 | 94 |
| Squash Rind | | * | * | 38 | 50 | 67 | 59 |
| Bottle Gourd | | | 2 | 10 | 82 | 67 | 59 |
| Cotton | | | | 57 | 67 | | 18 |
| Ricegrass | | 11 | 9 | 71 | 33 | 17 | |
| Dropseed Grass | | 3 | 7 | 52 | 17 | 11 | |
| Goosefoot | | 42 | 61 | 52 | 67 | 44 | 24 |
| Pigweed | | 1 | 17 | 28 | 33 | 28 | 12 |
| Purslane | | 6 | 34 | 14 | 50 | 39 | 18 |
| Tansy Mustard | | 1 | 4 | 33 | | | |
| Sunflower | | 1 | 1 | 5 | 83 | 72 | 65 |
| Beeweed | | 2 | 7 | 24 | 17 | 11 | 6 |
| Indian Buckwheat | | 7 | 1 | 5 | | | |
| Globemallow | | 12 | 1 | 14 | | | |
| Sedge | | | 3 | 14 | | | |
| Saltbush | | 2 | | | 17 | | 18 |
| Cholla | | | | 14 | | | |
| Prickly Pear | | 1 | 1 | | 17 | 11 | 6 |
| Hedgehog Cactus | | 1 | 12 | 19 | | | |
| Fishhook Cactus | | | | 5 | | | |
| Banana Yucca | | 5 | 14 | 48 | 50 | 11 | |
| Squawbush | | | 1 | 28 | 17 | 6 | 6 |
| Oregon Grape | | | 1 | 10 | | | |
| Groundcherry | | | | | 50 | 22 | 6 |
| One-seed Juniper | | * | * | 14 | * | * | * |
| Utah Juniper | | 3 | 16 | 38 | 100 | 78 | 76 |
| Piñon | | | 22 | 38 | 100 | 67 | 82 |
| Acorn | | | 1 | | 17 | | 6 |
| **Post-Contact Introductions** | | | | | | | |
| *Cucurbita maxima* | | | | | 17 | 50 | 59 |
| Chile | | | | | 17 | 11 | 18 |
| Peach | | | | | 100 | 89 | 76 |
| Watermelon | | | | | 100 | 89 | 82 |
| Cantaloupe | | | | | 100 | 72 | 82 |
| Peanut | | | | | 50 | 44 | 65 |
| Olive | | | | | | | 29 |
| Date | | | | | | | 12 |
| Pistachio | | | | | 67 | 17 | 35 |

*Taxon not distinguished in this study.

nately, with only charred kernels in the Homol'ovi II collection it is impossible to make any finer distinctions.

Metric data for maize cupules recovered by flotation from three rooms is summarized in Table 8.7. This table illustrates an important point that should be kept in mind when only maize remains recovered by flotation are available for study. The flotation process is extremely efficient for recovering small cob fragments that would be missed in macrobotanical samples. The net effect is that each measurement is shifted toward the

Table 8.7. Metric Data for Carbonized Cob Fragments Recovered from Flotation Samples

| | Room 211 | Room 212 | Room 215 |
|---|---|---|---|
| Number of fragments | 31 | 52 | 46 |
| Mean Row Number | 9.9 | 10.0 | 10.0 |
| % 6 Row | 0 | 2 | 0 |
| % 8 Row | 32 | 34 | 26 |
| % 10 Row | 39 | 34 | 48 |
| % 12 row | 29 | 23 | 24 |
| % 14 Row | 0 | 6 | 2 |
| Mean Cupule Width (mm) | | | |
| Mean | 5.5 | 5.3 | 5.0 |
| Standard deviation | 0.86 | 1.00 | 1.06 |
| Range | 3.2–6.8 | 3.1–7.4 | 2.8–7.1 |
| Mean Cupule Height (mm) | | | |
| Mean | 3.7 | 3.6 | 3.1 |
| Standard deviation | 0.81 | 0.75 | 0.39 |
| Range | 2.6–6.1 | 1.9–5.2 | 2.3–4.3 |
| Mean Rachis Diameter (mm) | | | |
| Mean | 9.0 | 8.9 | 8.5 |
| Standard deviation | 1.66 | 1.65 | 1.78 |
| Range | 5.8–12.2 | 4.7–11.9 | 5.3–11.9 |
| % Pueblo Flour | 22 | 13 | 13 |

*Note*: Not corrected for shrinkage.

Table 8.8. Metric Data for Charred Beans from Homol'ovi II Flotation Samples

| | Length (mm) | Width (mm) | Thickness* (mm) | Possible Type |
|---|---|---|---|---|
| Room | | | | |
| 212 | 8.2 | 5.2 | 3.9 | Small Common |
| | 12.1 | 5.0 | 4.8 | Kidney |
| 215 | 6.8 | 4.4 | 3.2 | Tepary |
| | 7.5 | 5.0 | 3.4 | Small Common |
| | 7.6 | 5.5 | 4.1 | Small Common |
| | 8.7 | 4.3 | 4.1 | Small Common |
| | 8.8 | 5.4 | 4.2 | Small Common |
| 217 | 7.9 | 5.0 | 4.7 | Small Common |
| | 7.9 | 6.0 | 3.8 | Small Common |
| Area | | | | |
| 221 | 6.5 | 3.6 | 2.7 | Tepary |
| | 6.6 | 4.7 | 4.1 | Tepary |
| | 6.7 | 5.2 | 2.6 | Tepary |
| | 6.8 | 3.9 | 3.2 | Tepary |
| | 7.0 | 4.3 | 3.9 | Tepary |
| | 7.2 | 4.3 | 3.5 | Small Common-Tepary |
| | 7.3 | 5.0 | 3.9 | Small Common-Tepary |
| | 7.5 | 5.6 | 4.3 | Small Common |
| | 7.7 | 5.0 | 4.6 | Small Common |
| | 7.9 | 5.7 | 4.8 | Small Common |
| | 8.0 | 5.4 | 3.5 | Small Common |
| | 8.3 | 5.7 | 4.6 | Small Common |
| | 8.6 | 5.0 | 4.5 | Small Common |
| | 8.8 | 4.9 | 4.3 | Small Common |
| | 8.8 | 5.5 | 4.4 | Small Common |
| | 9.0 | 5.6 | 4.6 | Small Common |
| | 9.1 | 5.4 | 4.4 | Small Common |
| | 9.7 | 6.2 | 4.6 | Common-Lima |
| | 10.3 | 6.8 | 4.1 | Lima |
| | 10.3 | 7.5 | 5.6 | Lima |
| | 10.4 | 6.8 | 5.1 | Lima |
| | 10.6 | 7.1 | 6.1 | Lima |
| | 11.7 | 7.0 | 7.0 | Lima |
| | 11.9 | 6.3 | 5.9 | Lima |

*Thickness is for two cotyledons.
*Note*: Not corrected for shrinkage.

small end of the size range. These smaller cupules come from tiller or immature ears or the tips of cobs. The percentage of large cobs is also slightly decreased. Otherwise, the two data sets are quite comparable.

The fasciated (flattened) cobs in the Activity Area 221 collection are interesting (Table 8.1). This is a genetic trait that I have seen in several maize collections from northeastern Arizona, especially those from Black Mesa. In extreme forms, fasciation can lead to bifurcated or branched (tassel-like) ears. Fasciation seems to become fixed in maize populations with a relatively small and isolated gene pool. Fasciation may also be enhanced by stress (temperature, moisture, or nutrient) during the critical period when the ear is developing. Fasciation may prove to be an interesting genetic marker for comparing maize from different prehistoric groups in the Southwest.

## Beans

Carbonized beans are even more difficult to classify than maize remains. Color, seed coat, and hilum (seed scar) characteristics are critical to identifying different types of beans but all of these characteristics are lost upon carbonization. Nevertheless it is often possible to distinguish tepary beans (*Phaseolus acutifolius*) because of their smaller size and squarish ends. Lima beans (*P. lunatus*) tend to have a lower length to width ratio (around 1.5:1) than common beans (*P. vulgaris*, 1.7:1 or greater). There may still be a great deal of overlap between these species and immature beans are easily misidentified. Table 8.8 contains metric data for a sample of beans from Homol'ovi II.

## Cucurbits

Both cushaw squash (*Cucurbita mixta*) and summer squash (*C. pepo*) were grown for food by the residents of Homol'ovi II. Twenty-eight percent of the Homol'ovi samples yielded *pepo* seeds whereas only five percent contained *mixta*. In addition, bottle gourds were probably cultivated for utilitarian purposes (containers and ceremonial rattles). In Table 8.6 there is an interesting pattern for the cultivated squashes. In prehistoric times summer squash is more common but is replaced by the cushaw in historic times. This same pattern is true in collections of plant remains from southern Arizona. In Hohokam samples *pepo* is more common but historic Pima and northern Mexican peoples grow more *mixta*. Cushaw squash is more resistant to some plant pests (such as vine borers) and diseases (viruses). Perhaps plant pests that spread after Spanish Contact times altered Southwestern agriculture in much the same way that European diseases affected indigenous human populations.

## Cotton

Fifty-seven percent of all the flotation samples from Homol'ovi II yielded cotton seeds, a higher proportion than that noted for any other data set in Table 8.6 except the earliest samples from Walpi. (The few samples analyzed from pre-1800 contexts at Walpi may not be representative). Cotton is a crop that requires abundant moisture and a long growing season. Located close to the floodplain of the Little Colorado River and with an average growing season of 172 days, Homol'ovi II is in an ideal setting for cotton cultivation. This crop may have been a major economic resource for the occupants of Homol'ovi II as suggested by Adams (Chapter 11). With a growing season of only 130 days (Hack 1942a) and without access to a perennial stream, cotton production around the Hopi Mesas to the northeast may have been much less dependable. Yellow ware ceramics from the Hopi Mesas may have been exchanged for cotton from the Homol'ovi area.

The abundance of cotton seeds in the Homol'ovi II collection is also noteworthy even when compared to Hohokam sites farther south. Cotton is usually identified in only about 10 percent of the flotation samples analyzed from sites in the Salt-Gila and Santa Cruz basins. Cotton was identified in 33 percent of the samples from the Hodges Ruin near Tucson (Huckell 1986). Escalante Ruin and Pueblo Las Fosas near Florence, Arizona also yielded rather high frequencies of cotton (43 percent and 30 percent respectively; Gasser and Miksicek 1985), but these values are still lower than Homol'ovi II.

The apparent ubiquity of cotton at Homol'ovi II may be inflated due to the unusually good preservation conditions that permitted the recovery and identification of uncharred seeds. Nevertheless 7 out of 21 flotation samples (33%) yielded charred cotton seeds, a value still within the range of the highest percentages from the Hohokam area. The value is still higher than any other figure for cotton in Table 8.6 except the earliest samples from Walpi. Suzanne Fish (Chapter 7) did not identify any cotton pollen in the Homol'ovi II samples, although maize was abundant and squash pollen was present. Cotton is an insect pollinated species that produces relatively low amounts of poorly dispersed pollen. Most of these grains adhere to the outer surfaces of floral parts or vegetative structures that would be removed before spinning and weaving the fiber. The absence of cotton pollen, perforated sherd disks, or spindle whorls (Hays, Chapter 3) and loom weights (Fratt, Chapter 5) may suggest that the cleaning, spinning, and weaving of cotton fiber occurred elsewhere, in untested parts of the pueblo. The cotton seeds recovered by flotation may reflect caches of seed reserved for future planting.

## HISTORIC AND PREHISTORIC VEGETATION NEAR HOMOL'OVI

The Little Colorado River has long been a favored route for travelers passing through east-central Arizona. Many journals contain descriptions of the local vegetation and the availability of fuel and water. These accounts should provide a useful data base for a comparison with the archaeological plant remains from Homol'ovi II.

Don Juan de Onate, the Spanish governor of the Territory of New Mexico between 1598 and 1610, sent a party of nine adventurers under the command of Captain Marcos Farfan de los Godos to explore settlements west of the Pueblo of Zuni and search for the silver mines near Jerome, Arizona. This party departed November 17, 1598 from the Hopi village of Awatovi.

They traveled six leagues [28.8 km] to the west over a sandy and woodless region and stopped for the night at a place where they found a small spring, which furnished enough water for the men but not the horses. Next morning they left this place, going in the same direction, and after proceeding about three leagues [14.4 km] came to a river which flowed toward the north [the Little Colorado], near Winslow, Arizona. It was fairly wide, carried considerable water, had many cottonwoods, level banks, and little pasture.

(Hammond and Rey 1953: 408)

Over 250 years later, Captain Lorenzo Sitgreaves was dispatched by the U.S. Corps of Topographical Engineers to find and map the junction of the Zuni and Little Colorado rivers and then follow the Colorado drainage to its mouth in the Gulf of California. This expedition departed from Zuni on September 24, 1851.

October 1, Camp No. 8 [west of Joseph City, Arizona] The river, winding to the north, gave us a straight course across the high land, soft and sandy, as usual and frequently intersected by deep ravines, until we again encountered it, flowing now between bluff sandy banks fringed with cottonwood trees, and presenting at length the appearance of a river, but with little water in its bed.

October 3, Camp No. 10 [near Winslow] Our course was interrupted by a deep bayou thickly overgrown with rushes [cattails or sedges], and which, on attempting to turn it, was found to lead to a rocky ravine or canon utterly impassable. We retraced our steps, therefore, and with much difficulty recrossed the river, which, making a bend to the north, winds through a broad plain resembling the bed of a great lagoon from which the water had just subsided, leaving it slimy and intersected with fissures and channels that often impeded our progress. Here and there only a bush of wild sage dotted its surface, and the surrounding hills appeared equally destitute of vegetation.

October 5, Camp No. 12 [near Leupp, Arizona] The country on the north bank presenting the same appearance of desolation as far as the eye could discern, we again crossed the river, and, passing on to the higher ground, encamped on a bayou near the edge of the valley. The grass upon the hills was invariably better and more abundant than on the river bottom, but the absence of wood and water in such places generally obliged us to make our camps near the river.
(Sitgreaves 1854: 7-8)

The Sitgreaves party probably camped on the Little Colorado very close to the location of Homol'ovi II on October 4, 1851, but the Report to Congress contains no entry for that date. Dr. S. W. Woodhouse was "surgeon and naturalist to the expedition" and he collected plants and animals along the route. Woodhouse described the country between Zuni and the San Francisco Peaks as follows:

Near our first camp on the Little Colorado [west of the junction of the Zuni and Little Colorado] there were lodges of the beaver to be seen, but no timber. On the banks of this stream were growing a species of swamp-willow, (*Salix*). The grass here was of good quality.

Much of this country presents a barren appearance, being covered with the *Obione canescens* [saltbush *Atriplex canescens*], and a species of artemisia, *Franseria acanthocarpa* [this could be bursage *Franseria acanthicarpa*, which is found in the area, but sagebrush *Artemisia tridentata* is more likely], and plants of this description. Deer, antelope, and the black-tailed hare [jackrabbit] are quite abundant.

After leaving Camp No. 6 [southeast of Holbrook, Arizona] about six miles, we passed over a beautiful rolling prairie covered with gramma-grass, and numerous large cedars, (*Juniperus*) the fruit of which is upwards of half an inch in diameter [Utah juniper]. This in all probability, Dr. Torrey will find to be a new species. The men killed a specimen of the porcupine. Thus far I have observed but few flowers or birds.

Near the first canon of this river, growing on the rocks were various varieties of cacti, and at the point where we first crossed were plenty of grape vines, (*Vitis*).

The vegetation along this stream varies but little. As we approached the San Francisco mountain, the cotton-wood (*P. monilifera*) [*Populus fremontii*] became more abundant; also scattered cedars along different parts of the route. Among the drift in one place I observed the remains of what appeared to be the black walnut, (*J. nigra*) [Arizona walnut *Juglans major*] showing that this tree must grow either on this stream or its tributaries. Gramma-grasses were found along different parts of the valley, and in some places quite abundant. Portions of agatized wood are found abundant along various portions of this stream. Among the quadrupeds deer, antelope, grizzly bear, and blacktailed hare, abound.
(Sitgreaves 1854: 36-37)

Two years after the Sitgreaves expedition, Lieutenant A. W. Whipple was assigned the task of surveying a route for the Santa Fe railroad from Fort Smith,

Arkansas to Los Angeles, California. His party reached Zuni late in November, 1853.

December 8 - Camp 81  We crossed the deep bed of a well-wooded tributary flowing from the northeast, called Cotton-wood Creek. Nearly opposite could be seen the junction of an affluent from the southeast. The *Colorado Chiquito* here branches into a net-work of channels, all bordered with *alamos* [cottonwoods]. Below camp is quite a forest, extending about four miles down the valley. From a hill two miles back from camp the river can be seen making a great bend, and sweeping northward.

December 9 - Camp 82  The camp-fires are bountifully supplied with fuel from the piles of drift-wood of pine, such as grows in this country only upon mountain slopes. It must, therefore, have been brought by freshets from spurs of Sierra Mogoyon [sic], among which the Colorado Chiquito takes its rise.

(Foreman 1941: 159-160)

Whipple was delayed by a mule stampede at Camp 82, just northeast of Winslow, Arizona for several days. Near Camp 82 he found the ruins of an ancient pueblo (Foreman 1941: 159), which could have been one of the Homol'ovis or another large site in the area.

In 1857, Lt. Edward F. Beale was charged with surveying a wagon route from Fort Defiance, Arizona to the Colorado River. His expedition used camels imported from the Near East as beasts of burden.

September 5. Camp No. 6 [west of Holbrook] Since we struck the river I have observed none of that salt ground, so characteristic of all the streams of this region; and the grass of the river bottom seems of a decidedly better quality, while the low hills which bound the view are everywhere covered with the best grama grass.

September 6. Camp No. 7 [junctions of Cottonwood Wash, the Little Colorado, and Clear Creek near Winslow] ... so I followed down the Cotton-wood, crossed the *Colorado Chiquito*, and after going a mile or two down it, encamped near

**Table 8.9. Wood Charcoal Recovered from Homol'ovi II Flotation Samples**
(Percent of Identified Fragments)

| Common name | Scientific name | (Number of fragments) | Room 211 (191) | 212 (145) | 215 (228) | 216 (50) | 217 (30) | Area 221 (235) | Total (879) |
|---|---|---|---|---|---|---|---|---|---|
| **Exotic** | | | | | | | | | |
| Douglas Fir | *Pseudotsuga menziesii* | | | | | | | 0.8 | 0.2 |
| Ponderosa Pine | *Pinus ponderosa* | | | | | | | 3.8 | 1.0 |
| Gambel's Oak | *Quercus gambelii* | | | | 0.4 | | | 0.4 | 0.2 |
| Piñon Pine | *Pinus edulis* | | | | | | | 1.3 | 0.3 |
| Juniper | *Juniperus* spp. | | | 0.7 | | 2.0 | | 2.1 | 0.8 |
| **Riparian** | | | | | | | | | |
| Reed | *Phragmites communis* | | 0.5 | 0.7 | | | | 1.3 | 0.6 |
| Willow | *Salix* sp. | | 6.3 | 8.3 | 4.4 | 2.0 | 6.7 | 14.5 | 8.1 |
| Cottonwood | *Populus fremontii* | | 23.6 | 53.1 | 32.0 | 40.0 | 70.0 | 59.1 | 42.7 |
| **Upland Shrubs** | | | | | | | | | |
| Greasewood | *Sarcobatus vermiculatus* | | 1.0 | 4.8 | 12.3 | 2.0 | | 0.4 | 4.4 |
| Saltbush | *Atriplex canescens* | | 39.8 | 13.1 | 26.3 | 24.0 | 6.7 | 8.1 | 21.4 |
| Rabbitbrush | *Chrysothamnus nauseous* | | 20.9 | 9.6 | 5.3 | 22.0 | 16.7 | 3.8 | 10.4 |
| Sagebrush | *Artemisia tridentata* | | 2.1 | | 1.3 | 6.0 | | | 1.1 |
| Mormon Tea | *Ephedra* sp. | | 1.0 | 2.1 | 4.8 | | | 0.4 | 1.9 |
| Squawbush | *Rhus trilobata* | | 0.5 | 2.8 | 7.9 | | | 3.0 | 3.4 |
| Rose Family | Rosaceae | | | 1.4 | 2.2 | 2.0 | | 0.8 | 1.1 |
| Yucca | *Yucca* spp. | | | 1.4 | | | | | 0.2 |
| Unknown | | | 4.2 | 2.1 | 3.1 | | | | 2.0 |

a singular stream coming in existence until you arrive directly on its banks, having neither cottonwood trees or willows to warn of its whereabouts. I explored it for some distance up, and found it issuing out of a rocky canon with precipitous sides. The water is clear, and the immense amount of driftwood, and its character, shows that it comes from a country where cypress [juniper] and pine of great size abound...[heading north along the Little Colorado again] Passed this evening more Indian trails, all going to the northward. Saw much beaver sign, and one fresh dead one, caught by Mr. Coyote last night, and only partly eaten. We saw large fires, Indian signals, in the Mogollon mountains this evening. Grass excellent and most abundant, and for water, the whole river.

(Lesley 1970: 197-201)

The journals of Farfan, Sitgreaves, Whipple, and Beale provide a composite description of the landscape near Homol'ovi prior to the late 1800s. The Little Colorado was a fairly permanent stream with rushes, cattails, willow, cottonwoods and in some places beaver. Salt and alkali buildup in the streambed was not a problem. The floodplain was littered with abundant pine, juniper, and cottonwood driftwood, carried down the Little Colorado, or from tributary streams that drained the Mogollon Rim, by occasional floods. Away from the river valley, the hillsides were essentially treeless, covered with a dense growth of grama grass and scattered shrubs such as saltbush or sagebrush. Deer, antelope, jackrabbits, and other game were abundant.

Wood charcoal (Table 8.9) and other plant remains identified from the Homol'ovi II excavations (Tables 8.3-8.5, 8.10) seem to confirm this picture. Cottonwood (42.7%) was the dominant type of charcoal. This was probably the major type of timber used for house construction and as an important fuel. Reed and willow charcoal, as well as sedge seeds (Room 215) and horsetail stems (Room 215) suggest marshlike conditions for parts of the Little Colorado floodplain near Homol'ovi. No cattail remains were recovered as macrofossils, but *Typha* pollen was present in many of the samples analyzed by Suzanne Fish (Chapter 7). The Douglas fir, ponderosa, piñon, juniper, and oak charcoal probably reflect driftwood gathered from the river.

Only a single grama grass seed was identified (Room 211), but the abundance of ricegrass and dropseed grains (both important wild foods), as well as grass stems, seem to confirm the lush grasslands reported by historic travelers.

Saltbush, greasewood, rabbitbrush, and squawbush

**Table 8.10. Macrobotanical Remains from Homol'ovi II**

| Provenience | | Material | |
|---|---|---|---|
| **Room 211** | | | |
| Charred Maize Cob | | | |
| **Room 212, Fill** | | | |
| 5 Carbonized Maize Cob Fragments | | | |
| Fused Corn Kernels | | | |
| 29 Wood Charcoal Fragments: | | Cottonwood | 69% |
| | | Saltbush | 14% |
| | | Rabbitbrush | 10% |
| | | Squawbush | 3% |
| | | Rose Family | 3% |
| **Room 215, Feature 2** | | | |
| 3 uncarbonized Piñon Nuts | | | |
| 12 uncarbonized *Cucurbita pepo* Squash Seeds | | | |
| Uncarbonized Maize Cob | | | |
| Charred Maize Kernels | | | |
| 17 Charcoal Fragments: | | Saltbush | 53% |
| | | Cottonwood | 24% |
| | | Rose Family | 18% |
| | | Rabbitbrush | 6% |
| **Room 216, Floor Fill** | | | |
| 7 Charred Maize Cob Fragments | | | |
| 17 Charcoal Fragments: | | Cottonwood | 65% |
| | | Rabbitbrush | 29% |
| | | Juniper | 6% |
| **Activity Area 221, Fill** | | | |
| Total Weight = 13.571 kg | | | |
| | | | |
| Cob Fragments = 1.902 kg | | | |
| Maize kernels = 10.974 kg | | | |
| Bean Remains | | | |
| 6 Small Common or Tepary Beans | | | |
| 2 Hopi Limas | | | |
| | | | |
| Wood Charcoal = 0.695 kg | | | |
| Analysis of 30% sample | | Cottonwood | 66% |
| by weight: | | Willow | 15% |
| | | Ponderosa Pine | 7% |
| | | Squawbush | 3% |
| | | Piñon Pine | 3% |
| | | Juniper | 2% |
| | | Saltbush | 1% |
| | | Rabbitbrush | 1% |
| | | Greasewood | 1% |
| | | Rose Family | 1% |
| | | Mormon Tea | 1% |

may be slightly overrepresented in the charcoal record in comparison to their prehistoric abundance in the local vegetation. Whiting (1939: 22, 38) describes these as the prescribed fuels for use in the kiva. In the past, these may have been more general-purpose indoor fuels as they are dense woods that burn hotter and longer than cottonwood.

Most of the animal bones identified by Szuter (Chapter 9) come from creatures that would have thrived in open grasslands or a mosaic of scrubland, prairie, marsh, and fields. Pronghorn antelope, the only positively identified artiodactyl, would have been far more common than deer in an open prairie setting. Cottontails, jackrabbits, and small rodents could have been hunted either in grassy scrub communities or fields around Homol'ovi II. Migratory waterfowl such as cranes, coots, geese, and pelicans would have been seasonal visitors to marshlands along the Little Colorado floodplain.

Today the vegetation around Homol'ovi II is radically different than that suggested by historical descriptions or the archaeobotanical record. In the washes, introduced plants such as saltcedar (*Tamarix pentandra*) and camelthorn (*Alhagi camelorum*) have replaced most of the cottonwoods, willows, rushes, and reeds found in the past. Unpalatable shrubs such as snakeweed (*Gutierrezia sarothrae*), rabbitbrush, and sagebrush have expanded greatly in the last century in response to grazing pressure that has removed much of the native grass cover. Today it is only possible to envision the lush grasslands of the past in the rare instances when a few years with significantly above average rainfall succeed one another.

## SUMMARY

Maize cobs and kernels were the most common plant remains recovered from Homol'ovi II. Between two and four distinct races of corn may have been cultivated. Tepary beans, limas, common beans, cushaw squash, summer squash, bottle gourds, and cotton were also included in the Homol'ovi crop assemblage. The ubiquity of cotton in flotation samples from Homol'ovi II suggests that this crop was an important economic resource for the ancient inhabitants. Wild plant foods such as grass seeds, cheno-am seeds, wild greens, yucca fruits, cactus fruits, juniper berries, and piñon nuts added variety and key nutrients to the diet. Cottonwood was the major type of wood used for construction and firewood. Other fuel types included saltbush, rabbitbrush, sagebrush, squawbush, and driftwood. The floodplain of the Little Colorado River probably supported a relatively lush riparian community that included cottonwoods, willows, sedges, cattails, and reeds. The uplands away from the river bottom probably had much denser grass cover and fewer shrubs than is characteristic of the over-grazed scrubland seen today. The local vegetation during the occupation of Homol'ovi II was probably similar to conditions described in the journals of 19th-century travelers.

# CHAPTER NINE

# Faunal Remains

Christine R. Szuter
University of Arizona

Although the inhabitants of Homol'ovi II pueblo were agriculturalists, the abundance of faunal remains recovered from the excavated rooms and Activity Area 221 (812 fragments) strongly indicates that hunting was an important activity. The animals not only provided food but also raw materials for clothing, bone tools, rattles, or bow strings. Beaglehole (1936: 3) has emphasized the role of hunting in Hopi society even though the economy was fundamentally agricultural. The abundance and degree of modification of the Homol'ovi II faunal remains attest to the significance of hunting among the pueblo's inhabitants.

This study presents a descriptive report of the unworked and worked faunal remains, discusses the exploitation of the riverine environment and the subsistence strategies of the Homol'ovi II inhabitants, and makes intrasite and intersite comparisons of faunal assemblages.

## METHODS

All of the 812 faunal remains recovered from the 1984 excavations were analyzed. For identifications I used the National Park Service faunal collection that is housed at the Arizona State Museum under the curatorship of Professor Stanley J. Olsen, and at times Professor Olsen and William Gillespie of the Department of Geosciences provided additional assistance.

Information on each bone was recorded on 5-by-8 inch notecards. Each card represented one taxon from one provenience unit (or bag). All provenience information on the bag was transferred onto each note card. In addition, ten variables were recorded: taxon, element, portion, side and percent of element, fusion, burning, butchering, weathering, relative size, and quantity. A few of these variables warrant discussion.

Burned bone was described according to color. Scorched bone was black or brown, and calcined bone was white or blue-gray. Butchering marks infrequently occurred and were both described and drawn. Degree of weathering was divided into three categories: good condition, slightly weathered, and heavily weathered. Bone in good condition has its cortical surface intact. Slightly weathered bone has slight root-etching on its surface, has a stained surface, or in other ways exhibits a weathered surface. Heavily weathered bone has a cracked or flaked cortical surface, a heavily root-etched surface, or a severely eroded surface. Estimates of the relative size of the skeletal element was made by comparing it to specimens in the comparative collection.

Taxonomic identifications were made on the basis of morphological characteristics, size, and geographic range. In four cases the elements were incomplete or lacked identifying characters and could only be placed as one of two species: (1) sandhill crane or turkey (*Grus canadensis* or *Meleagris* sp.), (2) prairie dog or squirrel (*Cynomys gunnisoni* or *Spermophilus variegatus*), (3) domestic dog or coyote (*Canis familiaris* or *C. latrans*), and (4) antelope or bighorn sheep (*Antilocapra americana* or *Ovis canadensis*).

As with most faunal assemblages, some bone could only be identified to class. These elements were put in different size groups for birds and mammals. Birds were grouped as small (sparrow size), medium (quail size), or large (eagle size). Mammals, being far more abundant, had a larger number of size categories, some of which overlapped. Generally, unidentified mammalian remains were the size of rodent, lagomorph, coyote, deer, or horse. If the fragment could not readily be placed into one of these size categories because it measured inbetween, it was placed in an intermediate size such as rodent-lagomorph, lagomorph-coyote, coyote-deer, or deer-horse. Additionally, bone fragments that were definitely mammalian but whose size could not be determined were labeled "size indeterminate." A final category included bone that could not be positively identified as either human or nonhuman.

Fragments that could be classified to order (that is, Rodentia, Artiodactyla, Carnivora) or below were considered "identified" bone. Identification to the level of order is different from Unidentified bone grouped by size classes.

The quantification of nonworked bone consisted of the NISP (number of identifiable specimens) and taxonomic indices comparing cottontails to jackrabbits and lagomorphs to artiodactyls. The lagomorph index is calculated by dividing the NISP of cottontails by the NISP of all lagomorphs. The artiodactyl index is calculated by dividing the NISP of artiodactyls by the sum of the NISP of lagomorphs and artiodactyls. Both of these indices have values that range from 0.0 to 1.0.

## UNWORKED BONE

Of the 812 bone and teeth fragments recovered, 15 are worked bone and 12 are human. Thirty unidentifiable large mammalian bones were classified as possibly human because of their size, morphology, and association with positively identified human bones. Of the remaining 755 nonworked bones, 437 (57.9 percent) are identifiable below the level of class. Table 9.1 is a taxonomic list of the recovered animal remains from Homol'ovi II. The quantity of bone and burned bone from each provenience unit within each room and the totals for each room are on file in the Arizona State Museum, University of Arizona, Tucson (Szuter 1985).

### Lagomorphs

Jackrabbits and cottontails comprise 73.9 percent (323 out of 437) of the identified faunal assemblage. The presence of lagomorphs was ubiquitous throughout the excavated features of the site. Not only were their remains associated with every room, but they were distributed throughout each provenience unit. Rodents, carnivores, artiodactyls, lizards, and birds together comprised the remaining 26.1 percent of the identifiable portion of the assemblage.

The sheer number as well as the presence of burning on the lagomorph elements attest to their economic importance. The presence of burned elements is often offered as evidence of cooking or roasting the animal. Although rabbits were undoubtedly eaten, burned elements are more likely a result of trash disposal and subsequent burning than the result of roasting a rabbit over a fire. The meat on a limb bone insulates the bone, thereby preventing it from being burned. Only portions of bone directly exposed to the fire usually show evidence of burning. Burned elements dating from the prehistoric occupation, however, do indicate cultural modification of the bone. Although most bone was not burned, lagomorph and unidentified lagomorph-size bone comprised a substantial portion of what was burned (68.3%; 127 of 186 elements).

**Table 9.1. Taxonomic List of Fauna from the 1984 Homol'ovi II Excavations**

| Scientific Name | Common Name |
|---|---|
| **Osteichthyes** | Fish |
| **Amphibia** | Amphibian |
| **Reptilia** | Reptile |
| Sauria | Lizards |
| **Aves** | |
| *Pelecanus* sp. | Pelican |
| *Branta canadensis* | Canadian Goose |
| *Aquila chrysaetos* | Golden Eagle |
| *Grus canadensis* | Sandhill Crane |
| *Grus canadensis* or *Meleagris* sp. | Sandhill Crane or Turkey |
| *Fulica americana* | American Coot |
| *Corvus corax* | Raven |
| **Mammalia** | |
| Leporidae | Leporids |
| *Lepus* sp. | Jackrabbit |
| *Lepus californicus* | Black-tailed Jackrabbit |
| *Sylvilagus* sp. | Cottontail |
| Rodentia | Rodent |
| Sciuridae | Squirrels and Allies |
| *Cynomys gunnisoni* | Gunnison's Prairie Dog |
| *C. gunnisoni* or *Spermophilus variegatus* | Gunnison's Prairie Dog or Rock Squirrel |
| *Ammospermophilus leucurus* | White-tailed Antelope Squirrel |
| Geomyidae | Pocket Gophers |
| *Thomomys bottae* | Valley Pocket Gopher |
| Heteromyidae | Kangaroo Rats and Pocket Mice |
| *Dipodomys ordii* | Ord's Kangaroo Rat |
| Cricetidae | Native Rats and Mice |
| *Peromyscus* sp. | Mouse |
| *Neotoma* sp. | Wood Rat |
| Carnivora | Carnivore |
| Canidae | Dogs and Allies |
| *Canis familiaris* or *C. latrans* | Domestic Dog or Coyote |
| Mustelidae | Weasels, Skunks, and Allies |
| *Taxidea taxus* | Badger |
| Artiodactyla | Artiodactyl |
| Cervidae | Deer and Allies |
| *Antilocapra americana* | Antelope |
| *A. americana* or *Ovis canadensis* | Antelope or Bighorn Sheep |

The constant exploitation of lagomorphs would offer a far more regular supply of meat than the larger game, even though the latter has more pounds of meat. The Hopi (Beaglehole 1936: 11) simply referred to the procurement of rabbits as "hunting," suggesting frequent though not necessarily regular hunting of lagomorphs.

Rabbit hunting also was associated with yearly as well as initiation ceremonies for youths (Beaglehole 1936: 14).

The Hopi used both communal and individual hunting techniques. Rabbit sticks were used to kill animals that were flushed from hiding. In a communal hunt both men and boys spread out, forming a two-winged circle. As they walked toward the center of the circle they beat the bush, thus moving rabbits out of hiding where they were killed. Rabbit hunting helped to protect agricultural fields from the destructive lagomorphs and provided meat for the Hopi and for their captive eagles (Beaglehole 1936: 11). Hunting, therefore, was practiced primarily in the early summer and fall and less frequently during the winter.

Cottontails and jackrabbits were recovered in nearly even proportions at Homol'ovi II, as indicated by the lagomorph index of 0.45. Both genera occur in similar environments. However, cottontails prefer more dense ground cover than do jackrabbits. Jackrabbits use wide, open spaces to flee from predators whereas cottontails use the dense vegetation to hide from theirs. Different hunting techniques can take advantage of these behavioral differences.

### Rodents

Although lagomorphs are generally considered to have economic importance prehistorically, rodents have been far more problematical. The burrowing habits of rodents are notorious and their presence at a site can be due to postabandonment activity. Although differentiating intrusive from cultural rodent remains is often difficult, the importance and probable inclusion of rodents in the prehistoric diet is highly likely. Arguments that they were eaten prehistorically are based on ethnographic reports of rodent use, the high portion of edible meat per carcass, the ease of capturing rodents, the benefits of clearing fields of rodents, and cultural modification of rodent remains (Stahl 1982; Seme 1984; Szuter 1984). The Hopi set traps around the edges of their fields to capture field mice. Ritual that was associated with setting traps for larger animals was not followed for rats, mice, or prairie dogs because these animals were not considered to possess a soul (Beaglehole 1936: 17-18).

Whereas sound arguments for the use of rodents can be made, archaeological evidence that they were indeed used for food is more difficult to find. One argument based on both ethnographic analogy and archaeological evidence is that rodents used as food would exhibit differential burning of skeletal elements. As mentioned above, burning generally is not a good criterion to indicate the animal was roasted. Rodents, however, may

**Table 9.2. Quantity and Type of Burned Skeletal Elements from Rodents**

| Provenience | Context | Taxa | Quantity | Skeletal Element |
|---|---|---|---|---|
| **Room** | | | | |
| 211 | Ash fill | Rodentia | 1 | Caudal vertebra |
| | | | 1 | Metatarsal |
| 212 | Fire pit | Rodentia | 5 | Caudal vertebrae |
| 215 | Hearth | Rodentia | 1 | Calcaneum |
| | | | 1 | Phalanx |
| | | | 1 | Femur |
| **Area** | | | | |
| 221 | Ext. fill | *A. leucurus* | 1 | Mandible |

be an exception because of their small size and methods used to prepare them. From ethnographic accounts, rodents are known to be eaten by boiling, roasting, or eating them whole, bones and all. Therefore, unless human coprolites are recovered, evidence of eating rodents is missing. The tail and feet of a rodent have a thin layer of skin and minimal muscle mass, and if an animal were placed on a spit and roasted, these peripheral elements may have burned more rapidly than the rest of the body and fallen into the fire pit. In this case, burned rodent bones would tend to be phalanges, metapodials, and caudal vertebrae. This pattern of differential skeletal burning has been observed for a series of Hohokam sites in south-central Arizona (Szuter 1984).

The Homol'ovi II rodent bones also exhibit a differential pattern of burning. Eleven rodent bones are burned. Ten of these were from hearths, fire pits, or ash fill from Rooms 215, 212, and 211. The other bone was from the exterior fill of Activity Area 221 (Table 9.2). With the exception of one femur and mandible, all of the elements are from caudal vertebrae, a metatarsal, phalanx, and calcaneum. If the rodents were intrusive and were inadvertently burned in these features, then a more representative sample of skeletal elements from the entire body would be expected. I do not suggest that all rodents recovered from the site were part of the diet, but it is possible that rodents comprised a portion of the diet and their overall economic importance needs to be evaluated.

### Carnivores

Carnivores were represented by the badger (*Taxidea taxus*) and by domestic dog or coyote (*Canis familiaris* or *C. latrans*). Overall, carnivores exhibit a much higher percentage of burned elements than do any other order

**Table 9.3. Burned Canis Skeletal Elements**

| Provenience | Element | Degree of Burning |
|---|---|---|
| Surface collection, Unit 37 | Humerus, shaft | Calcined |
| Room 211, Floor | Ulna, proximal and shaft | Scorched |
| | Radius, shaft | Calcined |
| Area 221, Exterior fill | Ulna, proximal and shaft | Scorched |
| | Metacarpal, complete | Calcined |
| | Tibia, shaft | Calcined |

of mammals, 7 of 12 (58%). For rodents, lagomorphs, and artiodactyls the percent of burned bone ranges between 20 to 23 percent. *Canis* remains account for six of the burned elements (Table 9.3). Five of the elements are forelimbs (humerus, ulna, and radius), whereas the remaining one is a tibia. The contrast in the quantity of burned carnivore bone compared to other orders of mammals suggests differential disposal or use of these animals.

**Artiodactyls**

Although not particularly abundant, 35 artiodactyl elements (8 percent of the identifiable bone) were recovered from Rooms 211, 212, 215, 216, 217, Activity Area 221, outside Room 206, and from surface collections. Some bone was more specifically identified as antelope and some antler was designated as Cervidae (Table 9.4). The skeletal elements represent major body segments: cranial, vertebral, and fore and hind limbs.

The abundance of artiodactyls relative to lagomorphs has been used as an indicator of small versus large game within an assemblage. The artiodactyl index based on NISP is 0.11 for the Homol'ovi II excavations. Artiodactyls are not particularly abundant when examining identifiable specimens. Another way to examine large versus small animal exploitation, however, is to look at bone that was unidentifiable but classified into small and large size categories. For this comparison, bone grouped into the unidentified small, lagomorph-size category and the unidentified large, artiodactyl-size category are used to make the index. The justification for examining this index of large to small unidentifiable bone is to examine any differences between it and the artiodactyl index. This large to small unidentifiable bone index is 0.25 for the Homol'ovi II excavations, suggesting that large game may be more common than indicated when only examining identifiable bone. The larger animals may have been processed by breaking up the

**Table 9.4. Artiodactyl Skeletal Elements Recovered from the 1984 Excavations of Homol'ovi II**

| Provenience | Quantity | Taxon | Skeletal Element |
|---|---|---|---|
| Room 206 | 3 | Antilocapra-Ovis | Phalanx |
| | 2 | Artiodactyla | Thoracic Vertebra |
| | 2 | Artiodactyla | Teeth |
| | 1 | Artiodactyla | Innominate |
| | 1 | Artiodactyla | Astragulus |
| | 1 | Artiodactyla | Metapodial |
| | 1 | Artiodactyla | Sesamoid |
| | 4 | Cervidae | Antler |
| 211 | 1 | *A. americana* | Radius |
| 212 | 1 | *A. americana* | Phalanx |
| | 1 | Artiodactyl | Calcaneum |
| 215 | 1 | Artiodactyl | Rib |
| | 1 | Artiodactyl | Metapodial |
| 216 | 1 | Artiodactyl | Metapodial |
| | 1 | *A. americana* | Phalanx |
| 217 | 1 | Artiodactyl | Tibia |
| Area 221 | 4 | Cervidae | Antler |
| | 2 | *A. americana* | Phalanx |
| | 1 | Artiodactyla | Metapodial |
| | 1 | Artiodactyla | Metatarsal |
| Surface Collect. | 1 | Artiodactyla | Calcaneum |
| | 1 | Artiodactyla | Thoracic Vertebra |
| | 1 | Artiodactyla | Innominate |
| | 1 | Artiodactyla | Phalanx |

bones, thus obscuring morphological features that would have aided more positive identification.

Antelope bone and Cervidae antler were the most specific artiodactyls identified at Homol'ovi II. Sitgreaves (1854: 13) and Whipple (Foreman 1941: 165) both observed antelope and deer herds during their expeditions in northern Arizona.

Beaglehole (1936: 4–8) details the hunting of deer and antelope by the Hopi. These animals were hunted communally and in pairs by running down the animal, then killing it by suffocation or with a bow and arrow. The animals were hunted from August through October when they were the fattest or from March to April when they had their young with them. After the animal was divided among the hunters and the meat was eaten or dried for later use, the bones of the animal received special treatment. They were marked with red ochre, kept from the dogs, and placed on a shrine. If similar practices were followed by the Homol'ovi II inhabitants, bone from artiodactyls might not be abundant because of cultural practices of bone disposal rather than the minimal hunting of these animals.

**Table 9.5. Quantity of Each Avian Body Part by Taxon for Surface Collected Material and from Activity Area 221**

| Provenience | Taxon | Quantity | Skeletal Element |
|---|---|---|---|
| Surface Collection | | | |
| | *Grus canadensis* | 1 | Carpometacarpus |
| | | 1 | Femur |
| | | 1 | Sternum |
| Activity Area 221 | | | |
| | *Aquila chrysaetos* | 1 | Carpometacarpus |
| | *Fulica americana* | 1 | Tibiotarsus |
| | *Grus canadensis* | 1 | Humerus |
| | | 1 | Sternum |
| | | 3 | Phalanges |
| | *Grus canadensis* or *Meleagris* sp. | 1 | Ulna |
| | *Corvus corax* | 1 | Tibiotarsus |
| | | 1 | Humerus |

### Aves

Bird remains account for 3.0 percent (13 of 437) of the identified elements. They include golden eagle, American coot, sandhill crane, and raven. Unworked bird bone was recovered from surface collections (3 sandhill crane fragments) and from Activity Area 221 (10 fragments of various species). Of the 13 fragments, 8 are from the wings of these birds (Table 9.5). Wing elements provided feathers and elements for the manufacture of bone tools (see Worked Bone below).

### Fish, Lizard, and Amphibian

Fish, lizard, and amphibian bones are not common. The two fish fragments (unidentified) were recovered from the exterior fill of Activity Area 221 and from the hearth of Room 215 (a fragment of a calcined small vertebra). The amphibian bone is an unidentified long bone from the fill outside of unexcavated Room 206. Although meager in number, these remains indicate exploitation of riverine resources. The lizard bone is a cranial fragment from the exterior fill of Activity Area 221. The bone is in excellent condition; it appears to be recent rather than prehistoric.

### WORKED BONE

The 15 worked bone artifacts are classified as awls or hairpins (8), bone tubes or stock for tubes or beads (4), and otherwise modified bone (3). Only one bone tube is nearly complete; the remaining artifacts are all broken (Fig. 9.1; Tables 9.6, 9.7).

### Awls, Hairpins, and Bodkins

Awls and hairpins are often fragmentary and hence difficult to classify. Olsen (1979) has attempted to distinguish these two types on the basis of tip morphology. Hairpins have a tip that is wider than it is thick, whereas awls can be either fine tipped (equal tip width and thickness) or blunt tipped (similar to hairpin tip morphology). Although fine-tipped awls may be easily separated on the basis of this criterion, the overlap of hairpins and blunt-tipped awls is more problematical. All of the awls and hairpins from Homol'ovi II are fragmentary and specific designations could not be made except for the canid metatarsal awl. Hairpins are considered ornamental and awls were used for basketry manufacture or for piercing hide or other materials. Determining the specific function of differently shaped awls has not been done. The fragmentary nature of the Homol'ovi II material makes the classification in general rather tentative, but the following variables were recorded for awls, hairpins, and bodkins: (1) taxon, (2) element, (3) portion, (4) presence of polish, striations, and burning, (5) length and width, (6) tip length and width, (7) manufacturing techniques, and (8) provenience (Table 9.6).

The worked element classified as a bodkin or blunt needle is from the exterior fill of Activity Area 221. The shaft of a long bone of a large mammal has two finished edges and the articular end has a hole drilled into it. Two complete bodkins were identified from the Awatovi materials (Wheeler 1978). The Homol'ovi II bodkin has the eye of the needle drilled through an articular surface, whereas the Awatovi bodkins are made from flat pieces of bone.

The most distinctive awl was made from a *Canis* metatarsal. The proximal end is ground and the lower shaft portion has two finished edges. This element is not burned nor does it have any visible striations or polish. The remaining awls and hairpins were made from long bones of large mammals. One artifact was made from an artiodactyl metatarsal (Fig. 9.1e). All of these bones have striations, one is polished, and three are burned. From marks on the bones, I believe these awls and hairpins were manufactured by the grooving and snapping technique (Olsen 1979).

### Bone Stock for Tubes, Rings, or Beads

Three of the bone stock pieces were made from the wing bones (ulna and humerus) of large birds. The fourth was made from an unidentified long bone of a large bird. Two elements were positively identified as Canadian goose and pelican. Only one of these artifacts has striations and none are burned (Table 9.7).

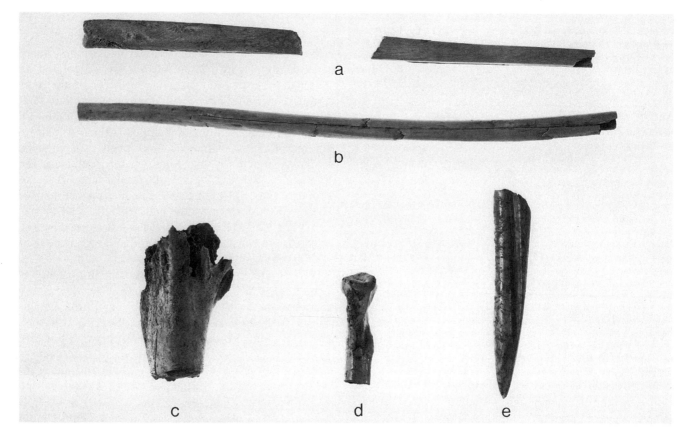

Figure 9.1. Bone artifacts: *a, b,* Artiodactyla ribs ground and smoothed from Room 216; *c, Branta canadensis* humerus bone tube or ring stock from surface; *d, Pelacanus* sp. ulna bone tube or ring stock from Room 215; *e,* Artiodactyla metatarsal awl from Activity Area 221. (Length of *e* is 6.9 cm.)

The pelican bone stock piece from Room 215 is a proximal ulna (Fig. 9.1*d*). Another ulna fragment from that same room, identified only as from a large bird like a sandhill crane or pelican, was manufactured into a bone tube. Both ends had been grooved and snapped. The unidentified bone stock specimen may be the end product of manufacturing this bone tube.

The bone stock fragment made from a humerus of a Canadian goose (Fig. 9.1*c*) is similar to an Awatovi one made from a pelican humerus (Wheeler 1978: 66, Fig. 19f). Both are the proximal end of a left humerus, are grooved and snapped, and have an incomplete groove along the shaft.

The pelican and the Canadian goose are migrant birds. The pelican is found during the winter and summer along the Little Colorado, whereas the Canadian goose winters in the area (S. J. Olsen 1978).

### Other Modified Bone

Other modified bone fragments have striations, an abraded surface, or a ground surface (Table 9.7). No

artifact type or functional designation could be made for these fragments. Two from Room 216 (Fig. 9.1*a, b*) were made from artiodactyl ribs and have striations or were ground and smoothed. A large mammalian fragment with striations is from Activity Area 221.

### INTRASITE VARIABILITY

The extensive pothunting of the site was not deep enough to destroy the floor assemblages of the rooms. Four of them (Rooms 211, 212, 215, and 217) had partially intact floor assemblages, all containing lagomorphs and unidentified small mammalian bones. In addition, Room 211 had two dog or coyote elements, one of which was burned; Room 212 had four prairie dog fragments; and Room 217 had one rodent and one artiodactyl fragment.

Intrasite variability in faunal remains is observable among different contexts such as fill, internal feature, and activity area. Floor assemblages were somewhat similar in terms of quantity and taxa recovered. Worked and unworked bird bone was concentrated in Activity

**Table 9.6. Awls and Hairpins from Homol'ovi II**

| Provenience | Taxon | Element | Articular end and shaft | Shaft | Tip | Shaft and tip | Polish | Crosswise striations | Longitudinal striations | Burned | Two finished edges, broken edge | One finished, one broken edge | Manufacturing technique unknown | Length (mm) | Width (mm) | Tip width (mm) | Tip thickness (mm) | Comments |
|---|---|---|---|---|---|---|---|---|---|---|---|---|---|---|---|---|---|---|
| Room 215 | Large Mammal | Long Bone | x | | | | | x | | | | | * | 121.0 | 8.2 | | | *Round in cross section |
| Area 221 | Artiodactyla | Metatarsal | | | | x | | | x | | x | | | | | 4.3 | 4.2 | |
| 221 | Large Mammal | Unknown | | | x | | | x | x | | | x | | | | 3.1 | 2.7 | |
| 221 | Large Mammal | Long Bone | | | | x | | x | x | | | | * | 15.8 | 5.3 | | | *Round in cross section |
| 221 | Large Mammal | Long Bone | x | | | | x | x | | | | x | | 51.4 | 13.2 | | | Hole drilled, articular end |
| 221 | Large Mammal | Long Bone | | x | | | | | x | x | x | | | 14.0 | 7.5 | | | |
| 221 | Large Mammal | Long Bone | | x | | | | | x | x | x | | | 23.2 | 7.6 | | | |
| 221 | *Canis* sp. | Metatarsal | x | | | | | | | | | x | | 55.5 | 7.8 | | | Awl, proximal end ground and smoothed |

* Information for this variable is provided in the text.
*Note*: An underlined measurement indicates the artifact had a fresh break. The artifact with a hole drilled into the articular end is classified as a bodkin.

**Table 9.7. Other Worked Bone from Homol'ovi II**

| Provenience | Taxon | Element | Artifact Type | Description |
|---|---|---|---|---|
| Surface Collect. | *Branta canadensis* | Humerus shaft | Bone Tube–Ring Stock | One end grooved and snapped, other end broken; proximal part of humerus shaft |
| Room 215 | *Pelecanus* sp. | Ulna, proximal and shaft | Bone Tube–Ring Stock | One end grooved and snapped; other end articular surface |
| 215 | Large Aves | Ulna shaft | Bone Tube | Two ends grooved and snapped; longitudinal striations along shaft |
| 216 | Artiodactyla | Rib, sternal end and shaft | Unknown | Sternal end ground and smoothed |
| 216 | Artiodactyla | Rib shaft | Unknown | Longitudinal striations along shaft |
| Area 221 | Large Aves | Long Bone | Bone Tube–Ring Stock | One end grooved and snapped, other end broken |
| 221 | Large Mammal | Unknown | Unknown | Burned fragment with crosswise striations |

Area 221 and in smaller quantities in Room 215. These two areas also contained the two fish remains, perhaps a fortuitous association. The quantity of bird bone concentrated in these contexts suggests manufacturing of bone tools or storage of material for making them. Bird bone in the form of finished tubes, bone stock, and unmodified bone indicates the entire process of manufacturing occurred nearby. The probability that at least the Area 221 material is secondary refuse means the exact area of manufacture cannot as yet be determined.

## COMPARISON WITH OTHER HOPI SITES

Comparisons with other sites are limited because so few sites from the same time period have been excavated. Both Walpi and Awatovi can be used for qualitative comparisons, but because of differences in the presentation of data few comparisons can be made on a quantitative level.

It is possible to discuss the presence of species identified at Homol'ovi II, Awatovi (Olsen 1978), and Walpi (Czaplicki and Ruffner 1981). Introduced and domestic animals are omitted from Table 9.8. Species diversity has been shown repeatedly to be correlated with NISP. The faunal remains analyzed for Walpi and Awatovi each totaled well over 10,000 fragments, compared to the 812 fragments from Homol'ovi II. For this reason alone diversity at Homol'ovi II is less. With this in mind, the similarities in the presence of particular species, rather than the absence, is discussed.

Cottontails, jackrabbits, and most rodent species were identified at Homol'ovi II, Walpi, and Awatovi. Rodents, such as the prairie dog, ground squirrel, pocket gopher, kangaroo rat, wood rat, and deer mouse occurred at the three sites. When only Awatovi and Walpi are compared (both sites have comparable sample sizes), mountain lion, bobcat, deer, antelope, and bighorn additionally are present.

The number of bird species at Awatovi is almost twice that at Walpi, whereas Homol'ovi has about half as many. Birds make up less than 10 percent of each assemblage, a figure that should be taken as a gross comparison because it is based on MNIs for Walpi, reported percents for Awatovi (no counts or NISP given), and NISP for Homol'ovi II. Nevertheless, the bird remains from these sites suggest the extensive use of avifauna.

**Table 9.8. Presence of Taxa at Walpi, Awatovi, and Homol'ovi II**

| Taxa | Walpi | Awatovi | Homol'ovi |
|---|---|---|---|
| Osteichthyes | | | x |
| Sauria | | | x |
| *Chrysemys picta* | x | | |
| *Podiceps caspicus* | | x | |
| *Branta canadensis* | x | x | |
| *Anas* sp. | x | x | |
| *Pelecanus* sp. | | x | x |
| *Ardea herodias* | | x | |
| *Cathartes aura* | | x | |
| *Accipiter cooperii* | | x | |
| *Circus cyaneus* | | x | |
| *Buteo regalis* | | x | |
| *Buteo jamaicensis* | | x | |
| *Buteo swainsoni* | | x | |
| *Aquila chrysaetos* | x | x | x |
| *Falco mexicanus* | x | x | |
| *Grus canadensis* | | x | x |
| *Fulica americana* | | | x |
| *Zenaida macroura* | x | x | |
| *Otus flameolus* | x | | |
| *Otus asio* | x | x | |
| *Bubo virginianus* | | x | |
| *Asio otus* | x | x | |
| *Colaptes cafer* | x | | |
| *Eremophila alpestris* | x | | |
| *Corvus corax* | x | x | x |
| Fringillidae | x | | |
| *Lepus californicus* | x | x | x |
| *Sylvilagus* sp. | x | x | x |
| *Cynomys gunnisoni* | x | x | x |
| *Spermophilus variegatus* | | x | |
| *Ammospermophilus leucurus* | x | x | x |
| *Thomomys bottae* | x | x | x |
| *Dipodomys ordii* | x | x | x |
| *Castor canadensis* | x | | |
| *Onychomys leucogaster* | | x | |
| *Peromyscus* sp. | x | x | x |
| *Neotoma* sp. | x | x | x |
| *Erethizon dorsatum* | x | x | |
| *Canis* sp. (dog or coyote) | x | x | x |
| *Canis lupus* | x | | |
| *Urocyon cinereoargenteus* | | x | |
| *Taxidea taxus* | x | | x |
| *Felis concolor* | x | x | |
| *Lynx rufus* | x | x | |
| *Odocoileus hemionus* | x | x | |
| *Antilocapra americana* | x | x | x |
| *Ovis canadenis* | x | x | |

## SUMMARY

Limited excavations at Homol'ovi II yielded 812 bone fragments. Nearly 60 percent of the bone is identifiable below the level of class. Lagomorphs dominate the assemblage, comprising over 70 percent of the identifiable remains, with rodents, carnivores, artiodactyls, birds, and one lizard fragment forming the remainder. Unidentifiable bone consists of remains of mammals, fish, birds, and amphibians.

Although not numerically abundant, the presence of fish, amphibian, and several bird species indicate exploitation of riverine resources. Remains of cottontail are as abundant as jackrabbit, indicating a dense ground cover where they could hide (Miksicek, Chapter 8). The abundance of jackrabbits and cottontails along with several species of rodents points to a reliance on these animals. Small game could be exploited easily by all members of the society, offering a minor but steady supply of protein to supplement both wild and domesticated foodstuffs. The faunal assemblage suggests a focus on hunting animals that avoided scheduling conflicts with agricultural pursuits.

Intrasite differences in the distribution of bird bone existed. The Activity Area had the greatest diversity and number of worked and unworked bird bone. The artiodactyl remains were scattered throughout the excavated areas.

Comparisons with other sites can only be made on the presence of species. A variety of lagomorph and rodents, along with antelope, was recovered from Walpi, Homol'ovi II, and Awatovi. Bird bone at the three sites comprised less than 10 percent of each assemblage. Differences in species diversity between Homol'ovi II and the other two sites is probably due to sample size rather than cultural preferences.

The fragmentary nature of the 15 pieces of worked bone meant that many could only be classified as awls and hairpins or bone tubes and ring stock. Large mammals and large bird elements were most frequently used to manufacture the tools.

The local riverine environment along with the surrounding countryside was the source of animals hunted by the inhabitants of Homol'ovi II. For the Hopi (Beaglehole 1936: 3–4) hunting provided a contrast to the monotonous and routine demands of agriculture, just as it may have for the residents of Homol'ovi II. Hunting fulfilled ritual, social, and subsistence needs. The ceremonial aspects of hunting mirrored the significance of ritual in Hopi daily life. Communal hunting methods were not only well adapted to the open country, but provided group protection from enemies that solitary hunts could not offer. Finally, meat, hide, and bone supplied protein and tool resources. Surely for the inhabitants of Homol'ovi II hunting provided a thread in their lives that tied together subsistence, technological, ritual, and social needs.

# CHAPTER TEN

# Shell

Sharon Urban
Arizona State Museum

Archaeological excavations and surface collections at Homol'ovi II yielded 14 pieces of freshwater and marine shell, representing five artifact categories. This material was obtained from ten different proveniences within the site area: five excavation units, two surface collection units outside the pueblo, and three specimens from plaza surfaces. This report discusses the shell species and their origins, artifact classes represented, provenience locations, the collection and its analysis, and conclusions.

## SPECIES AND SOURCES

The shell material either was obtained locally from the Little Colorado, as in the case of *Anodonta* (a freshwater, edible clam), or was brought in from the Gulf of California (Table 10.1). Bequaert and Miller (1973: 222) report *Anodonta* from the Little Colorado as late as 1956. This genus requires a free flowing, freshwater stream to grow and reproduce. It has also been reported from the Chevelon drainage at about the same time. Due to the seasonality of the flow in these two drainages today, *Anodonta* is no longer found in a living state.

The marine pieces included *Conus* sp., *Glycymeris* sp., *Olivella dama*, and one fragment that was not identifiable as to genus. These specimens live in moderately shallow waters in the Gulf of California and would have been easily obtained by beachcombing. It is also possible these shells were traded through a route that connected the coastal areas with the shell working industries of southern Arizona that in turn supplied the Greater Southwest with shell products. Traded shells may appear either in the natural, unaltered state, or they may be worked into a finished artifact. Most prehistoric communities at a distance from the shell source and its manufacturing center received finished products. The only exception to this is the freshwater *Anodonta*, which was obtained and worked locally. Homol'ovi appears to fit this general pattern, especially because

**Table 10.1. Frequency of Shell Species at Homol'ovi II**

| Species | Frequency |
|---|---|
| Freshwater | |
| *Anodonta californiensis* | 2 |
| Unidentified | 1 |
| Marine | |
| *Conus* sp. | 3 |
| *Glycymeris* sp. | 6 |
| *Olivella dama* | 1 |
| Unidentified | 1 |
| Total shell | 14 |

4 Identified species
2 Unidentified species
6 Species total represented

the pueblo was some 600 miles from the source. However obtained, shell does seem to have been an item sought after by the inhabitants of Homol'ovi II.

## ARTIFACT CATEGORIES

Shell is divided into five categories: raw material, worked material, utilized pieces, ornament, and blanks (Table 10.2). *Raw Material* is a piece of shell that either has been left unaltered and is in its natural shape, or it has been broken to shape but shows no sign of alteration. *Worked Material*, on the other hand, has an area that has been altered in some way. It may contain an edge that has been cut, ground, carved, or drilled. Usually this category contains those pieces that may have broken during "manufacture," such as in the reworking of a broken piece, or is a fragment of a once completed piece.

The *Utilized* category is perhaps the most rare. These shell pieces served a useful function in daily life; in other words, they are tools.

**Table 10.2. Distribution of Shell by Species, Provenience, and Modification**

| Provenience | Raw Material | | Worked Material | | | Awl | Beads | Ornaments Bracelets | Tinkler | Blank | Total |
|---|---|---|---|---|---|---|---|---|---|---|---|
| | *Anodonta* | Unidentified | *Conus* | *Glycymeris* | Unidentified | *Glycymeris* | *Olivella dama* | *Glycymeris* | *Conus* | *Anodonta* | |
| Surface | | | | | | | | | | | |
|   Unit #2 | | | 1 | | | | | | | | 1 |
|   Unit #39 | | | | | | | | 1 | | | 1 |
|   NE¼, Central Plaza | | | 1 | | | | | | | | 1 |
|   NW¼, East Plaza | | 1 | | 1 | | | | | | | 2 |
|   West end, roomblocks, East Plaza | | | | | | | | | | 1 | 1 |
| Room | | | | | | | | | | | |
|   211, East half | 1 | | | | | | | | | | 1 |
|   212, West half | | | | | | 1 | | | | | 1 |
|   215, East half | | | | | | | 1 | | | | 1 |
|   216, Fill | | | | | | | | 1 | | | 1 |
| Activity Area | | | | | | | | | | | |
|   221, Exterior fill | | | | 1 | | 1 | | 1 | 1 | | 4 |
| Total | 1 | 1 | 2 | 2 | 1 | 1 | 1 | 3 | 1 | 1 | 14 |

*Ornament* is usually the largest shell category at any site, offering some insight as to the use of shell. At Homol'ovi subcategories include beads, bracelets, and tinklers. Beads and bracelets are more common than tinklers.

The *Blank* category is composed of those pieces that have been worked into a geometric shape, including circular, square, rectangular, or triangular, along with any of the associated subgroupings. These pieces are generally well finished and could function as is, or perhaps they were awaiting perforation to be turned into pendants. In either case, their immediate function is not readily discerned.

## DISTRIBUTION

Shell artifacts were found in a few surface collected areas of the site (Fig. 10.1), but all clustered within the pueblo unit itself or, in one instance, was immediately to the exterior of the pueblo. Five of these provenience areas are surface collections, each of which yielded one piece of shell with the exception of the northwest quarter of the East Plaza that contained two fragments. From the excavated rooms all but Room 217 produced shell artifacts. Activity Area 221 contained the most shell, with four recovered pieces.

## DISCUSSION

Distribution of shell at the site is, as expected, widely dispersed. If the excavated rooms had not been pothunted they probably would have yielded more shell. It is not surprising to see a lack of shell on the surface. It would be collected by pothunters or visitors to the site. One would not expect to see shell scattered on the surface the same way it appears on Hohokam sites farther to the south and west where shell items were more easily available. Generally, the greater the distance from the source of marine shell, the better the material is curated. Pieces are considered more precious and are not usually thrown away when broken but rather reworked. It is possible that rodent activity, pothunting, or erosion brought these pieces to the surface.

The genera represented are those to be expected, with *Glycymeris* and *Olivella* being the most commonly found at sites in the Southwest. *Conus* is slightly more rare, but only at sites with a pre-1350 date (Hammack and Sullivan 1981: 320). *Conus* and *Olivella* could easily

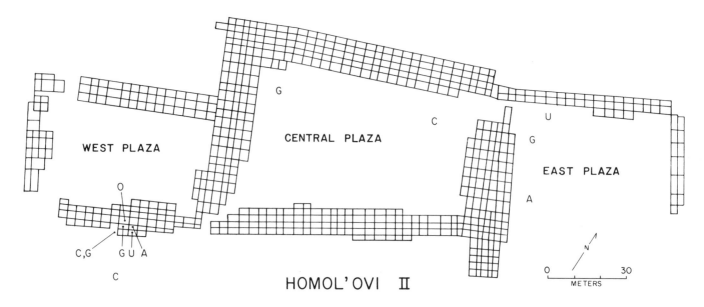

WEST PLAZA

CENTRAL PLAZA

EAST PLAZA

G

C

U

G

A

O

C,G    G U A

C

N

0        30
METERS

HOMOL'OVI II

Figure 10.1. Location of shell. A = *Anodonta*, C = *Conus*,
G = *Glycymeris*, O = *Olivella dama*, U = unidentified.

be traded as raw material as they are simply worked into artifacts requiring a minimum amount of effort to produce. *Glycymeris*, on the other hand, is thought to be traded as a completed piece in either bracelet or pendant form. Quite frequently when a bracelet shattered, pieces were reworked into another form, as is the case with the awl from Activity Area 221.

It is not surprising to see *Anodonta* at Homol'ovi, as it is usually present at sites some distance from the source of the more desired marine genera. Because this clam is edible, it is generally assumed to be a food source first, then a piece of workable material second. *Anodonta*, when completely dried, is very fragile and transporting it would be difficult.

A wide variety of artifact categories is found at Homol'ovi II (Fig. 10.2). Materials include nonworked pieces, partially worked pieces, and finished artifacts. The categories of Geometric and Utilized are more rare in that they do not occur or are not found at every site. Shell awls could represent some specialized function or craft, because a bone or stone tool would be more readily available.

Although any genera of shell can be found within the Raw and Worked Material categories, those classified as Geometrics, Ornaments, and Utilized are of a more prescribed character. The Geometric category requires a shell that has a large surface area that lacks sculpture and is relatively flat. Clam shells are generally the best, such as *Anodonta*, *Glycymeris*, and *Laevicar-*

Figure 10.2. Enlargement of shell artifacts: *a*, geometric, *b-d*, ornaments. *a*, *Anodonta californiensis* (west end of roomblocks, East Plaza); *b*, *Glycymeris* sp. (Room 216, fill); *c*, *Olivella dama*, (Room 215, east half); *d*, *Conus* sp. (Area 221, fill). Length of *b* is 2.5 cm.

*dium*. Of the Ornament class, beads and bracelets are the most common. Beads can be constructed on a variety of shells, but *Olivella* is always the most common genus used. Bracelets are only made of *Glycymeris* shells and tinklers are solely constructed of the gastropod *Conus*. For most of the utilized artifacts a good sturdy shell is needed. Of the awls and needles found at sites, they are made from reworked bracelet fragments of *Glycymeris*.

## CONCLUSIONS

Judging from the shell types and artifact categories present at the site, the material seems to fit into a later time period. Unfortunately there is not enough shell in this collection to estimate a date, but the presence of *Conus* is generally associated with a post-1350 time frame (Hammack and Sullivan 1981: 320). Along with the appearance of *Conus*, one usually expects to see large amounts of *Laevicardium*, which is a large bivalve from the Gulf of California that was often used to make small pendants. Its absence may be due to the small sample size. *Laevicardium* has been found at other large sites in the area (Fewkes 1904: 91), so it is safe to assume its probable presence here as well.

The sites of Chevelon, Chavez Pass, and the others within the Homol'ovi Ruin Group (Andrews 1982: 147; Dosh 1982: 27; Fewkes 1904: 88–91; and Jennings 1980: 155) indicate the presence of shell of a wider variety both in artifact types and, to some extent, in genera (based, of course, on a larger shell artifact inventory per site). Unfortunately, some of the shell in the early reports (Fewkes 1904) was not identified as to genus, but an educated guess from the photographs can add at least two genera to the list as published. The potential for greater quantities of shell and a wider variety of shell types is certainly warranted. This could easily be determined by future excavations at the site.

The only common marine shell that is missing is *Laevicardium*. The marine specimens of *Conus*, *Glycymeris*, and *Olivella* are all most typical, representing the usual shell genera from any Southwestern site. Not only were these genera present, but so were the most general types of artifacts, in particular beads and bracelets, and, for this time period, tinklers. The presence of these types indicates a link to the Hohokam, via trade routes. Other common distinct genera, but of less frequent occurrence, may not have reached these people so far north, but the mainstay of the shell trade (*Conus*, *Glycymeris*, and *Olivella*) certainly did.

*Anodonta* on the other hand, serves in a different manner. It is a local shell, utilized for adornment as well as a possible training medium for the shell-working process. Marine shells do break, the supply is short, so reworking to salvage material is a must. Skills learned on the local resource may be applied toward the more valuable marine piece in need of remodeling.

From the material at hand it can be inferred that some knowledge of shell working was present at the site. The freshwater *Anodonta* was collected and the shell worked. Also the broken *Glycymeris* bracelet from Room 216 is another example of manufacture, even though it is a reused piece. Shell evidently carried enough value as a status marker in the society to make it a sought after item, no matter its source. Perhaps the *Anodonta* pieces were only temporary "replacements" until the "real thing" was once again obtained through trade.

The Hohokam are generally thought to be master craftsmen in shell working (Haury 1976: 306) and the suppliers of shell for the Southwest. At Hohokam sites in southern Arizona dating to A.D. 1300-1400, one finds large quantities of shell. For some reason this shell appears not to be disseminated from the manufacturing centers (or at least at a fast pace), because it does not appear in quantity at northern sites such as Homol'ovi II. The shell reaching Homol'ovi may not have been of the broadest selection nor of the best quality that was available earlier in the shell trade network. However, the presence of shell at the pueblo indicates a desire for shell pieces as items of personal adornment or as status symbols. The quantity of shell and the genera represented may never have been great, mainly because of the distance from the source and because of the time period represented at the site (A.D. 1300-1400). To qualify this last statement, the sample size should be taken into consideration because the work done at Homol'ovi II was mainly for stabilization purposes, and the site itself was not completely and systematically excavated. Additionally, judging from the size of the pueblo, one would expect more shell to be present in other rooms and features. Only after a systematic excavation of the site would a definitive statement on its shell content be apropos.

After the collapse of the shell trade network, perhaps sometime around A.D. 1450, shell continued to be traded, but through new channels and from different sources, both in terms of the trader and the geographic source of the material. A hint of this continued trade in shell can be seen at sites that were occupied from the 1500s on into the present. An example of continued trade is reflected in the shell from Walpi (Nations and Adams 1980), a Hopi village in northeastern Arizona that has been occupied since 1690.

# CHAPTER ELEVEN

# Homol'ovi II in the 14th Century

E. Charles Adams
Arizona State Museum

Homol'ovi II functioned as a central place in the Western Pueblo world of the 14th century. The people of Homol'ovi II traded widely. Nonlocal ceramics, obsidian, and shell indicate trade extended into the Verde Valley, Tonto Basin, the Salt-Gila River Valleys, upper Little Colorado River Valley, the Hopi Mesas, the Zuni area, and the Flagstaff area. Presence of yellow ware at small sites, as well as large pueblos, in some of these areas suggests the trade was in items needed or desired by both groups and were not items of symbolic status. The model best describing the regional trade system is down-the-line following a distance-decay falloff, with individual large pueblos such as Homol'ovi II acting as supply zones. At the community level, exchange with other pueblos or areas is best viewed as reciprocal.

Internally, the subsistence base seems dominated by domestic crops and local flora and fauna. The presence of cotton and riverine flora and fauna in abundance suggests some of the local items that could be exported to nonriverine areas, including the Hopi Mesas and Nuvakwewtaqa. Numerous items available only in the Little Colorado River area, such as turtles and birds, are resources collected historically by the Hopi. The surface lithics suggest specific activity spaces within and outside the pueblo. Surface ceramics indicate concentrations of earlier ceramics in the eastern plaza area and later ceramics in the western plaza area, supporting the interpretation of possible temporal difference in occupation of the plazas made by Weaver and others (1982). Excavations in five rooms and an outside work area in the south roomblock of the West Plaza were conducted to evaluate the nature of the late occupation of Homol'ovi II. Two dated radiocarbon samples and the dominant yellow ware ceramic assemblage clearly date the use of the rooms to the 1300s. The frequency of various tree-ring dated yellow wares corroborate the calibrated means of the radiocarbon samples at A.D. 1350. This places the latest occupation and use of the rooms as midden areas to the 1350-1375 period.

Presence of a katsina face on a Paayu Polychrome bowl on the floor of Room 215 suggests the presence of the katsina cult (compare Hays 1989). Pond's (1966) excavation of a kiva with murals in the West Plaza of Homol'ovi II certainly supports this contention, as do the extensive rock art panels having katsina faces or figures on the mesa edge west of the pueblo (Cole 1989). The apparent proliferation of piki stones in the ground stone assemblage may also be associated with the katsina cult (Adams 1991). Piki is an important element in food distribution at modern Hopi katsina dances. It seems probable that the cult was present at Homol'ovi II by the mid 1300s (Adams 1991).

## THE CERAMIC ASSEMBLAGE AND DATING

The Homol'ovi II ceramic assemblage underscores the problems with the yellow ware typology. Colton (1956) assigns only general dates to the yellow ware types, with their production lasting from 1300 or 1400 to the Mission Period, or about 1625. Nevertheless, Colton recognizes two distinct "styles" in both Sikyatki Polychrome and Jeddito Black-on-yellow that he refers to as early geometric and late "free treatment." The latter refers to the curvilinear, asymmetric life forms and abstract bird designs recovered by Fewkes (1919) at Sikyatki and elsewhere. Although the validity of this scheme seemingly has merit, no systematic, controlled set of data has been analyzed to determine this. The identification of an intermediate type, Paayu Polychrome, is an initial attempt to "bridge-the-gap" in refining the broad temporal range of the yellow ware types. An earlier contribution to refining Colton's scheme was made by Smith (1971). Although continuing Colton's reliance on stylistic differences in separating the yellow wares, Smith emphasized the technological attributes of paste and color to separate Awatovi Black-on-yellow from Jeddito Black-on-yellow. The Homol'ovi II data seem to support this approach. Because he concentrated on the ceramic assemblage from the western mound at Awatovi, Smith does not consider the later yellow ware types.

Thus the restorable vessel assemblage is comprised of one major type, Awatovi Black-on-yellow that is nearing the end of its production, and two other types, Sikyatki (Paayu) Polychrome and Jeddito Black-on-yellow at the beginning of their manufacture. The convergence of dates for these three types offered by Breternitz (1966), Colton (1956), and Smith (1971) would be 1350 to 1375.

On the basis of two calibrated radiocarbon dates and archaeomagnetic dates, the excavated rooms at Homol'ovi II certainly date to the 1300s with the mean at 1350. These radiocarbon dates should indicate the time of use rather than the fill of the rooms, which is represented in the ceramics. The tree-ring dated ceramic assemblage also supports a mid 14th-century date. A date of 1350 applied to the excavated remains offers major implications for the artifactual assemblage, in particular the pottery. Considering only the partially reconstructible vessels discussed in Chapter 3, there are 12 Awatovi Black-on-yellow vessels, 2 Jeddito Black-on-yellow vessels, 2 Paayu Polychrome vessels (a possible intermediate type between Jeddito Black-on-yellow and Sikyatki Polychrome), 2 Bidahochi Polychrome vessels, and 1 vessel each of Jeddito Engraved, Jeddito Yellow Ware, Jeddito Corrugated, Huckovi Black-on-orange, and Homolovi Polychrome. The assemblage generally supports the dates assigned various yellow ware types by Colton (1956) and Smith (1971). Nonetheless, refinement of the chronology is in order. Awatovi Black-on-yellow is the dominant ceramic type, which suggests its production persisted to after 1350. The Paayu Polychrome vessels would have previously been designated Sikyatki Polychrome. Appearance of both Jeddito Black-on-yellow and Sikyatki Polychrome by the mid 14th century is much earlier than suggested by either Colton or Smith. Although this is not really surprising, much more excavation is needed to substantiate the designation of a new type and refinement of time of production of all of the types. The presence of Bidahochi Polychrome, Jeddito Engraved, and Jeddito Corrugated is not surprising and is in line with dates suggested by Colton.

The problems related above can be used to argue for using both stylistic and technological studies in ceramic analysis, and for using attribute-oriented analyses in addition to typologically based ones. Such an approach is being used by the Homol'ovi Research Program. One promising area of research has found significant variation in framing line size and distance from rim and major design field. It is too early to determine what may be the causes of the variation. Excavations at Homol'ovi III and Homol'ovi IV, both late 13th-century

pueblos within 5 km of Homol'ovi II, indicate the framing lines are narrower and much closer to the rim than in the Homol'ovi II collection. These clear chronological differences lend hope that a major factor in the variation in attributes of the framing lines is due to time. It is still too early to evaluate trends in other attributes of style.

A possible second major influence on framing line morphology could be divergent origins of the manufacturer. Substantial evidence has now been gathered from the Homol'ovi III and Homol'ovi IV ceramic data to make clearcut statements about affinities to other non-Homol'ovi assemblages. The nonlocal ceramics at Homol'ovi III are dominated by White Mountain Red wares and Cibola White wares. This assemblage means that the founders of Homol'ovi III were probably immigrants from the upper Little Colorado River drainage. At Homol'ovi III the Winslow Orange Ware polychromes evolved out of the White Mountain Red Ware and Cibola White Ware stylistic traditions. Framing lines for these two traditions, even for types contemporary with the Jeddito Yellow wares, are always much closer to the rim and narrower than for the Jeddito wares.

Homol'ovi IV provides an interesting ceramic contrast to Homol'ovi III. The assemblage is dominated by Jeddito Black-on-orange, Bidahochi Black-on-white, Tusayan White wares, Little Colorado White wares, Tusayan Gray wares, and Little Colorado Gray wares. The founders of Homol'ovi IV almost certainly came from the vicinity of the Hopi Mesas. Surface collections from Homol'ovi IV strongly suggest that Tuwiuca Black-on-orange, a Winslow Orange Ware, evolved from Jeddito Black-on-orange. Although there are more clearcut ties to the roots of the Jeddito Yellow Ware tradition on the Hopi Mesas, the relationship of framing line attributes on Homol'ovi IV orange ware to Homol'ovi II yellow ware may not be direct enough to substantiate a clear evolutionary sequence of change. The best solution to the stylistic conundrum would appear to be additional excavations at Homol'ovi II. The excavations must be in an area without architecture that was probably used over most of the life of the pueblo. The most likely source of these data would be in the Central Plaza. When excavations resume at Homol'ovi II, stratigraphic tests in the Central Plaza will be a top priority.

The other major trend noted in the reconstructible vessel assemblage at Homol'ovi II was the predominance of yellow wares in the assemblage. Only one of the 23 reconstructible vessels was not a yellow ware and it was Homolovi Polychrome. The assemblage demonstrates the complete reliance of the Homol'ovi II people on imports from the Hopi Mesas. Numerous experiments on the Jeddito Yellow wares from Homol'ovi II and Homol'ovi III in contrast to the Winslow Orange wares from the same sites demonstrate: (1) that the vessels were not manufactured of the same clay nor fired with the same fuel; (2) that the yellow ware vessels that could be sourced were coal fired; and (3) that the yellow ware vessels that could be sourced were made of clay from the Hopi Mesas (Bishop and others 1988; De Atley and others 1986; Block 1985; Bhattacharyya 1985; Vaitkus 1986). Bishop and others (1988) have analyzed and sourced over 20 yellow ware sherds from Homol'ovi II. All that could be sourced came from Awatovi, a Hopi village on Antelope Mesa. There are no outcrops of coal near the Homol'ovi sites. The nearest coal that could have been mined by prehistoric technology is at the Hopi Mesas, also the source of the yellow ware clay (Hack 1942b; De Atley and others 1986). There is little doubt that most of the yellow-firing pottery at Homol'ovi II was traded from Hopi villages, over 80 km to the north.

The almost exclusive use of yellow ware pottery by the Homol'ovi people by the mid 1300s is certainly a surprise. The implication is that production of at least the decorated Winslow Orange Ware ceramics had all but ended by 1350. Therefore, the decorated Winslow Orange Ware tradition offers a tight chronological control to sites on which it is located. Period of manufacture for the Winslow Orange wares, the decorated central Little Colorado River Valley ceramic tradition, apparently is restricted to 1275 to 1350. Comparable to this surprise are nagging questions as to why the Homol'ovi people imported so many yellow wares and how they were able to "pay" for them.

To answer these questions one need only look at the wood resources of the central Little Colorado River Valley. Today, excluding introduced species such as tamarisk and camelthorn, the dominant tree is the cottonwood and the dominant bush is willow, both riparian species, although the desert olive is relatively abundant in areas on the floodplain. There are also numerous upland shrubs; however, with the exception of the greasewood, none exceed a meter high. Therefore, local wood resources are restricted to the narrow riverine environment and are dominated by wood that burns at a relatively low temperature in contrast to juniper, oak, and most pines.

A comparison of the wood charcoal recovered from Homol'ovi II (see Table 8.9) to the partial list above is revealing. No apparent variation in species from those in existence today is noted, nor is there any change in plant dominance. Outside of species available today in the area only 2.5 percent of the wood assemblage could be considered exotic. The figure for exotics, including juniper, indicates that access to, or at least use of, these trees was limited. At present, the nearest dense growth

of a nonriparian tree, the juniper, is 20 km to the south in the vicinity of Sunset Mountain.

Wood use at Homol'ovi II was primarily of local plants. None of the locally available species produce a hot enough fire for a long enough period to fire prehistoric pottery well. It is unlikely the local plants would have been in enough abundance to provide building material, firewood, and fuel to fire pottery for the populations inhabiting the central Little Colorado River Valley in the 14th century. Whereas recycling was possible for roofing material and local plants and driftwood could have served as fuel to heat rooms, the local plants were neither adequate in quality nor available in quantity to be used to fire pottery. Instead of traveling the 20 km or so to collect wood for firing their pots or carrying the pots to the fuel source, the Homol'ovi people instead may have opted to trade for their pottery needs. The nearest source of pottery was not the Hopi Mesas. Nuvakwewtaqa (Chavez Pass) is located only 58 km to the southwest in an area dense with piñon and juniper. Whereas Alameda Brown wares, which occur fairly frequently at Homol'ovi II, may have been traded from Nuvakwewtaqa, the vast majority of the ceramics originated at the Hopi Mesa pueblos. From the technological standpoint, the occupants of the Hopi villages manufactured perhaps the finest pottery in the southwestern United States. This quality could have been a major factor in deciding who to trade with, but a critical factor remained. What commodities did the Homol'ovi people trade?

## EXCHANGE SYSTEMS

Cotton (*Gossypium hirsatum*) was recovered from 57 percent of the flotation samples collected at Homol'ovi II. This indicates a major commitment to growing cotton near the Homol'ovi pueblos. Cotton was a major crop at Hopi when the Spanish arrived (Brew 1949). The Hopi farming village of Moenkopi was reestablished in the 1870s partly as a good location to grow cotton, and this may have been true of the original village founded in the 14th or 15th century (Nagata 1970: 143-144). The elevation of the Moenkopi Valley near present Moenkopi is 1463 m (4800 feet), with a growing season of over 150 days (Nagata 1970: 17). Moenkopi Wash is a perennial stream with extensive irrigation used to water the crops by the Hopi. The Little Colorado River floodplain below Homol'ovi II is at 1474 m (4830 ft), with a growing season of 172 days (Smith 1945). The Little Colorado River is nearly a perennial stream capable of being used for irrigation. Not only do the Homol'ovi flotation samples have charred and uncharred cotton seeds in 57 percent of the samples, but climatically and hydrologically the area is excellently suited for growing cotton.

The expansive acreage devoted to cotton agriculture noted by early Spanish explorers to the Hopi Mesas in the 16th and 17th centuries suggests a need for the product. The Hopis' ability to give 600 cotton blankets to Espejo when he visited in 1583 suggests cotton items were a major Hopi export (Hammond and Rey 1929). This is supported by Father Garces' diary that noted Hopi blankets were in use in southwestern Arizona (Coues 1900). Given the Hopi use of cotton in early historic times, such use probably existed 200 years earlier. Given the high potential for cotton production in the central Little Colorado River Valley and its abundance in the Homol'ovi II perishable remains, it seems that cotton was grown by the inhabitants of Homol'ovi II. Although considerably more research must be conducted, a working hypothesis is that the inhabitants of Homol'ovi II, and probably of the contemporary Homol'ovi I and Chevelon ruins, were exchanging cotton for yellow-firing pottery manufactured at the Hopi Mesas. A reciprocal exchange network was established because it benefited both populations.

A second possible exchange item to the Hopi Mesas, and to other areas with no extensive riparian habitats, could have been flora and fauna associated with the Little Colorado River. Using modern Hopi society as a model, almost any plant or animal associated with water is significant in ritual (Tyler 1964, 1979; Whiting 1939; Parsons 1936). Conversations with numerous Hopi confirm their historic use of the Homol'ovi area to collect turtles and various birds or bird feathers for their ceremonies. The Homol'ovi II faunal assemblage suggests some of the diversity in avifauna available in the area. More extensive excavations at Homol'ovi III have considerably expanded the bird assemblage, suggesting the diversity of the resource base. Wetland fauna found in abundance in both the Awatovi and Walpi assemblages may have originated in the Little Colorado River Valley (see Table 9.8). These include the white pelican, blue heron, sandhill crane, mallard duck, teal, and Canadian goose. From the Homol'ovi II remains were recovered the Canadian goose, white pelican, and sandhill crane. Although there may have been wetland areas around the Hopi Mesas, these would have been much more restricted in extent than the Little Colorado River Valley.

In addition to the intensive exchange indicated between the Hopi Mesa pueblos and the Homol'ovi pueblos, other aspects of the assemblage point to more far-reaching trade. In particular, Salado polychromes, Zuni Glaze wares, and White Mountain Red wares provide a small, but steady, contribution to the total ceramic inventory at Homol'ovi II collected from the surface. These ceramics indicate contact with Western Pueblo groups to the south, southeast, and east just above and below the Mogollon Rim. Interestingly, distribution of yellow ware contemporary with Homol'ovi II is found in locations from which all of the trade pottery originates.

Yellow ware pottery provides a small, but consistent, increment to contemporary ceramic assemblages from the Zuni area on the east to the Verde Valley on the west, including sites in the upper Little Colorado River Valley and in the Tonto Basin. It is these very areas that provide small, but consistent, contributions to the Homol'ovi ceramic assemblage, in particular White Mountain Red Ware, Zuni Glaze Ware, and Roosevelt Red Ware. The analysis by Crown and Bishop in this report suggests a multiple origin for the Roosevelt Red Ware type, Gila Polychrome. From the distribution and frequency of imports at Homol'ovi II it would appear that although yellow wares are probably being exchanged to the upper Little Colorado River, to the Zuni area, to the Tonto Basin, and to the Verde Valley, ceramics are also being traded in reciprocal fashion from these areas to Homol'ovi II. This suggests that the Homol'ovi pueblos could have acted as intermediaries in the exchange of yellow wares in down-the-line fashion, as opposed to direct exchange between manufacturers of these wares and their Hopi Mesa counterparts (compare Upham 1982).

Obsidian provides a steady increment to the lithic assemblage. At Homol'ovi III, obsidian is found almost exclusively with proveniences having yellow ware ceramics and is rare to nonexistent in earlier proveniences (Harry 1989). The relatively broad spectrum of shell recovered from Homol'ovi II added to that recovered by Fewkes (1904) and by subsequent excavation at Homol'ovi III suggests contacts with Hohokam people. David Doyel indicated in 1986 that Jeddito Yellow Ware vessels had been found at Pueblo Grande within modern Phoenix. Perhaps the pottery, or its contents, was exchanged for finished and unfinished shell products, such as were found at Homol'ovi II. These data indicate that the people at Homol'ovi II were participating in a broad and diverse trade system. In some cases the trade was probably reciprocal, such as yellow pottery for cotton. In other cases the Homol'ovi traders probably acted more as middlemen.

Examination of survey collections at the Museum of Northern Arizona and the Arizona State Museum taken from the upper and middle Verde Valley has shown both Winslow Orange wares and Jeddito Yellow wares were present. Because Winslow Orange Ware was produced only in the central Little Colorado River Valley, the implication is that acquisition of yellow ware pottery by people in the Verde Valley was accomplished through people at the Homol'ovi villages. The probable restricted time of manufacture of the Winslow Orange wares and their occasional occurrence on Verde Valley sites without Jeddito Yellow wares suggests that contacts between the Homol'ovi people and Verde Valley people were established before yellow wares entered the exchange system.

Winslow Orange Ware at protohistoric Anderson Mesa sites contemporary with Homol'ovi II indicates possible contact prior to the presence of yellow wares in the exchange system. The absence or low level of obsidian in pre-yellow ware proveniences at Homol'ovi sites means either that yellow ware provided the medium of exchange for obsidian from Anderson Mesa sites or that obsidian was obtained directly or by using means other than through the contemporary Anderson Mesa pueblos.

From the vantage point of the manufacturing area for yellow pottery, the Hopi Mesas, the 14th-century exchange system would best be characterized as down-the-line exchange following a distance-decay falloff from the source. Within such an exchange system with respect to the Hopi Mesa villages, the yellow ware ceramics at Homol'ovi II could best be viewed as a result of a supply zone effect. Homol'ovi II trade relations were basically reciprocal. Upham (1982) has suggested that Jeddito Yellow Ware and White Mountain Red Ware were status wares (Feinman and others 1981), implying elite control of a broad or regional exchange system throughout the Western Pueblo area east to Acoma.

A central element to Upham's argument that sociopolitical organization of Western Pueblo people in the 14th century was different and in fact more centralized than in modern groups lay in his analysis of decorated ceramic assemblages. For example, according to Upham, the large sites had qualitatively different ceramic assemblages than the small sites because the leadership, or elite, resided in the large pueblos. As control became more centralized these elites accumulated wealth to support their status and to bank for future exchange opportunities with elite from other villages. Hallmarks of wealth and status were ceramics requiring considerably more labor, such as polychromes (especially White Mountain Red wares). Upham reasoned that the low frequency of White Mountain Red wares and Jeddito Yellow wares at his study site, Nuvakwewtaqa, was because of this restricted access to the products. Upham then describes the network as a system of pueblos having elites who participated in the exchange of these status commodities. Central to this system are the Homol'ovi pueblos.

There are numerous assumptions about ceramic manufacture that Upham applies throughout the study area, such as frequency of decorated sherds in a ceramic assemblage (1982: 151-153) and the significance of

frequency of decorated Jeddito Yellow Ware to total decorated pottery (1982, Fig. 41) that appear to distort data basic to his conclusions. Additionally, Upham's assumption that the small sites in the Chavez Pass area are contemporary with the Nuvakwewtaqa pueblo is seriously flawed. Nevertheless, Homol'ovi II does fit some aspects of Upham's model. It does appear to be a participant in a broad system of exchange with contemporary groups throughout the southwestern Plateau area and below the Mogollon Rim to the Phoenix Basin. There are at present no data at Homol'ovi II that cannot be explained as the product of reciprocal exchange between each area and Homol'ovi II. The hallmark status ware, Jeddito Yellow Ware, is ubiquitous at Homol'ovi II and occurs on hundreds of small and large sites within a 10-km radius of the pueblo. In fact, the combination of excavation and survey data recently compiled in the Homol'ovi II area best fits a model that considers the artifact distribution at Homol'ovi II to be a result of the supply zone effect (Renfrew 1977). In this model Homol'ovi II as a trade center would receive outside goods and distribute them to nearby settlements.

The serious flaws in Upham's assumptions and the radical divergence of Homol'ovi II ceramics from the predicted distribution based on the Nuvakwewtaqa data clearly indicate that Upham's model is in need of major revision. There is no question that a regional exchange system flourished in most areas surrounding Homol'ovi II. There is no evidence of elite control of this exchange or its manipulation to increase status and power among a few within each pueblo or pueblo cluster.

There is no question that by southwestern U.S. standards, a sophisticated regional exchange system was operative in the 14th century involving the Western Pueblo people from the middle Verde Valley on the west, to the Tonto Basin on the south, to Zuni on the east, and to Hopi on the north. The socioeconomic and politicoeconomic systems operative at the Hopi Mesas historically could provide a model of village organization capable of operating such a trade system. Ceramic data at Homol'ovi II do not suggest major economic ties to groups other than at the Hopi Mesas. The generalized distribution of the ceramics on the surface of Homol'ovi II does not suggest elite access to these goods. Burial data would undoubtedly contribute to our understanding of access to the trade wares. These data are not and, due to vandalism, may never be available to archaeologists.

The term elite has prompted considerable discussion and misunderstanding among archaeologists. Upham (1982: 120) refers to the modern sociopolitical structure of the Hopi as a "decision-making elite." Given this definition there can be little argument that such an elite existed in the 1300s at Homol'ovi II. However, considering the nature of the use of yellow ware pottery at Homol'ovi II and the absence of evidence for agriculture intensification around the Homol'ovi sites, the evidence for a cooperative, multiple village, elite organization based on restrictive control of regional exchange cannot be supported with the Homol'ovi II data. Excavations at Walpi Pueblo (Adams 1982) uncovered trade items from throughout the Southwest in the 18th-century deposits, including sillimanite axes from Picuris, Zuni pottery, Paiute and Apache basketry, obsidian from the Flagstaff area, turquoise, Gulf of California and Pacific coast shell, and others. Yet, given Upham's (1982) characterization of historic Pueblo regional and village sociopolitical organization combined with Spanish documents of the 18th century, there is no evidence of the existence of a decision-making elite any different from that documented in the late 19th-century ethnographies of the Hopi (Parsons 1936). The apparent operative sociopolitical system at Hopi throughout the contact period consisted of a theocracy of several males from the leading clans and lineages of each village. The leading clans tended to be similar from village to village, but were not identical.

Thus a regional exchange system does not imply a region-wide elite on a scale different from historic Pueblos. In a cluster of villages the size of the Homol'ovi group, the presence of trade items from throughout the Western Pueblo area would be expected. Participation in a regional exchange system with yellow ware, and other artifacts, as symbolic of elite status is not indicated and cannot be demonstrated with the Homol'ovi II data. Many more in-depth and systematic collections from contemporary pueblos, distributional studies of artifacts on these sites, and ceramic style analyses are required to support or reject Upham's model.

## FUTURE RESEARCH PRIORITIES

Research priorities for future excavations at Homol'ovi II include more in-depth understanding of the local resource base available to the Homol'ovi II people and identification of items not locally available. Survey of a 30-square-mile area in the vicinity of the Homol'ovi pueblos (Lange 1989) suggests a continued expansion away from the river in searching for arable land. As population expanded and land became scarce, boundaries of ownership within and between pueblos developed (compare Preucel 1988). The perishable or semiperishable items in the Homol'ovi assemblage probably hold keys to unraveling the complex economic ties between Homol'ovi and other nearby pueblos.

A second research priority is to obtain a clearer understanding of the nature and role of the katsina cult in the sociopolitical structure of Homol'ovi II. This understanding will allow us to evaluate the potential for the cult to act as an integrative sociocultural device as suggested by Titiev (1944) and Eggan (1950). The cult could provide the sociopolitical tool for integrating the diverse membership within each village that resulted from their rapid growth. Other more local research priorities include sorting out the local evolution of the Winslow Orange wares, obtaining temporal understanding of the Jeddito Yellow wares, defining the founding and development of the pueblo, and evaluating the historic Hopi as a model for understanding the social, political, ceremonial, and subsistence structure of Homol'ovi II.

The 1984 Arizona State Museum research program at Homol'ovi II accomplished its purpose, to establish baseline data for future research programs to be conducted at the pueblo. In addition to excavations at Homol'ovi II, we realize that future research must include excavations at the smaller pueblos of the Homol'ovi group, intensive and regional survey of the Homol'ovi area, location and evaluation of collections taken from the ruins in the past, and interviews with elderly Hopi who best understand the oral histories of their people and the structure of their culture. Such a broad anthropological approach to research at Homol'ovi II will provide the best opportunity for understanding the function of this pueblo in the 14th-century Western Pueblo world.

# Turquoise, Bead, Hematite, Textile, and Cordage

Kelley Ann Hays
Arizona State Museum

## TURQUOISE

Two fragments of turquoise were recovered (Fig. A.1b, c). The first, from surface collection unit 5, is a light blue tab bead fragment, broken across the drilled hole. It is square or rectangular in shape, and measures 6 mm across its unbroken axis. It is 1.7 mm thick. The second piece, from Room 212, exterior vandals' spoil, is a small flat chip of greenish blue stone with rounded edges and an irregular shape. It measures 4.5 mm by 3.7 mm by 1.2 mm thick. It was probably a mosaic piece.

## BEAD

A flat disc bead (Fig. A.1a) was recovered on the floor of Room 212. It is dark brown stone, of unknown type, and measures 3.0 mm in diameter and 1.0 mm thick.

## HEMATITE

A small flat piece of ground hematite (Fig. A.1d) was recovered from Area 221, fill. It is ground on both surfaces and two edges, and snapped on the other two edges. There are three deeply incised straight lines on one surface, which is dark red (10R 3/6) in a freshly spalled area. The opposite surface is blackened, probably by burning. The piece measures 25 mm by 27 mm and is 4 mm thick.

## TEXTILE AND CORDAGE FRAGMENTS

Three small, fragile fragments of charred textile and cordage were recovered from Area 221 fill (Fig. A.1e, f). This deposit probably represents debris cleared from a burned storage room that also contained burned corn, other plant materials (Chapter 8), and ceramics. The textile fragment measures about 3 cm by 1 cm. It appears to have a twilled weave of cotton thread. Two short (about 1 cm long) lengths of single ply cordage of a rougher vegetable fiber were found in the same deposit.

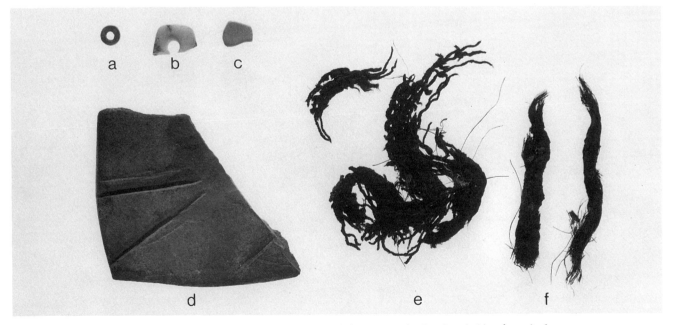

Figure A.1. Miscellaneous artifacts: a, bead; b, c, turquoise bead and chip; d, worked hematite; e, f, charred textile and cordage. Maximum width of d at bottom is 27 mm.

# Provenience and Measurement Information for Certain Illustrated Vessels

Kelley Ann Hays
Arizona State Museum

Fig. 3.1  *a*, Rye Creek Ruin, ASM GP 11270, rim diameter about 12 cm
*b*, Homol'ovi II kiva (see Pond 1966), ASM 89-39-6, rim diameter about 20 cm
*c*, Old Mishongnovi, FMNH 75738, rim diameter about 25 cm

Fig. 3.2  *a*, USNM 156579, not to scale
*b*, FMNH 72624, rim diameter 19 cm
*c*, USNM 157459, not to scale
*d*, USNM 156630, not to scale
*e*, FMNH 72652, rim diameter 23 cm
*f*, FMNH 73107, diameter about 15 cm

Fig. 3.11 (not to scale)
*a*, from Homol'ovi, FMNH 75605
*b*, from Homol'ovi, USNM 157043
*c*, from Homol'ovi, FMNH 75319
*d*, from Sikyatki, USNM 15554

---

ASM = Arizona State Museum
FMNH = Field Museum of Natural History
USNM = United States National Museum

# References

ADAMS, E. CHARLES
  1979  Native Ceramics from Walpi. *Walpi Archaeological Project, Phase II*. Vol. 3. Flagstaff: Museum of Northern Arizona.
  1980  An Archaeological Assessment of Homolovi I Ruin Near Winslow, Arizona. Report submitted by the Museum of Northern Arizona to the Bureau of Land Management, Phoenix District Office, Phoenix. MS, Museum of Northern Arizona, Flagstaff.
  1982  *Walpi Archaeological Project: Synthesis and Interpretation*. Flagstaff: Museum of Northern Arizona.
  1983  The Appearance, Evolution, and Meaning of the Katsina Cult to the Pre-Hispanic Pueblo World of the Southwestern United States. Paper presented in the symposium entitled: "Models of Pueblo Prehistory" at the 11th International Congress of Anthropological and Ethnological Sciences, Vancouver. MS, Homolovi Research Program, Arizona State Museum, University of Arizona, Tucson.
  1989a  Passive Resistence: Hopi Responses to Spanish Contact and Conquest. In *Columbian Consequences*, Vol.1, *Archaeological and Historical Perspectives on the Spanish Borderlands West*, edited by David Hurst Thomas, pp. 77–92. Washington: Smithsonian Institution.
  1989b  The Homol'ovi Research Program. *Kiva* 54(3): 175–194.
  1991  *The Origin and Development of the Pueblo Katsina Cult*. Tucson: University of Arizona Press.

ADAMS, E. CHARLES, DEBORAH S. DOSH, AND MIRIAM T. STARK
  1986  Spatial Organization in the Hopi Mesas–Hopi Buttes–Middle Little Colorado River Valley, A.D. 1300–1600. Paper presented at the 59th Annual Pecos Conference, Shoofly, Arizona. MS, Homol'ovi Research Program, Arizona State Museum, University of Arizona, Tucson.

ADAMS, JENNY L.
  1979  Stone Implements, Miscellaneous Groundstone and Natural Objects. In "Stone Artifacts from Walpi," by Jenny L. Adams and David Greenwald. *Walpi Archaeological Project–Phase II*, Volume 4, Part I. Flagstaff, Museum of Northern Arizona.
  1986  A Use Wear Analysis Comparing Handstones Used to Process Hides and Corn. MS, Master's thesis, Department of Anthropology, University of Colorado, Boulder.
  1989a  Experimental Replication of the Use of Ground Stone Tools. *Kiva* 54(3): 261–271.
  1989b  Methods for Improving Ground Stone Artifacts Analysis: Experiments in Mano Wear Patterns. In "Experiments in Lithic Technology," edited by Daniel S. Amick and Raymond P. Mauldin, pp. 259–276. *BAR International Series* 528. Oxford: BAR.

ANDREWS, MICHAEL J.
  1982  An Archaeological Assessment of Homolovi III and Chevelon Ruin, Northern Arizona. MS, prepared for the Arizona State Land Department, Phoenix, by Northern Arizona University, Flagstaff.
  1983  An Archaeological Survey near Chevelon Ruin, Northern Arizona. Final report submitted to the Arizona State Land Department, Phoenix, by Northern Arizona University, Flagstaff.

BARTLETT, KATHARINE
  1933  Pueblo Milling Stones of the Flagstaff Region and Their Relation to Others in the Southwest. *Museum of Northern Arizona Bulletin* 3. Flagstaff: Northern Arizona Society of Science and Art.
  1943  A Primitive Stone Industry of the Little Colorado Valley. *American Antiquity* 8(3): 266–268.

BEAGLEHOLE, ERNEST
  1936  Hopi Hunting and Hunting Ritual. *Yale University Publications in Anthropology* 4: 1–26.

BEQUAERT, JOSEPH C., AND WALTER B. MILLER
  1973  *The Mollusks of the Arid Southwest*. Tucson: University of Arizona Press.

BHATTACHARYYA, MANDRIA
  1985  Homolovi Ceramics Technology. MS, Laboratory of Traditional Technology, University of Arizona, Tucson.

BISHOP, RONALD L., AND HECTOR NEFF
  1989  Compositional Data Analysis in Archaeology. *Archaeological Chemistry IV, Advances in Chemistry Series*, pp. 57–86. Washington: American Chemical Society.

BISHOP, RONALD L., GARMAN HARBOTTLE, AND EDWARD V. SAYRE
  1982  Chemical and Mathematical Procedures Employed in the Maya Fine Paste Ceramics Project. In "Excavations at Seibal," edited by Jeremy A. Sabloff, pp. 272–282. *Memoirs of the Peabody Museum of Archaeology and Ethnology* 15(2). Cambridge: Harvard University.

BISHOP, RONALD L., ROBERT L. RANDS, AND GEORGE R. HOLLEY
  1982  Ceramic Compositional Analysis in Archaeological Perspective. In *Advances in Archaeological Method and Theory*, Vol. 5, edited by Michael B. Schiffer, pp. 275–330. New York: Academic Press.

BISHOP, RONALD L., VELETTA CANOUTS, SUZANNE P. DE ATLEY, ALFRED QOYAWAYMA, AND G. W. AIKENS
1988    The Formation of Ceramic Analytical Groups: Hopi Pottery Production and Exchange, A.C. 1300-1600. *Journal of Field Archaeology* 15(3): 317-337.

BLACKMAN, M. JAMES
1986    Precision in Routine I.N.A.A. Over a Two Year Period at the NBSR. *NBS Reactor: Summary of Activities July 1985 Through June 1986, NBS Technical Note* 1231, edited by Frederick J. Shorten, pp. 122-126. Gaithersburg, MD: National Bureau of Standards.

BLOCK, REBECCA
1985    Thermal Expansion Measurements of Ceramics at Homolovi II. MS, Laboratory of Traditional Technology, University of Arizona, Tucson.

BOYER, KENT
1986    Ground Stone Analysis. MS, Arizona State Museum Library, University of Arizona, Tucson.

BREED, CAROL S., AND WILLIAM J. BREED, EDITORS
1972    Investigations in the Triassic Chinle Formation. *Museum of Northern Arizona Bulletin* 47. Flagstaff: Northland Press.

BRETERNITZ, DAVID A.
1966    An Appraisal of Tree-ring Dated Pottery in the Southwest. *Anthropological Papers of the University of Arizona* 10. Tucson: University of Arizona Press.

BREW, J. O.
1949    The History of Awatovi. In "Franciscan Awatovi: The Excavation and Conjectural Reconstruction of a 17th Century Spanish Mission Establishment at a Hopi Indian Town in Northeastern Arizona," by R. G. Montgomery, W. Smith, and J. O. Brew. *Papers of the Peabody Museum of American Archaeology and Ethnology* 36: 1-43. Cambridge: Harvard University.

BURTON, JEFFERY F.
1990    Archeological Investigations at Puerco Ruin, Petrified Forest National Park, Arizona. *Western Archeological and Conservation Center Publications in Anthropology* 54. Tucson: National Park Service.

CAMERON, CATHERINE M.
1985    An Analysis of Manos from Chaco Canyon, New Mexico. MS, prepared for the Division of Cultural Research, Southwest Regional Office, National Park Service.

CARLSON, ROY L.
1970    White Mountain Redware: A Pottery Tradition of East-Central Arizona and Western New Mexico. *Anthropological Papers of the University of Arizona* 19. Tucson: University of Arizona Press.

CAYWOOD, LOUIS RICHARD
1972    *The Restored Mission of Nuestra Señora de Guadalupe de Zuni, Zuni, New Mexico.* St. Michaels: St Michaels Press.

CHRISTENSON, ANDREW L.
1987    Perforated and Unperforated Plates as Pottery Manufacture Tools. In "A Functional and Technological Study of the Ceramics of Black Mesa, Arizona," edited by Marion F. Smith, Jr. *Center for Archaeological Investigations Occasional Paper Series.* Carbondale: Southern Illinois University.

COLE, SALLY J.
1989    Katsina Iconography in Homol'ovi Rock Art. *Kiva* 54(4): 313-329.

COLTON, HAROLD S.
1937    Some Notes on the Original Condition of the Little Colorado River. *Museum of Northern Arizona Notes* 10(6): 17-20. Flagstaff: Museum of Northern Arizona.
1939    Prehistoric Culture Units and Their Relationships in Northern Arizona. *Museum of Northern Arizona Bulletin* 17. Flagstaff: Museum of Northern Arizona.
1943    Reconstruction of Anasazi History. Proceedings of the American Philosophical Society 86(2): 264-269. Philadelphia: American Philosophical Society.
1955    Pottery Types of the Southwest. *Museum of Northern Arizona Ceramic Series* 3A. Flagstaff: Museum of Northern Arizona.
1956    Pottery Types of the Southwest. *Museum of Northern Arizona Ceramic Series* 3C. Flagstaff: Museum of Northern Arizona.

COUES, ELLIOT
1900    *On the Trail of a Spanish Pioneer: The Diary and Itinerary of Francisco Garces in his Travels through Sonora, Arizona and California, 1775-1776.* New York. 2 Vols.

COURLANDER, HAROLD
1971    *The Fourth World of the Hopis.* New York: Crown Publishers.

CROWN, PATRICIA L.
1981    *Variability in Ceramic Manufacture at the Chodistaas Site, East-Central Arizona.* Doctoral dissertation, University of Arizona, Tucson. Ann Arbor: University Microfilms.
1983    An X-ray Fluorescence Analysis of Hohokam Ceramics. In "Hohokam Archaeology along the Salt-Gila Aqueduct, Central Arizona Project," Vol. 8, "Material Culture," edited by Lynn S. Teague and Patricia L. Crown. *Arizona State Museum Archaeological Series* 150. Tucson: University of Arizona.
1990    Converging Traditions: Salado Polychrome Ceramics in Southwestern Prehistory. Paper presented at the 55th Annual Meeting of the Society for American Archaeology, Las Vegas.

CROWN, PATRICIA L., AND RONALD L. BISHOP
1987    The Manufacture of the Salado Polychromes. *Pottery Southwest* 14(4): 1-4. Albuquerque.

CROWN, PATRICIA L., LARRY A. SCHWALBE, AND J. RONALD LONDON
1988    An X-ray Fluorescence Analysis of Material Variability in Las Colinas Ceramics. In "Excavations at Las Colinas, Phoenix, Arizona," Vol 4, "Material Culture," edited by David A. Gregory and Carol Heathington. *Arizona State Museum Archaeological Series* 162. Tucson: University of Arizona.

CZAPLICKI, N. J., AND GEORGE A. RUFFNER
1981    An Analysis of the Vertebrate Fauna of Walpi. *Walpi Archaeological Project, Phase II*, Vol. 8, Part I. Flagstaff: Museum of Northern Arizona.

DANSON, EDWARD B., AND ROBERTS M. WALLACE
1956    A Petrographic Study of Gila Polychrome. *American Antiquity* 22: 180-183.

DEAN, JEFFREY S., ROBERT C. EULER, GEORGE J. GUMERMAN, FRED PLOG, RICHARD H. HEVLEY, AND THOR N. V. KARLSTROM
1985 Human Behavior, Demography and Paleoenvironment on the Colorado Plateaus. *American Antiquity* 50(3): 537–554.

DE ATLEY, SUZANNE P., RONALD L. BISHOP, VELETTA CANOUTS, ALFRED GOYAWAYMA, AND C. W. AIKENS
1986 Hopi Social Boundary Maintenance and Exchange Relationships. Paper presented at the 51st Annual Meeting of the Society for American Archaeology, New Orleans. MS, Homol'ovi Research Program, Arizona State Museum, University of Arizona, Tucson.

DI PESO, CHARLES C.
1976 Gila Polychrome in the Casas Grandes Region. *The Kiva* 42: 57–64.

DOCKSTADER, FREDERICK J.
1954 The Kachina and the White Man: A Study of the Influence of White Culture on the Hopi Kachina Cult. *Cranbrook Institute of Science Bulletin* 35. Bloomfield Hills, Michigan: Cranbrook Institute of Science.

DOELLE, WILLIAM H.
1980 *Past Adaptive Patterns in Western Papagueria: An Archaeological Study of Nonriverine Resource Use.* MS, Doctoral dissertation, University of Arizona, Tucson. Ann Arbor: University Microfilms.

DOSH, STEVEN G.
1982 The Emergency Protection of Homolovi I Ruin. Final report submitted to the Bureau of Land Management, Phoenix, by the Museum of Northern Arizona, Flagstaff. MS, Museum of Northern Arizona, Flagstaff.
1984 Backfilling and Stabilization of Homolovi II Ruin. Final report submitted to the Arizona State Land Department, Phoenix, by the Museum of Northern Arizona, Flagstaff. MS, Museum of Northern Arizona, Flagstaff.

DOYEL, DAVID E.
1976 Classic Period Hohokam in the Gila River Basin, Arizona. *The Kiva* 42(1): 27–37.

DOYEL, DAVID E., AND EMIL W. HAURY, EDITORS
1976 Summary of Conference Discussion. The 1976 Salado Conference. *The Kiva* 42(1): 127–134.

EGGAN, FRED
1950 *Social Organization of the Western Pueblos.* Chicago: University of Chicago Press.

EULER, ROBERT C., GEORGE J. GUMERMAN, THOR N. V. KARLSTROM, JEFFREY S. DEAN, AND RICHARD H. HEVLY
1979 The Colorado Plateaus: Cultural Dynamics and Paleoenvironment. *Science* 205(4411): 1089–1101.

FAO
1961 Food Composition Table for Use in Latin America. Rome: Food and Agriculture Organization of the United Nations.

FEINMAN, GARY M., STEADMAN UPHAM, AND KENT G. LIGHTFOOT
1981 The Production Step Measure: An Ordinal Index of Labor Input in Ceramic Manufacture. *American Antiquity* 46(4): 871–884.

FERG, ALAN
1982 14th Century Katchina Depictions on Ceramics. In "Collected Papers in Honor of John W. Runyan." *Papers of the Archaeological Society of New Mexico* 7. Albuquerque: Archaeological Society of New Mexico.

FEWKES, JESSE W.
1904 Two Summers' Work in Pueblo Ruins. *Twenty-second Annual Report of the Bureau of Ethnology,* Part I, pp. 3–196. Washington.
1919 Designs on Prehistoric Hopi Pottery. *Thirty-third Annual Report of the Bureau of American Ethnology,* pp. 207–284. Washington.

FOREMAN, GRANT
1941 *A Pathfinder in the Southwest.* Norman: University of Oklahoma Press.

FRANKLIN, HAYWARD H., AND W. BRUCE MASSE
1976 The San Pedro Salado: A Case of Prehistoric Migration. *The Kiva* 42(1): 47–56.

FRATT, LEE
1991 Ground Stone Artifacts from Homol'ovi II: A Descriptive and Analytical Report. MS on file, Arizona State Museum Library, University of Arizona, Tucson.

GASSER, ROBERT E.
1981 Archaeobotanical Remains from Walpi. *Walpi Archaeological Project, Phase II,* Vol. 7, Part I. Flagstaff: Museum of Northern Arizona.
1982 The Specialist's Volume: Biocultural Analyses. The Coronado Project Archaeological Investigations. *Coronado Series* 4, *Museum of Northern Arizona Research Paper* 23. Flagstaff: Museum of Northern Arizona.

GASSER, ROBERT E., AND CHARLES MIKSICEK
1985 The Specialists: A Reappraisal of Hohokam Exchange and the Archaeobotanical Record. In "Proceedings of the 1983 Hohokam Symposium, Part II," edited by Alfred E. Dittert, Jr. and Donald E. Dove. *Arizona Archaeological Society Occasional Paper* 2: 483–498. Phoenix: Arizona Archaeological Society.

GIFFORD, JAMES C., AND WATSON SMITH
1978 Gray Corrugated Pottery from Awatovi and Other Jeddito Sites in Northeastern Arizona. *Papers of the Peabody Museum of Archaeology and Ethnology* 69. Cambridge: Harvard University.

GILPIN, DENNIS
1988 The 1987 Navajo Nation Investigations at Bidahochi Pueblo, a Fourteenth Century Site in the Hopi Buttes, Navajo County, Arizona (NNAD-88-299). Paper presented at the 1988 Pecos Conference, Cortez, Colorado.

GRAYSON, DONALD K.
1973 On Methodology of Faunal Analysis. *American Antiquity* 38(4): 432–439.

GREBINGER, PAUL
1976 Salado–Perspectives from the Middle Santa Cruz Valley. *The Kiva* 42: 39–46.

GUMERMAN, GEORGE J.
1966 Two Basketmaker II Pithouse Villages in Eastern Arizona: A Preliminary Report. *Plateau* 39(2): 80–87.
1969 The Archaeology of the Hopi Buttes District. MS, Doctoral dissertation, Department of Anthropology, University of Arizona, Tucson.

GUMERMAN, GEORGE J., AND JEFFREY S. DEAN
1989    Prehistoric Cooperation and Competition in the Western Anasazi Area. In *Dynamics of Southwestern Prehistory*, edited by Linda S. Cordell and George J. Gumerman, pp 99–148. Washington: Smithsonian Institution.

GUMERMAN, GEORGE J., AND S. ALAN SKINNER
1968    A Synthesis of the Prehistory of the Central Little Colorado Valley, Arizona. *American Antiquity* 33(2): 185–199.

HACK, JOHN T.
1942a    The Changing Physical Environment of the Hopi Indians of Arizona. *Papers of the Peabody Museum of American Archaeology and Ethnology* 35(1). Cambridge: Harvard University.
1942b    Prehistoric Coal Mining in the Jeddito Valley, Arizona. *Papers of the Peabody Museum of American Archaeology and Ethnology* 35(2). Cambridge: Harvard University.

HAMILTON, W. R., A. R. WOOLEY, AND A. C. BISHOP
1974    The Larousse Guide to Minerals, Rocks, and Fossils. New York: Larousse.

HAMMACK, LAURENS C., AND ALAN P. SULLIVAN, EDITORS
1981    The 1968 Excavations at Mound 8, Las Colinas Ruins Group, Phoenix, Arizona. *Arizona State Museum Archaeological Series* 154. Tucson: University of Arizona.

HAMMOND, GEORGE P., AND AGAPITO REY
1929    *Expedition into New Mexico made by Antonio de Espejo, 1582–1583, as Revealed in the Journal of Diego Perez de Luxam, a Member of the Party.* Los Angeles: The Quivira Society.
1953    *Don Juan de Onate, Colonizer of New Mexico 1595–1628.* Albuquerque: University of New Mexico Press.

HANTMAN, JEFFREY L.
1978    Modelling Prehistoric Colonization: The Mormon Case Example, 1876–1896. Paper presented at the 22nd Annual Meeting of the Arizona-Nevada Academy of Science meetings, Tempe. MS, Arizona State Museum Library, University of Arizona, Tucson.
1982    A Long Term Management Plan for Significant Sites in the Vicinity of Winslow, Arizona. Prepared for the Arizona State Land Department, Phoenix, by Soil Systems Inc., Phoenix. MS, Arizona State Museum Library, University of Arizona, Tucson.

HANTMAN, JEFFREY L., AND KENT G. LIGHTFOOT
1978    The Analysis of Ceramic Design: A New Approach to Cultural Resource Management. In "The Little Colorado Planning Unit," edited by Fred Plog. *Arizona State University Anthropological Research Papers* 13. Tempe: Arizona State University.

HARBOTTLE, GARMAN
1976    Activation Analysis in archaeology. In *Radiochemistry: A Specialist Periodical Report*, edited by G. W. A. Newton, pp. 33–72. Burlington, London: The Chemical Society.

HARRY, KAREN G.
1989    The Obsidian Assemblage from Homol'ovi III: Social and Economic Implications. *Kiva* 54(4): 285–296.

HAURY, EMIL W.
1945    The Excavation of Los Muertos and Neighboring Ruins in the Salt River Valley, Southern Arizona. *Papers of the Peabody Museum of American Archaeology and Ethnology* 24(1). Cambridge: Harvard University.
1976    *The Hohokam Desert Farmers and Craftsmen: Excavations at Snaketown, 1964–1965.* Tucson: University of Arizona Press.

HAYS, KELLEY ANN
1989    Katsina Depictions on Homol'ovi Ceramics: Toward a Fourteenth-Century Pueblo Iconography. *Kiva* 54(4): 297–312.

HAYS, KELLEY ANN, RICHARD C. LANGE, AND JOHN MADSEN
1984    Excavation and Surface Collection of Homolovi II Ruin. MS, Arizona State Museum Library, University of Arizona, Tucson.

HENRY, DON O., C. VANCE HAYNES, AND BRUCE BRADLEY
1976    Quantitative Variation in Flaked Stone Debitage. *Plains Anthropologist* 21(75): 57–61.

HEVLY, RICHARD H.
1968    Studies of the Modern Pollen Rain in Northern Arizona. *Journal of the Arizona Academy of Science* 5(2): 116–126.

HOLMES, WILLIAM H.
1896    Manufacture of Pecked-abraded Stone Implements– A Study of Rejectage. *The American Antiquarian* 17(6): 309–313.

HUCKELL, LISA W.
1986    Botanical Remains. In "The 1985 Excavations at the Hodges Site, Pima County, Arizona," edited by Robert W. Layhe. *Arizona State Museum Archaeological Series* 170: 241–269. Tucson: University of Arizona.

JELINEK, ARTHUR J.
1976    Form, Function, and Style in Lithic Analysis. In *Cultural Change and Continuity: Essays in Honor of James Bennett Griffin*, edited by Charles E. Cleland, pp. 19–33. New York: Academic Press.

JENNINGS, CALVIN H.
1980    Further Investigations at the Puerco Site, Petrified Forest National Park, Arizona. MS, Laboratory of Public Archaeology, Colorado State University, Fort Collins.

JETER, MARVIN D.
1980    Analysis of Flaked Stone Artifacts and Debitage. In "Prehistory in Dead Valley, East-Central Arizona: The TG&E Springerville Report," edited by David E. Doyel and Sharon S. Debowski. *Arizona State Museum Archaeological Series* 144: 235–304. Tucson: University of Arizona.

KELLER, DONALD R.
1984    Gray Mountain: A Prehistoric Chert Source Site in Coconino County, Arizona. *The Arizona Archaeologist* 19. Phoenix: Arizona Archaeological Society.

KELLER, DONALD R., AND SUZANNE M. WILSON
1976    New Light on the Tolchaco Problem. *The Kiva* 41(3–4): 225–239.

KIDDER, ALFRED V.
1927    Southwestern Archaeological Conference. *Science* 66(11): 489–491.

1973 *An Introduction to the Study of Southwestern Archaeology with a Preliminary Account of the Excavations at Pecos (1924)*. New Haven: Yale University Press.

KINTIGH, KEITH W.
1985 Settlement, Subsistence, and Society in Late Zuni Prehistory. *Anthropological Papers of the University of Arizona*. Tucson: University of Arizona Press.

KOLBE, TOM
1991 The Geomorphology and Alluvial Chronology of the Middle Little Colorado River Valley, Arizona. MS, Master's thesis, Department of Quaternary Studies, Northern Arizona University, Flagstaff.

LANGE, RICHARD C.
1989 A Survey of the Homolovi Ruins State Park. *Kiva* 54(3): 195–216.

LANGE, RICHARD C., AND BARBARA A. MURPHY
1987 Archaeomagnetic Dates and Data from Arizona and New Mexico: A Discussion of a Large Set of Archaeologist-collected Samples. *Colorado State University Technical Series* 2. Fort Collins: Colorado State University.

LANGE, RICHARD C., LISA C. YOUNG, AND LEE FRATT
1986 The First Season's Survey by the Arizona State Museum in the Vicinity of the Homol'ovi Ruins. MS, Arizona State Museum Library, University of Arizona, Tucson.

LEBLANC, STEVEN, AND BEN NELSON
1976 The Salado in Southwestern New Mexico. *The Kiva* 42: 71–80.

LESLEY, LEWIS BURT, EDITOR
1970 *Uncle Sam's Camels*. Glorieta, New Mexico: The Rio Grande Press.

LEVIN, JANE R.
1990 Design in the Service of Dating: Chronological Refinement of Jeddito Yellow Ware. MS, Homol'ovi Research Program, Arizona State Museum, University of Arizona, Tucson, Arizona.

LIGHTFOOT, KENT
1984 *Prehistoric Political Dynamics: A Case Study from the American Southwest*. Dekalb, Illinois: Northern Illinois University Press.

LIGHTFOOT, KENT G., AND ROBERTA JEWETT
1984 Late Prehistoric Ceramics Distributions in East Central Arizona: An Examination of Cibola, White Mountain, and Salado Wares. In "Regional Analysis of the Cibola Whitewares," edited by Alan P. Sullivan and Jeffrey L. Hantman, pp. 36–73. *Arizona State University Anthropological Research Papers* 31. Tempe: Arizona State University.

LINDSAY, ALEXANDER J., JR., AND CALVIN H. JENNINGS
1968 Salado Red Ware Conference, Ninth Ceramic Seminar. *Museum of Northern Arizona Ceramic Series* 4. Flagstaff.

LOGIN, ERIK
1990 A Preliminary Analysis of the Occurrence of Pigment on the Ground Stone from Homol'ovi III. MS on file at the Arizona State Museum, University of Arizona, Tucson.

MARTIN, PAUL S., AND JOHN B. RINALDO
1960 Table Rock Pueblo, Arizona. *Fieldiana: Anthropology* 51(2).

MARTIN, PAUL S., AND ELIZABETH S. WILLIS
1940 Anasazi Painted Pottery in the Field Museum of Natural History. *Field Museum of Natural History Anthropology Memoirs* 5. Chicago: Field Museum of Natural History.

MAYRO, LINDA L., STEPHANIE M. WHITTLESEY, AND J. JEFFERSON REID
1976 Observations on the Salado Presence at Grasshopper Pueblo. *The Kiva* 42: 85–94.

MEHRINGER, PETER J.
1967 Pollen Analysis of the Tule Springs Area, Nevada. In "Pleistocene Studies in Southern Nevada," edited by H. Marie Wormington and D. Ellis. *Nevada State Museum Anthropological Papers* 13: 130–200.

MINDELEFF, COSMOS
1901 Localization of Tusayan Clans. *Nineteenth Annual Report of the Bureau of American Ethnology*. Washington.

NAGATA, SHUICHI
1970 *Modern Transformations of Moenkopi Pueblo*. Urbana: University of Illinois Press.

NATIONS, J. DALE, AND JENNY L. ADAMS
1980 Analysis of Shell Material from the Walpi Archaeological Project. In *Walpi Archaeological Project, Phase II*, Vol. 6, Part III. Flagstaff: Museum of Northern Arizona.

NEQUATEWA, EDMUND
1936 Truth of a Hopi and Other Clan Stories of Shungopovi. *Museum of Northern Arizona Bulletin* 8. Flagstaff: Museum of Northern Arizona.

NEWCOMER, MARK H.
1971 Some Quantitative Experiments in Handaxe Manufacture. *World Archaeology* 3(1): 85–93.

NICKERSON, NORTON H.
1953 Variation in Cob Morphology among Certain Archaeological and Ethnological Races of Maize. *Annuals of the Missouri Botanical Garden* 40: 78–111.

O'KANE, WALTER C.
1950 *Sun in the Sky*. Norman: University of Oklahoma Press.

OLSEN, SANDRA L.
1979 A Study of Bone Artifacts from Grasshopper Pueblo, AZ P:14:1. *The Kiva* 44(4): 341–373.

OLSEN, STANLEY J.
1978 The Faunal Analysis. In "Bones from Awatovi, Northeastern Arizona." *Papers of the Peabody Museum of Archaeology and Ethnology* 70(1): 1–34. Cambridge: Harvard University.

PARSONS, ELSIE C., EDITOR
1936 The Hopi Journal of Alexander M. Stephen. *Columbia University Contributions to Anthropology* 23. New York: Columbia University Press.

PLOG, FRED T., JAMES HILL, AND DOUGLAS REED, EDITORS
1976 Chevelon Archaeological Research Project. *UCLA Archaeological Survey Monograph* 2. Los Angeles: University of California.

POND, GORDON G.
1966 A Painted Kiva near Winslow, Arizona. *American Antiquity* 31(4): 555–558.

PREUCEL, ROBERT W.
1988 *Seasonal Agricultural Circulation and Residential Mobility: A Prehistoric Example from the Pajarito Plateau, New Mexico.* Doctoral dissertation, Department of Anthropology, University of California, Los Angeles. Ann Arbor: University Microfilms.

RATHJE, WILLIAM L., AND MICHAEL B. SCHIFFER
1982 *Archaeology.* New York: Harcourt, Brace, and Jovanovich.

REED, ERIC
1948 The Western Pueblo Archaeological Complex. *El Palacio* 55(1): 9–15.

REINHART, THEODORE R.
1965 The Metate and Mano at Sapawe. The University of New Mexico Seminar paper for Anthropology 594. MS, Department of Anthropology, University of New Mexico, Albuquerque.

RENFREW, COLIN
1977 Alternative Models for Exchange and Spatial Distribution. In *Exchange Systems in Prehistory*, edited by Timothy K. Earle and Jonathan E. Ericson, pp. 71–90. New York: Academic Press.

RICE, PRUDENCE M.
1987 *Pottery Analysis: A Sourcebook.* Chicago: University of Chicago Press.

RIPPEY, CHARLES D.
1969 Rabbit Hill Village: A Basketmaker III–Pueblo I Pit House Village East of Winslow, Arizona. MS, Museum of Northern Arizona, Flagstaff.

ROBBINS, WILFRED W., JOHN P. HARRINGTON, AND BARBARA FREIRE-MARRECO
1916 Ethnobotany of the Tewa Indians. *Bureau of American Ethnology Bulletin* 55. Washington.

ROZEN, KENNETH C.
1979 Lithic Analysis and Interpretation. In "The Aepco Project," by Deborah A. Westfall, Kenneth Rozen, and Howard M. Davidson. *Arizona State Museum Archaeological Series* 117(2): 209–321. Tucson: University of Arizona.
1981 Patterned Associations among Lithic Technology, Site Content, and Time: Results of the TEP St. Johns Project Lithic Analysis. In "Prehistory of the St. Johns Area, East-Central Arizona: The TEP St. Johns Project," by Deborah A. Westfall. *Arizona State Museum Archaeological Series* 153: 157–232. Tucson: University of Arizona.
1984 Flaked Stone. In "Hohokam Habitation Sites in the Northern Santa Rita Mountains," by Alan Ferg, Kenneth C. Rozen, William L. Deaver, Martyn D. Tagg, David A. Phillips, Jr., and David A. Gregory. *Arizona State Museum Archaeological Series* 47(2): 421–604. Tucson: University of Arizona.

SCHIFFER, MICHAEL B.
1987 *Formation Processes of the Archaeological Record.* Albuquerque: University of New Mexico Press.

SCHROEDER, ALBERT
1957 Comments on Gila Polychrome. *American Antiquity* 23: 169–170.

SCOTT, LINDA J.
1980 Pollen Analysis in Selected Rooms at Walpi and Along Modern Transects Near First Mesa. In "Arch-aeobotanical Remains from Walpi," by Robert E. Gasser and Linda J. Scott. *Walpi Archaeological Project Phase II*, Vol. 7, Part II. Flagstaff: Museum of Northern Arizona.

SEME, MICHELE
1984 The Effect of Agricultural Fields on Faunal Assemblage Variation. In *Papers on the Archaeology of Black Mesa, Arizona*, Vol. 2, edited by Steven Plog and Shirley Powell, pp. 139–157. Carbondale: Southern Illinois University Press.

SIEBERT, SARA
1987 An Analysis of the Hoes. In "The Second Season's Survey of the Homol'ovi Ruins State Park, Northeastern Arizona," prepared by Richard C. Lange, Miriam T. Stark, Lee Fratt, Lisa C. Young, and Sara L. Seibert. MS, Arizona State Museum Library, University of Arizona, Tucson.

SIMS, JACK R., JR., AND D. SCOTT DANIEL
1967 A Lithic Assemblage near Winslow, Arizona. *Plateau* 39(4): 175–188.

SITGREAVES, CAPTAIN LORENZO
1854 *Report on an Expedition Down the Zuni and Colorado Rivers.* U.S. Senate Executive Document, 33rd Congress, 1st Session, Washington.

SMITH, H. V.
1945 The Climate of Arizona. *University of Arizona Agricultural Experimental Station Bulletin* 197. Tucson: University of Arizona.

SMITH, WATSON
1971 Painted Ceramics of the Western Mound at Awatovi. *Papers of the Peabody Museum of American Archaeology and Ethnology* 39(1). Cambridge: Harvard University.

SNEATH, PETER H., AND ROBERT R. SOKAL
1973 *Principles of Numerical Taxonomy.* San Francisco: W. H. Freeman.

STAHL, PETER W.
1982 On Small Mammal Remains in Archaeological Context. *American Antiquity* 47(4): 822–829.

SULLIVAN, ALAN P., III
1980 *Prehistoric Settlement Variability in the Grasshopper Area, East-Central Arizona.* Doctoral dissertation, University of Arizona. Ann Arbor: University Microfilms.
1984a Patterns of Preceramic and Ceramic Period Lithic Technology on Voigt Mesa. In "The Prehistoric Occupation of Voigt Mesa, Arizona: The 1983 TEP Springerville Project," by Katharina J. Schreiber and Alan P. Sullivan, III. *Arizona State Museum Archaeological Series* 166: 23–54. Tucson: University of Arizona.
1984b Sinagua Agricultural Strategies and Sunset Crater Volcanism. In "Prehistoric Agricultural Strategies in the Southwest," edited by Suzanne K. Fish and Paul R. Fish. *Arizona State University Anthropological Research Papers* 33: 85–100. Tempe: Arizona State University.
1987 Probing the Sources of Lithic Assemblage Variability: A Regional Case Study Near the Homol'ovi Ruins, Winslow, Arizona. *North American Archaeology* 8(1): 41–71

1988 Prehistoric Southwestern Ceramic Manufacture: the Limitations of Current Evidence. *American Antiquity* 53(1): 23–35.

SULLIVAN, ALAN P., III, AND KENNETH C. ROZEN
1985 Debitage Analysis and Archaeological Interpretation. *American Antiquity* 50(4): 755–779.

SZUTER, CHRISTINE R.
1984 Faunal Exploitation and the Reliance on Small Animals among the Hohokam. In "Hohokam Archaeology along the Salt-Gila Aqueduct Central Arizona Project," Vol. 7, "Environment and Subsistence," edited by Lynn S. Teague and Patricia L. Crown. *Arizona State Museum Archaeological Series* 150(7): 139–170. Tucson: University of Arizona.
1985 The Faunal Remains from Homol'ovi II. In Excavation and Surface Collection at Homol'ovi II Ruin, edited by Kelley Ann Hays and E. Charles Adams, Appendix C, pp. C1–28. MS, Archaeology Section, Arizona State Museum, University of Arizona, Tucson.

TITIEV, MISCHA
1944 Old Oraibi: A Study of the Hopi Indians of Third Mesa. *Papers of the Peabody Museum of American Archaeology and Ethnology* 22. Cambridge: Harvard University.

TYLER, HAMILTON A.
1964 *Pueblo Gods and Myths.* Norman: University of Oklahoma Press.
1979 *Pueblo Birds and Myths.* Norman: University of Oklahoma Press.

UPHAM, STEADMAN
1982 *Polities and Power: An Economic and Political History of the Western Pueblo.* New York: Academic Press.

VAITKUS, ROBERT
1986 Experimental Replication of Winslow Orange Wares: A Prehistoric Assemblage at Homol'ovi II and Homol'ovi III. MS, Laboratory of Traditional Technology, University of Arizona, Tucson.

WALLACE, ROBERTS M.
1954 Petrographic Analysis of Pottery from University Indian Ruins. Appendix F in "Excavations, 1940, at University Indian Ruin," by Julian Hayden. *Southwestern Monuments Association Technical Series* 5 (1957). Globe.

WEAVER, DONALD E., JR., STEVEN G. DOSH, AND KEITH E. MILLER
1982 An Archaeological Assessment of Homolovi II Ruin. Final report submitted to the State Historic Preservation Office, Phoenix, by the Museum of Northern Arizona, Flagstaff. MS, Museum of Northern Arizona, Flagstaff.

WENDORF, FRED, AND TULLY H. THOMAS
1951 Early Man Sites near Concho, Arizona. *American Antiquity* 17(2): 107–114.

WENTWORTH, C. K.
1922 Scale of Grade and Class Terms for Clastic Sediments. *Journal of Geology* 30(5): 388.

WHEELER, RICHARD PAGE
1978 Bone and Antler Artifacts. In "Bones from Awatovi, Northeastern Arizona," by Stanley J. Olsen and Richard P. Wheeler. *Papers of the Peabody Museum of American Archaeology and Ethnology* 70(2): 35–69. Cambridge: Harvard University.

WHITING, ALFRED
1939 Ethnobotany of the Hopi. *Museum of Northern Arizona Bulletin* 15. Flagstaff: Museum of Northern Arizona.

WILCOX, DAVID
1987 Frank Midvale's Investigation of the Site of La Ciudad. *Anthropological Field Studies* 16. Tempe: Arizona State University.

WISEMAN, REGGE N.
1970 Hypothesis for Variation Observed in Late Pueblo Manos and Metates. *Southwest Lore* 36(3): 46–50.

WOOD, J. SCOTT
1987 Checklist of Pottery Types for the Tonto National Forest: An Introduction to the Archaeological Ceramics of Central Arizona. *The Arizona Archaeologist* 21. Phoenix: Arizona Archaeological Society.

WOODBURY, RICHARD B.
1954 Prehistoric Stone Implements of Northeastern Arizona. *Papers of the Peabody Museum of American Archaeology and Ethnology* 34. Cambridge: Harvard University.

YOUNG, LISA C.
1989 Mobility and Farmers: Adaptive Diversity in the American Southwest. MS, NSF Dissertation Improvement Proposal, Arizona State Museum, University of Arizona, Tucson.

YOUNG, LISA C., AND KAREN G. HARRY
1989 A Preliminary Analysis of Temporal Changes in the Homol'ovi III Chipped Stone Assemblage. *Kiva* 54(4): 273–284.

ZIER, ANNE H.
1981 An Experiment in Ground Stone Use-Wear Analysis. MS, Master's thesis, Department of Anthropology, University of Colorado, Boulder.

# Index

# Abstract

Homol'ovi II is a 14th-century pueblo with over 700 rooms that is located along the Little Colorado River five miles north of the modern town of Winslow in northeastern Arizona. Although known by archaeologists since J. Walter Fewkes' work in 1896, no systematic archaeological excavations were conducted at the pueblo until 1984. Excavations were initiated because the pueblo had been ravaged by a century of vandalism. This vandalism threatened the integrity of the pueblo and had become a concern of professional archaeologists, avocational archaeologists, citizens of Winslow, and the Hopi, who consider Homol'ovi II to be ancestral to many of their clans.

The excavation of five rooms and an outside activity area in 1984 by the Arizona State Museum, University of Arizona was initiated to evaluate the damage to the pueblo, to open an area that could be viewed by the public following a self-guided trail, and to assess the viability of developing a new state park around Homol'ovi II.

This report summarizes the findings of the 1984 excavations, which clearly demonstrate that many of the archaeological deposits are undamaged by the vandalism. Significant information on the age of the deposits, the nature and direction of exchange between Homol'ovi II occupants and their neighbors, and the subsistence base of the people was recovered and is reported herein. The extensive surface collection proved useful in discovering trends in activities and age between the village's plazas and between plaza and extra-village areas.

The significant findings reported in this volume are that the excavated deposits date between A.D. 1340 and 1400, that nearly all the decorated ceramics during this period were imported from villages on the Hopi Mesas, that cotton was a principal crop which probably formed the basis of Homol'ovi II's participation in regional exchange, that chipped stone was a totally expedient technology in contrast to ground stone which was becoming more diverse, and that the katsina cult was probably present or developing at Homol'ovi II.

The areas uncovered in the 1984 excavations have been stabilized and form the core of the interpretive program for the Homolovi Ruins State Park, which was established in 1986. The research findings form the basis for future excavations at Homol'ovi II that should broaden our knowledge of the developments taking place in 14th-century Pueblo society, connecting the people whom archaeologists term the Anasazi with those calling themselves Hopi.

# Resumen

El sitio de Homol'ovi II es uno pueblo del siglo catorce que consiste de más de 700 cuartos y que está localizado a lo largo del Río Little Colorado (Colorado Chico), cinco millas al norte de la actual ciudad de Winslow en el noroeste de Arizona. Aunque ha sido conocido desde el trabajo de J. Walter Fewkes en 1896, no se hicieron excavaciones arqueológicas sistemáticas en el pueblo hasta 1984. Las excavaciones se empezaron porque el pueblo había sido saqueado por un siglo de vandalismo. Este vandalismo amenazaba la integridad del pueblo y era causa de inquietud entre arqueólogos profesionales, arqueólogos aficionados, ciudadanos de Winslow, y los hopi, que consideran Homol'ovi ser ancestral a muchos de sus clanes.

La excavación de cinco cuartos y un area exterior de actividad en 1984 por el Arizona State Museum (Museo Estatal de Arizona) de la Universidad de Arizona se empezó para evaluar el daño al pueblo, para abrir un area que se pudiera visitar por el público siguiendo un camino sin guía, y para evaluar la posibilidad del desarrollar un parque estatal alrededor de Homol'ovi II.

Este reportaje resume las conclusiones de las excavaciones de 1984 que claramente demuestran que muchos de los depósitos arqueológicos no han sido dañados por el vandalismo. La información signicativa sobre la edad de los depósitos, el tipo y la dirección del intercambio entre los habitantes de Homol'ovi II y sus vecinos, y el base de sustentación de la gente se recuperó y aquí mismo se reporta. La extensa colección superficie ha sido muy útil para descubrir las tendencias de actividades y la edad entre las plazas del pueblo y entre la plaza y areas fuera del pueblo.

Las conclusiones signicativas que se reportan en este volumen son que los depósitos excavados fechan entre 1340 hasta 1400 A.C., que la mayoría de las cerámicas decoradas durante esta época fueron importadas de las viviendas en las mesas hopi, que el algodón era un producto principal que probablemente formaba el base de la participación de Homol'ovi II en el intercambio regional, que la piedra lascada se estaba convertiendo en una tecnología expediente por constraste con la de le piedra molida que se estaba haciendo más diversa, y que el culto katsina estaba probablemente presente o se estaba desarrollando en Homol'ovi II.

Los areas descubridos por las excavaciones de 1984 se han estabilizados y forman el corazón del programa interpretivo para Homol'ovi Ruins State Park (Parque Estatal del las Ruinas Homol'ovi) el cual fue establecido en 1986. Las conclusiones de las investigaciones forman el base para excavasiones futuras en Homol'ovi II que ensancharan nuestro conocimiento de los desarrollos que sucedieron entre la socied de este pueblo del siglo catorce, haciendo la conección entre la gente que los arqueólogos nombran anasazi y los que ellos mismos se nombran hopi.